BOOKS BY HANNAH ARENDT

Nonfiction

Between Past and Future: Six Exercises in Political Thought
Crises of the Republic
Eichmann in Jerusalem: A Report on the Banality of Evil
Essays in Understanding, 1930–1954
The Human Condition
The Jew as Pariah: Jewish Identity and Politics in the Modern Age
Lectures on Kant's Political Philosophy
The Life of the Mind
Love and Saint Augustine
Men in Dark Times
On Revolution
On Violence
The Origins of Totalitarianism
Rahel Varnhagen: The Life of a Jewish Woman
Responsibility and Judgment

Correspondence

Between Friends: The Correspondence of Hannah Arendt and
Mary McCarthy, 1949–1975
Correspondence, 1926–1969 (with Karl Jaspers)
Letters, 1925–1975 (with Martin Heidegger)
Within Four Walls: The Correspondence Between Hannah Arendt and
Heinrich Blücher, 1936–1968

RESPONSIBILITY AND JUDGMENT

RESPONSIBILITY

❖❖❖ AND ❖❖❖

JUDGMENT

Hannah Arendt

Edited and with an Introduction
by Jerome Kohn

SCHOCKEN BOOKS, NEW YORK

Portions of this work have previously appeared in the following
publications: *Dissent; The Listener; New York Herald Tribune
Magazine; New York Review of Books; Social Research; The
American Experiment*, edited by S. B. Warner; *Amor Mundi*,
edited by James Bernauer; and *Auschwitz* by Bernd Naumann.

Library of Congress Cataloging-in-Publication Data
Arendt, Hannah.
    Responsibility and judgment / Hannah Arendt; edited and
with an introduction by Jerome Kohn.
        p. cm.
    Includes bibliographical references.
    ISBN 0-8052-4212-0
        1. Political ethics. 2. Responsibility. 3. Judgment.
4. Political participation. I. Kohn, Jerome. II. Title.
    JA79.A73 2003
    172—dc21   2003045737

www.schocken.com
Book design by Peter A. Andersen
Printed in the United States of America
First Edition
2   4   6   8   9   7   5   3   1

CONTENTS

INTRODUCTION
BY JEROME KOHN

"Particular questions must receive particular answers; and if the series of crises in which we have lived since the beginning of the century can teach us anything at all, it is, I think, the simple fact that there are no general standards to determine our judgments unfailingly, no general rules under which to subsume the particular cases with any degree of certainty." With these words Hannah Arendt (1906–75) encapsulated what throughout her life she regarded as the problematic nature of the relation of philosophy to politics, or of theory to practice, or, more simply and precisely, of thinking to acting. At the time she was addressing a large audience that had gathered from across the nation in Manhattan's Riverside Church to attend a colloquium on "The Crisis Character of Modern Society."* The year was 1966 and a particular political crisis, the escalation of the war in Vietnam, was uppermost in the minds of the citizens who had come together to express their concern over America's policy in Southeast Asia and to deliberate on what they, individually and collectively, could do to change that policy. Believing that their nation's devastation of an ancient culture and of a people who posed no threat to it was

---

*Arendt's brief remarks were later published in *Christianity and Crisis: a Christian Journal of Opinion* vol. 26, no. 9 (May 30, 1966): 112–14.

morally wrong, they turned to Arendt and the other speakers whose experience of past crises would, they hoped, shed light on the present one.

At least with Arendt they were in for something of a disappointment. Despite the fact that totalitarianism and other crises of the twentieth century had been the focus of her thought for many years, she offered them "no general standards" to measure the wrong that had been done, much less any "general rules" to apply to the wrong that was now being done. She said nothing to substantiate the convictions they already held, or to render their opinions more convincing to others, or to make their antiwar efforts more effective. Arendt did not believe that analogies derived retrospectively from what had or had not worked in the past would avert the pitfalls of the present situation. As she saw it, the spontaneity of political action is yoked to the contingency of its specific conditions, which renders such analogies unavailing. That "appeasement" had failed in Munich in 1938, for instance, did not entail that negotiations were pointless in 1966. And while Arendt believed that the entire world, for its own sake, must remain vigilant in resisting such elements as racism and global expansionism which had crystallized in totalitarianism, she objected to the indiscriminate, analogizing application of the term "totalitarian" to whatever regime the United States might oppose.

Arendt did not mean that the past as such was irrelevant—she never tired of repeating William Faulkner's epigram "The past is never dead, it's not even past"—but that applying "so-called lessons of history" to indicate what the future holds in store is only slightly more useful than examining entrails or reading tea leaves. In other words, her view of the past, clearly stated in "Home to Roost," the last piece included in *Responsibility and Judgment,* was more complicated and less confident than that contained in Santayana's frequently repeated remark, "Those who cannot remember the past are condemned to repeat it." On the contrary, Arendt believed that "for better or worse" our world has *"become"* what in reality it is: "the world we live in at any given moment *is* the world of the past." Her belief is hardly a historical "lesson," and it raises the question of how the past—past *action*—can be *experienced* in the present. In "Home to Roost" she did not answer that question with a theory, but her bittersweet judgment of the state of the Republic in 1975 provided an example of what she meant by the presence of the past. Although its "beginnings two hundred years ago" were "glorious," she said, the betrayal of America's "institutions of liberty" *"haunts"* us today. The *facts* have come home to roost, and the only way we can remain true to our origins is not by blaming "scapegoats," or by escaping into "images, theories, or sheer follies," but by trying to make those facts "welcome." It is we as a people who are responsible for them now.

The sole advice, if it can be called that, she ever offered was embedded in the "particular answers" she gave to "particular questions," which the following anecdote may illustrate.* When in the late 1960s her students asked her if they ought to cooperate with labor unions in opposing the war in Vietnam, to their surprise, unhesitatingly and with considerable common sense Arendt answered, "Yes, because that way you can use their mimeograph machines." Another anecdote from the same period exemplifies an entirely different perspective, one that has nothing to do with giving advice. When students demonstrating against the war occupied the New School's classrooms, the faculty called a special meeting to address the question of whether the police should be summoned to restore order. Arguments pro and contra were

---

*I am grateful to Elisabeth Young-Bruehl for recalling this incident.

presented, which ambled, as the meeting wore on, toward a positive resolution. Arendt said nothing until one of her colleagues, a friend she had known since her youth, reluctantly concurred that the "authorities" probably had to be informed. She turned on him sharply, saying "For God's sake, they are students not criminals." There was no further mention of the police, and in effect those eight words ended the discussion. Spoken spontaneously and based on her own experience, Arendt's words reminded her colleagues that the matter they addressed lay between them and their students and not between their students and the law.* Arendt's response was a judgment of a particular situation in its particularity, which the many words of argumentation had obscured.

No one was more aware than Arendt that the political crises of the twentieth century—first the outbreak of total war in 1914; then the rise of totalitarian regimes in Russia and Germany and their annihilation of entire classes and races of human beings; then the invention of the atomic bomb and its deployment to obliterate two Japanese cities in World War II; then the cold war and the unprecedented capacity of the post-totalitarian world to destroy itself with nuclear weapons; then Korea; then Vietnam; and on and on, events "cascading like a Niagara Falls of history"—can be viewed in terms of a breakdown in morality. That there had been such a collapse was obvious. But the controversial, challenging, and difficult heart of what Arendt came to see was that the moral breakdown was not due to the ignorance or wickedness of men who failed to recognize moral "truths," but rather to the inadequacy of moral "truths" as standards to judge what men had

*Arendt enjoyed telling the story of being arrested for her work on behalf of a Zionist organization in Berlin in 1933. The policeman in whose custody she was placed immediately saw that she was not a criminal, not someone who should be in jail, and arranged for her release. She left Germany forthwith.

become capable of doing. The only general conclusion that Arendt allowed herself pointed, ironically, to the generality of the sweeping change in what the long tradition of Western thought had held sacrosanct. The *tradition* of moral thought had been broken, not by philosophical ideas but by the political facts of the twentieth century and could not be put back together again.

Arendt was neither a nihilist nor an amoralist, but a thinker who followed where her thinking led. Following her, however, imposes a task on her readers—not so much on their intelligence or knowledge as on their ability to think. It is not theoretical solutions she advances but an abundance of incentives to *think for oneself.* She found immensely significant Tocqueville's insight that when in times of crisis or genuine turning points "the past has ceased to throw its light upon the future, the mind of man wanders in obscurity." At such moments (and to her the present was such a moment), she found the mind's obscurity to be the clearest indication of the need to consider anew the meaning of human responsibility and the power of human judgment.

In 1966 Hannah Arendt was famous, which is not to gainsay that to some her fame appeared as infamy. Three years earlier, in 1963, the publication of her book *Eichmann in Jerusalem: A Report on the Banality of Evil* created a storm of controversy that wrecked a number of close friendships and alienated her from almost the entire Jewish community worldwide. This was grievous to Arendt, who was born a German Jew, a fact she considered a "given" of her existence, a gift of a specific kind of experience that proved crucial in the development of her thought. To give a single example: When one is attacked as a Jew, Arendt found it necessary to respond as a Jew. To respond in the name of humanity, claiming the Rights of Man, was absurdly beside the point, the denial but not the refutation of the accusation that Jews were less than human, were nothing but vermin and like vermin should be gassed. The only feasible response was: I am a Jew, and I defend myself as a Jew to show that I have as much right to belong to the world as anyone else. Arendt's responsibility as a Jew issued in her call for a Jewish army to fight the enemies and destroyers of Jews.*

What were the reactions to *Eichmann?* The outrage of Jews can be summed up in their reaction to the less-than-a-dozen pages Arendt devoted to the "cooperation" given to Adolf Eichmann by some leaders of European Jewish communities in selecting those of their coreligionists, the less "prominent" ones, to precede them to the gas chambers. That this happened is a factual matter, brought up at the trial and corroborated both before and since the trial. But that Arendt's concept of the banality of evil trivialized what Eichmann had done and even exculpated him, made him less guilty, less "monstrous" than his victims, which was what was charged, was patently absurd. Whatever "cooperation" the Jewish leadership offered, it was Hitler and his henchmen, with the support of such a man as Eichmann, who initiated and carried out the "final solution" to the question of Jewish existence: systematic, industrialized murder. To be sure, what the Jewish leadership had done was a telling sign of the general moral breakdown, but no Jew bore any responsibility whatsoever for the genocidal policy itself, which was as self-evident to Arendt as it was to anyone else.

Ingenuous or disingenuous, the failure of her Jewish readership to recognize where specific responsibility lay, and where it did not, indicated to Arendt the complete reversal of the Socratic

---

*The much misunderstood importance of Arendt's experience as a Jew, including her views on Zionism and the formation of the state of Israel, will be the subject of a forthcoming volume in this series of her unpublished and uncollected writings.

proposition, "It is better to suffer wrong than to do wrong." For now it seemed not only understandable and acceptable but also "responsible" (so it was said) under Nazi rule for the Jewish elders to have done wrong, to have chosen the less "famous" to be sent first to their deaths, rather than to have suffered wrong themselves. When popular opinion sentenced him to death, Socrates judged his situation and decided to stay and die in Athens rather than to escape and live a meaningless life elsewhere, and for Arendt his example, more than any argument, established his proposition as the founding principle of Western moral thought.* Socrates lived in the distant past, under a regime that may have been corrupt but certainly was not evil in the sense of Hitler's Germany. Yet, are not moral principles meant to transcend historical time and the contingencies of this world?

Eichmann elicited different reactions, no less perplexing to Arendt. It was frequently said, for instance, that there is an Eichmann in all of us, meaning that under the conditions in which we live everyone, willy-nilly, is nothing but a "cog" in a machine, thereby collapsing the distinction between responsible and irresponsible behavior. For Arendt the chief virtue of the trial in Jerusalem, as of any trial, was that it did not treat the defendant Eichmann, the desk murderer par excellence, as a cog but as an individual on trial for his life, a particular man to be judged for his specific responsibility in the murders of millions of human beings. He himself had not committed the murders but had made

---

*In "Some Questions of Moral Philosophy" Arendt made it clear that she did not consider Socrates' life "political," although his death would prove momentous for Plato's political philosophy. When called upon to do so, he fulfilled his duty as an Athenian citizen, fighting as a soldier and at least once acting in an official capacity for Athens. But he preferred thinking with himself and with his friends to interacting with the "multitude," and in this sense his judgment and action when sentenced to death were moral rather than political.

them possible by supplying the victims, herding and shipping them to the factories of death at Auschwitz. Ultimately the court found Eichmann more guilty—and in this Arendt agreed with the court—than those who actually wielded the instruments of physical destruction.

Not in reference to Eichmann, yet strangely akin to this reaction, was another (mentioned in "Personal Responsibility Under Dictatorship") suggesting that in the terror of Nazi domination the temptation not to do right was tantamount to being forced to do wrong, and in such circumstances no one could be expected to behave like a saint. But if what Arendt wrote in *Eichmann* is read, it is clear that not she but the Israeli prosecutor raised the question of why Jews had not resisted and in some cases had even facilitated the processes of extermination. To her the introduction of the notion of temptation was a further indication of the displacement of morality, for it flies in the face of every notion of human freedom. Morality depends on freedom of choice, in which temptation and force are never the same; temptation cannot be, as Arendt said, "a moral justification" of any deed, whereas force has little if any moral implication for those subjected to it.

At least once it was said that, since "the murder of six million European Jews" was "the supreme tragic event of modern times," *Eichmann* was "the most interesting and moving work of art of the past ten years."* Arendt found the logic of this reaction extraordinarily inappropriate. She had not, like Dostoevsky or Melville, created a tragedy from her thought but had scrutinized the facts that unfolded during a particular trial. For her the only pertinent issue of the trial was a judgment (ultimately her own

---

*Susan Sontag, *New York Herald Tribune*, March 1, 1964.

and not the court's) that made manifest Eichmann's responsibility in having violated the plurality "of mankind in its entirety . . . human diversity as such . . . without which the very words 'mankind' or 'humanity' would be devoid of meaning." In other words, in the trial of Eichmann, Arendt discerned the sense in which his crime could rightfully be judged as a crime against humanity, against the human status, against every human being.

It was also said that the concept of the banality of evil presented a hard theory to refute because of its *plausibility*, a reaction echoed today in the term's incessant usage in newspaper accounts of common and petty criminal acts. To Arendt the banality of evil was not a theory or doctrine but signified the factual nature of the evil perpetrated by one thoughtless human being—by someone who never thought about what he was doing, either in his career as a Gestapo officer in charge of the transportation of Jews or as a prisoner in the dock. The whole course of the trial bore out and confirmed this. The brute fact of the banality of evil surprised and shocked her because, as she said, "it contradicts our theories concerning evil," pointing to something that though it is "true" is not in the least "plausible." In *Eichmann* Arendt had not dreamed up, or imagined, or even thought through the concept of the banality of evil. It was, she said, "thought-defying."

With one exception, the addresses, lectures, and essays collected in this volume date from after the trial and in different ways represent Arendt's struggle to understand the significance of Eichmann's inability to think. Eichmann stood out from the vast historical context she had explored in *The Origins of Totalitarianism* and *The Human Condition* as a particular man, an ordinary, normal man, a "buffoon," and as such an altogether unlikely perpetrator of evil. Arendt, alone, was struck by the fact that Eichmann's banality, his total lack of spontaneity, made him neither a "monster" nor a "demon" but nevertheless an agent of the most extreme evil. That perception was the catalyst of Arendt's final understanding of the primary topics of the present volume: responsibility and judgment.

Is there something that was not said but somehow lies behind these misunderstandings, as well as many others that have not been mentioned, of what Arendt wrote in *Eichmann*?* If there is one thing, I suspect that it is the truly bewildering problem of Eichmann's conscience, which no one apart from Arendt either saw, understood, or cared to broach. This failure is noteworthy in at least two respects: first, in his testimony Eichmann presented ample evidence that he possessed what is ordinarily called a "conscience." When examined by the Israeli police, he declared "that he had lived his whole life according to Kant's moral precepts," that he had acted "according to a Kantian definition of duty," that he had not simply obeyed the law of Hitler's Germany but had identified his will "with the principle behind the law."† Second (although this is almost always denied), nothing shows more conclusively that in confronting Eichmann's evidence Arendt was doing exactly what she claimed, reporting on what emerged during the trial, though admittedly at a level of complexity that is seldom reached in such reporting. That Eichmann's "conscience" came to light in the course of the trial is integral to the meaning of the banality of evil—it was the evidence for the former that culminated in the concept of the latter—but by the same token it has

*For a full account of the many articles and books that contributed to the controversy in the years immediately following the publication of *Eichmann* see R. L. Braham, *The Eichmann Case: A Source Book* (New York: World Federation of Hungarian Jews, 1969). Since 1969 practically all of the multifold works on Arendt have dealt with the concept of the banality of evil without achieving anything like a consensus as to its meaning, making *Eichmann* one of the most disputed books ever written.
†Eichmann's "principle" was Hitler's will and not Kant's practical reason.

to be added that, in its ongoing career in theoretical studies of evil, the banality of Eichmann has revealed the reluctance of philosophers, psychologists, and others whose intelligence is beyond question, to analyze the phenomenon of human conscience. They tend, on the contrary, to conceive it as the rationalization of a motive, or as an irresistible emotion, or as a "prescription" for action, or, more subtly, as an intention submerged in the unconscious. For whatever reason, the phenomenon of conscience seems recalcitrant to analysis.

However that may be, without intending to make a theory of the concept of the banality of evil, in "Thinking and Moral Considerations" Arendt asked herself the Kantian question "with what right did I possess and use [the concept]?" It is no accident that there, and in greater detail in the lectures that constitute "Some Questions of Moral Philosophy," Arendt proceeded by looking at the experiences embedded in the Latin etymology of the word "conscience" and its Greek cognates, by noting the crucial change from a negative to a positive function of conscience that occurred with the advent of Christianity and the discovery of the will, and finally by implying that the phenomenal reality of conscience may be discovered where it has seldom been sought, in the exercise of the faculty of judgment. It is almost as if she put the word "conscience" on trial, peppering it with questions whose living roots, though buried in the historical past, were nourished in her mind. That trial, in which Arendt appears as passionate inquirer and impartial judge, began in Jerusalem but did not end there and has not yet ended. There is certainly much more at stake in these investigations, which include Arendt's unfinished, posthumously published *The Life of the Mind,* than an attempt to put to rest the controversy surrounding *Eichmann,* which in any case they have not succeeded in doing.

At stake is Arendt's effort to understand anew the meaning of morality as the knowledge of the difference between right and wrong, between good and evil. It was Friedrich Nietzsche, the thinker and philologist with whom Arendt's profound rapport was due to a similar cast of mind rather than to intellectual influence—to a shared capacity for sudden insight rather than systematic philosophy—who suggested that morality and ethics are no more than what they denote: *customs and habits.* In her native land Arendt saw what she and many others had taken for granted, a seemingly sound and secure moral structure, collapse under Nazi rule, in the most extreme instance by reversing the commandment "Thou shalt not kill" to "Thou shalt kill"; and then after the end of World War II she saw another reversal in which the former structure was reinvoked. But then how sound and secure could it be? Had not Nietzsche finally been proved right in holding that the principles from which the norms and standards of human conduct are derived are *exchangeable* values? However much one might expect Arendt to have agreed, she did not. She believed that Nietzsche's "abiding greatness" lay not in having shown morality for what it is but in having "dared to demonstrate how shabby and meaningless [it] had become," which is something quite different. Like Nietzsche she rejected the imposition and acceptation of norms and values whose source is divine or natural law, under which all particular cases can be subsumed, but unlike him Arendt was genuinely astonished that in twenty-five hundred years "literature, philosophy, and religion" had not come up with "another word" for morality, or for its "preachings about the existence of a 'conscience' that speaks with an identical voice to all men." More than anything else her astonishment was due to the fact that some people do distinguish right from wrong and, which is more important, under any circumstances, as long as they *can,* will act according to the distinctions they themselves have made. Though they are neither saints nor heroes, and though they do not hear the voice of God or see by the universal light of nature *(lumen naturale)*, they know and abide by the difference between good and evil. In the world that had been revealed in the twentieth century, this fact was too portentous for Arendt to let pass as a matter of innate "nobility" of character.

From the 1940s at least until Stalin's death in 1953 the leitmotif of Arendt's work was what she called the "radical" or "absolute" evil of totalitarianism: the mass annihilation of human beings undertaken by Nazism and Bolshevism for no humanly comprehensible purpose. Totalitarianism defied and ravished human reason and, by exploding the traditional categories for understanding politics, law, and morality, tore apart the intelligible fabric of human experience. The possibility of demolishing the human world, although entirely without precedent, was demonstrated in the "experiments" conducted in the "laboratories" of totalitarian concentration camps. There the existence of distinct human beings, the substance of the idea of humanity, was obliterated; individual lives were made "superfluous" by transforming them into "inanimate" matter to fuel the engines of extermination, which accelerated the movement of the ideological laws of nature and history.* The evil of twentieth-century totalitarian domination was of course unknown to Nietzsche or anyone before him who had reflected on the age-old problem of human evil. By naming it "radical" Arendt meant that evil's root had for the first time appeared in the world.

But what Arendt herself had not realized before encountering

*In Nazi Germany the "law" of nature was to create one master race, which logically entails the extermination of all races declared "unfit to live"; in Bolshevism the "law" of history was to create one classless society, which logically entails the liquidation of all "dying" classes, i.e., of classes consisting of those "condemned to death." The reader will find little mention of Bolshevism in the present collection, because there the moral issue was masked by hypocrisy. Morally, though not socially, Nazism was the more revolutionary movement.

Eichmann's inability to reflect on what he had done, which she distinguished from stupidity, was that such evil could spread *limitlessly* across the earth, the most startling aspect of which was that its distension need not be rooted in an ideology of any kind. Human evil is limitless when it brings forth no remorse, when its acts are forgotten as soon as they are committed. It was only then that for her the disposition of individual persons, not necessarily to resist but to refrain from doing evil, to reject or not even be tempted by evil, demanded the attention of everyone, not only philosophers and other intellectuals, to what "for want of a better term," as she put it, "we call morality." In other words, in these late writings Arendt was intent to salvage moral phenomena, and at the same time to show that conscience is not, as Nietzsche thought, merely a late epiphenomenon in the "genealogy of morals." In one way or another all the pieces in this collection can be read as tales of the missing "better term," just as one of them, "*The Deputy:* Guilt by Silence?," can also be read as the tale of a missing pope. Arendt wrote *Eichmann* in a state of "euphoria," not because rootless evil could be thought but because it could be overcome by *thinking*.

But how unfamiliar and strange all this must sound to readers who rightly consider politics to be the overall focus of Arendt's work. In many places she distinguished politics from morality, much as Machiavelli had done long before her in the Renaissance. Here, in "Collective Responsibility," she makes that distinction unequivocally: "In the center of moral considerations of human conduct stands the self; in the center of political considerations stands the world." This case can be made still stronger by adding that morality and also religion tend to negate (though not destroy, as totalitarianism did) the fundamental political propensity, rooted in the condition of human plurality, to care more for the world than for either oneself or the salvation of one's soul. Are not moral and religious "truths" and "true standards," regardless if they are fruits of philosophical contemplation or spiritual meditation, actualized in the mind, "seen" by the mind's eye in what, from the point of view of the world, is the most intensely private of experiences? Theoretically, from that viewpoint, these truths deprive those who hold them as "absolutes" from participating in public affairs, since genuine political activity, which by definition depends on the uncoerced agreement of others, cannot easily accommodate anyone who answers to "higher" than publicly enacted and publicly amendable laws. Here Arendt was close indeed to Machiavelli: when moral and religious commandments are pronounced in public in defiance of the diversity of human opinions they corrupt both the world and themselves.

Moreover, if human freedom, as Arendt believed, is the raison d'être of politics, and if the experience of freedom is unambiguous only in action, which despite Kant she also believed, then in distinguishing thinking from acting she is pointing out two activities that differ essentially from one another. Thinking is *self*-reflective, whereas an agent can act only with others than himself; and the activity of thinking, which takes place in solitude, stops when a thinker begins to act, just as the activity of acting, which requires the company of others, stops when an agent begins to think with himself. But in her concern with the *activities* themselves rather than with the results of either thinking or acting, Arendt took a step in the direction of Kant. Because the outcome of our acts are determined contingently and not autonomously, most often by the reactions of others to what we intend to accomplish, in his moral philosophy Kant located freedom in our motivation to act, our uncoerced conscious decision to obey the law of which we ourselves are the author, the "law of freedom" and its categorical imperative. For the same reason, because we cannot know in advance the results of what we are doing when we act with others, Arendt found the experience of freedom actualized in the process of initiation, in bringing something new, whatever it turns out to be, into the world. Arendt found that what Kant meant by human freedom, that is, autonomy, does not depend on obedience to law, which by definition denies freedom, but on the *appearance* in the world of the moral person or personality who embodies the law. Arendt agreed that this Kantian person (here the word "moral" is redundant) is self-constituted in the activity of self-reflection, and therein lay her problem. When that person appears amidst his fellow men he stands apart from them in the sense that he is responsible only to himself: to him every inclination, to do right as well as wrong, is a temptation that leads him "astray" from himself and into the world, and for that reason must be resisted. The categorical imperative may indeed be the most compelling account ever offered of the traditional notion of moral consciousness or conscience; Kant himself thought of it as a "compass" derived from the universal law of pure practical reason, pointing out right from wrong and available to every rational creature. But to Arendt it was insufficiently political, because the dutiful agent takes no responsibility for the consequences of his acts, because Kant's notion of duty, as Eichmann showed, can be perverted, and because (although of course Kant knew nothing of this) the limitlessness of thoughtless evil eludes its conceptual grasp.

Another ingredient that should be added to this cursory view of Arendt's concern with what we are accustomed to think of as morality is the example of Jesus of Nazareth. In his love of action, of doing good—of effecting the unprecedented by performing "miracles," and of making new beginnings possible by

forgiving trespasses—which in its sheer energy she compared to
Socrates' love of thinking, Arendt pointedly distinguished Jesus
from Christ the Savior of sinners in the Christian religion. What
matters most in this context is Jesus' insistence that in order to do
good the goodness of what is done must be hidden not only from
others but also from the doer (his left hand must not know what
his right hand does), which to Arendt signified the doer's selflessness, the absence of the doer's self and not merely of his self-
righteousness. In this sense the doer of good is more alone in
the world than even the thinker, since he has not even himself
for company. How then are we to comprehend the distinction
between good and evil, on which the Nazarene also insisted,
unless its origin lies in selfless action and not, as Kant thought, in
self-reflective thought? Jesus' sublime and revolutionary carelessness (when asked What should we do? he answered, Follow me,
do as I do, do not worry about tomorrow) implies a lack of concern for stabilizing institutions, perhaps even for life itself, both of
which are clearly reflected in the eschatological beliefs of early
Christians. But they also bring to mind and may in part explain
Arendt's interpretation of Machiavellian *virtù* as virtuosity.*

There was surely no greater virtuoso of action than Jesus. The
distinguishing mark of Arendt's conception of action, as opposed
to behavior, is that it is its own end. Because the goals set by some
agents inevitably conflict with those set by others, the meaning of
action, if it has any, must lie within itself. For Arendt this distinguished action not only from laboring for the sake of life but also
from any kind of making, since making's end lies not in the

*To see across two millennia and of all people Jesus and Machiavelli in somewhat the
same light casts light on the daring as well as the danger, the iconoclastic quality, of
Arendt's way of thinking after the rupture of the tradition of Western thought.

activity but outside and beyond it in whatever is made, including works of productive art which add to and embellish the world. Arendt believed that Machiavelli shared her understanding of action as the one perfect, pure activity of active life, and that Jesus in his "carelessness," which is to say his *goal-lessness,* exemplified it. The problem in all of this is *who* is good, particularly since Jesus denied that he himself was, but also because Machiavelli considered himself obliged to teach princes how *not* to be good. According to Arendt the uniqueness of the agent, revealed in action, can appear to others as "glory" or "greatness," yet he cannot appear as uniquely good. The reason he cannot is twofold: if what is taken for morality is rule-defined, as it was for both Jesus and Machiavelli, there is nothing unique about adhering to those rules; and, again to both Jesus and Machiavelli, and in much the same sense, if doing good is to be good it must not appear as such in the world.

Whence then is good? When Jesus enjoined us to turn the other cheek when we are struck, to give not just our coat, which is demanded, but our cloak as well, and in short to love not only our neighbor as ourself but also our enemy, he cast aside the rules of traditional morality, or, rather, judged them inadequate. Neither Jesus nor Machiavelli were bound by conventional standards, and both offered examples of action whose principles shone forth in the action itself. Those principles included faith and courage, but they did not include distrust or hatred, which cannot appear as either glorious or great. Of course the foregoing comparison of Jesus and Machiavelli has its limits. What I have tried to show is that both were selfless actors (in Machiavelli's case a frustrated actor, a would-be founder of republics) and that neither was a philosopher, which points to their lack of interest in the will, the mental faculty that moves us to act. With the advent of Christianity, theologians looked on the faculty of the will as crucial in determining the bliss of heaven or the torment of hell as the condition of an individual's *future* life, his eternal life after death. Arendt viewed Paul, as opposed to Jesus, as the founder not only of the Christian religion, but of Christian *philosophy,* who in his effort to become worthy of salvation discovered that he could not do the good he willed; what he discovered, in other words, was that the *I-will* was split from the *I-can.* While Paul saw this split as a contradiction between spirit and body, which required divine Grace to be healed, Augustine later radicalized his doctrine. Augustine situated the contradiction within the will itself, within the will's freedom *as its own cause.* For him it was not the body that disobeyed the will but the will that disobeyed itself. As *conscience,* being conscious of the difference between good and evil, the will is positive: it commands what ought to be done, but at the same time, in its freedom, it prevents what it commands.

Arendt, on whom Augustine exerted great influence, saw that the inability of the will to effect the good that it itself wills raised troubling moral questions: if it is divided against itself can the will do any good at all? "And yet without a will how could I ever be moved to act?" Arendt was deeply indebted to Augustine for his experience of *thinking* as an activity guided by love of the goodness of what exists. Because thinking cannot be guided by evil, since evil destroys what exists, she came to believe that the activity of thinking conditions whoever engages in it against evildoing. As important as that was to her, she knew better than to suggest that thinking determines the goodness of specific acts,* which is to say that thinking in itself does not resolve the problem

---

*Heidegger provides a case in point, but by no means the only one. Arendt believed that in part the *déformation professionelle* of philosophers was a proclivity for tyranny.

of action as it appears in the inner contradictoriness of the will. In regard to the spontaneity of action, the will's freedom is an *abyss*.

In a late (1973) sketch for remarks delivered to the American Society of Christian Ethics,* Arendt said that "for the first time since antiquity" we are living in a world that lacks the stability of authority, and, as far as moral action is concerned, especially the authority of the church.† For centuries the church's authority held the will's oscillations in abeyance, constraining action by the threat of damnation, but now, she said, hardly anyone, and certainly not the masses, still believes in that authority. Since, to her, action and beginning were one and the same, Arendt then drew attention to the fact that all beginnings contain "an element of utter arbitrariness," and related this arbitrariness to natality as the accidental condition of our birth. She meant, on the one hand, that the meetings of our parents, grandparents, and progenitors, as far back as we care to look, are contingent or chance events having no necessary cause. On the other hand, she meant that our contingency as beginnings is the price we pay for being free, for being able to experience freedom as beginning. For Arendt the contingency of human freedom is the real crisis in which we live today; it cannot be avoided, and the only meaningful question that can be asked is whether or not our freedom pleases us, whether or not we are willing to pay its price.

In her remarks Arendt went on to say that Socratic thinking, thinking in its "maieutic function" or "midwifery," *corresponds* to our crisis by preparing us to meet whatever appears, whatever comes to us, so to speak, from the future. In questioning the opin-

---

*These remarks apparently were Arendt's response to several papers presented on her work.
†Arendt's much-debated "preference" for antiquity over modernity here appears as their *similarity*; looking to antiquity it is possible to see ourselves from a distance, that is, with impartiality.

ions and prejudices (pre-judgments) of his interlocutors, Socrates never discovered "any child . . . that was not a wind egg," which to Arendt meant that when such thinking ended not only his interlocutors but also Socrates was "empty." "Once you are empty," she said, "you are prepared to judge" *without* subsuming particular cases under rules and standards that have vanished in the gale of thought. There is, however, no necessity that you will judge. If judgment is exercised the phenomena are met "head-on" in their contingent reality: *this* is good, *that* bad, *this* right, and *that* wrong. Arendt believed that we *can* judge moral and political phenomena as in fact we do judge a particular rose that has appeared in our garden, and not another rose, to be beautiful. In other words, our judgment in these matters is free, which is the reason that Arendt, in "Some Questions of Moral Philosophy," viewed it as linked to the free choice *(liberum arbitrium)* of the will, the arbitrating function Augustine discerned in the will before he found and concentrated on the will's inner contradiction. Arendt understood the judge to be an arbiter of the "utter arbitrariness" of all beginnings, and judgment to be a faculty distinct from the will, a faculty that Kant, many centuries after Augustine, discovered in the realm of aesthetics. It would be interesting to speculate, though this is not the place, on the relevance to these matters of Augustine's role in establishing the authority of the church, as well as on the fact that Kant made his discovery during an unprecedented event, the French Revolution, which profoundly interested him.

In her remarks Arendt indicated that the "imperishability" of works of productive art, the fact that we can and do judge them as beautiful after hundreds or thousands of years, brings the durability of the past and hence the stability of the world into our experience. But unlike the productive arts which bolster the structure of the world, action, without any plan or paradigm, *changes* it. Action, as the twentieth-century bore witness, demonstrates the fragility and the malleability of the world which lurk in the will's abyssal freedom. Yet, according to Arendt, despite its "haphazard" and "chaotic" contingency, *after it is over* a story can be told that "makes sense" of action. How, she asked, is that possible? As opposed to philosophers of history, who typically read either progress or decline in the results of action, Arendt's concern was with free action, of which the results are unknown while it is being enacted. If the faculty of judgment stands apart from action to fit it into a story, it must also be operative in the actor, whom Arendt likened to a performer. Although the actor's performance disappears as soon as it ends, while it lasts it "lightens up" the principle that inspires it. The actor spontaneously judges that principle fit to appear in the world: it pleases him, and his action is an appeal to others, a plea that it will also please them. The actor who is too busy to think while acting is not mindless, and all mental activity, according to Arendt, reflects back on itself. Unlike thinking and willing, however, judging is closely connected to the sense that corresponds to it, that is, to taste. The reflectivity of judging is qualified by the "it-pleases" or "it-displeases" of taste, and when judgment reflects the taste of other judges, the immediacy of the judge's own taste is transcended. The act of judging transforms taste, the most subjective of our senses, into the specifically human *common sense* that orients men, men who judge, in the world.

Judgment, then, is a sort of balancing activity, "frozen" in the figure of the scales of justice that weigh the stability of the world in which its past is present *against* the world's renewal, its openness to action, even if that may shake the world's very structure. In her unwritten volume on *Judging* Arendt may have crossed some of the *t*'s and dotted some of the *i*'s she mentioned at the end of "Some Questions of Moral Philosophy." No one of course can say what that volume would have contained, or whether it would have resolved the many problems of action Arendt distinguished in the writings that compose the first part, "Responsibility," of the present volume. With some degree of confidence it may be said that the ability to think, which Eichmann lacked, is the precondition of judging, and that the refusal as well as the inability to judge, to imagine before your eyes the others whom your judgment represents and to whom it responds, invite evil to enter and infect the world. It may also be said that the faculty of judgment, unlike the will, does not contradict itself: the ability to formulate a judgment is not split from its expression, in fact they are virtually the same in speech as in deed. As to Arendt's "better term" one might say that the phenomenon of conscience is real in listening and attending to the voices of the living, and of the no longer and not yet living, who share in common a mutually pleasing and enduring world, the possibility of which both instigates and is the result of judgment. One might also say that the ability to respond by judging impartially—considering and treating with consideration as many different points of view as possible—the fitness or unfitness of particular phenomena to appear in the world seamlessly joins politics and morality in the realm of action. The second part of this volume, "Judgment," offers examples of Arendt's formidable capacity to respond in that manner. Finally, it may be asked if Arendt was not referring to the strictly moral power of judgment when at the end of "Thinking and Moral Considerations" she wrote that judging "may indeed prevent catastrophes, at least for myself, in the rare moments when the chips are down"?

A NOTE ON THE TEXT

All the texts—lectures, addresses, and essays—included in *Responsibility and Judgment*—were written by Hannah Arendt in English, a language she learned when she was already thirty-five years old and had arrived in America as a refugee from Nazi-dominated Europe. Within a year, by 1942, she was writing in her newly acquired language, but as long as she lived she submitted her English works for "Englishing" prior to publishing them, a process that has been continued here. Arendt was a natural writer; after having *thought,* she once said, she sat down and *typed* as fast as she could move her fingers. That worked brilliantly when she wrote in German, her mother tongue, but anyone who has pored over her English manuscripts knows that her speed in writing brought difficulties in its wake. She had an enormous vocabulary, enhanced by her knowledge of ancient Greek and Latin, but in English the immediacy of her voice, its unique quality, resulted in overly long sentences whose wording and punctuation often do not accord with accepted usage. Another problem is that the manuscripts contain lots of cuttings and pastings (she wrote before personal computers) and handwritten additions whose legibility and intended location are frequently far from clear. The editor's mandate is to make Arendt's English writings coherent without altering what she wanted to say or how she wanted to say it: to modify her syntax when necessary but to preserve her style that reflects the sinuosity of her mind.

The text of the "Prologue" is a speech Arendt delivered in Copenhagen in 1975, upon accepting the Danish government's Sonning Prize for her contribution to European civilization. Arendt was the first American citizen to win the prize and the first woman—past winners had included Niels Bohr, Winston Churchill, Bertrand Russell, and Albert Schweitzer. In her acceptance speech, she asked the unusual question of why she, "who is neither a public figure nor has the desire to become one," should be awarded a "public honor," since thinkers "live in hiding," as far as possible from the light of publicity. This was not modesty, which differs from humility and is always false: twenty years earlier she had written to her husband that appearing in "the public eye" was a "misfortune." It made her "feel as if I have to go around looking for myself."* In the speech Arendt performed in public the rare and difficult act of self-judgment, thereby indicating that the ability to judge *this* right and *that* wrong first and foremost depends on the self-understanding of the judge. Arendt judged herself and in doing so exemplified the ancient injunction to Know Thyself as the condition of judgment. She used the Latin noun *"persona,"* derived from the verb *"per-sonare,"* which originally referred to the voice sounding through a stage actor's mask. She used it not as the Romans had, metaphorically referring to the political person as distinguished from "a member of the human species," but in her own metaphorical sense of a *somebody* who is "identifiable" without being "definable," a unique *thisness* that perdures within the exchangeable masks the actor dons for his role in "the great play of the world," one of which she was wearing as

Within Four Walls: The Correspondence between Hannah Arendt and Heinrich Bluecher 1936–1968, ed. Lotte Kohler (New York: Harcourt, 2000), p. 236.

she spoke. It is hard to imagine how Arendt could have suggested more transparently that the judge cannot be severed from the self-less actor, whose uniqueness appears only to others, as his inner, invisible, audible other side.

The most daunting task in this volume was presented by "Some Questions of Moral Philosophy." In 1965 and 1966 Arendt gave two courses, the first at the New School for Social Research, which bore the present title, and the second at the University of Chicago, called "Basic Moral Propositions." The New School course consisted of four long lectures, and the Chicago course of seventeen sessions that for the most part utilized the lecture material. The edited lectures make up the body of the text included here, while significant variants of her thought in "Basic Moral Propositions" have been incorporated in the endnotes. In this text the reader has the opportunity to listen to Arendt as a teacher, and perhaps visualize her in that role. I want to thank Elizabeth M. Meade for her help in preparing successive drafts of "Some Questions of Moral Philosophy." Needless to say, any gaffes that remain in the final version are my responsibility.

"Personal Responsibility Under Dictatorship," "Collective Responsibility," "Thinking and Moral Considerations" and "Home to Roost" were also originally prepared by Arendt as pieces to be spoken, either as lectures or public addresses. Since the "Prologue" and "Home to Roost" were delivered in the last year of Arendt's life, this collection begins and ends with her last two appearances in public. "Personal Responsibility Under Dictatorship" is known to some of Arendt's readers in a much shorter form broadcast in England and America and published in *The Listener* in 1964. The full manuscript is published here for the first time. "Collective Responsibility" was not Arendt's title but rather the title of a symposium, held on December 27, 1968, at a meeting of the American Philosophical Society. In responding to a paper

presented there, she was intent to distinguish *political* from personal responsibility and to point out different nuances of meaning in the ways the word "responsibility" is used. Except in three
cases, mentioned in the endnotes, references to the paper to which
she responded have been deleted. The choice was either that or to
include the other paper, which was not deemed advisable. On
December 21, 1968, she wrote to Mary McCarthy: "Your letter
came just when I was trying to figure out what to say as discussant
about a paper on Collective Responsibility next week in Washington, Philosophical Society, without losing my temper and becoming outrageously impolite. The irrelevancies of academe are
beyond belief and expectation."*

The remaining pieces included in *Responsibility and Judgment*
are essays. "Reflections on Little Rock" is included as a prime
example of Arendt's judgment. It is the only pre–Eichmann piece
in this collection and as such merits some explanation. After long
delays, Arendt withdrew "Reflections" from *Commentary,* which
had commissioned it, and published it in *Dissent,* accompanied by
the following editorial disclaimer: "We publish [this essay] not
because we agree with it—quite the contrary!—but because we
believe in freedom of expression even for views that seem to us
entirely mistaken." The vitriol of the reactions to "Reflections,"
anticipating the controversy that erupted four years later over
Eichmann, was due to its having struck a raw liberal nerve, which
it continues to do today. Arendt was neither a liberal nor a conservative, but here questioned the tendency of liberals to subsume
the particular question of black children's education under the
general political rule of "equality." She opposed racial legislation
in any form, particularly antimiscegenation laws, but also the

Between Friends: the Correspondence of Hannah Arendt and Mary McCarthy 1949–1975,
ed. Carol Brightman (New York: Harcourt Brace, 1995), p. 228.

Supreme Court's decision to legally enforce a policy of school desegregation. To her that abrogated the private right of parents to select their children's schools and flew in the face of the preeminently discriminatory character of the social realm. The photograph that is reproduced had exemplary status in Arendt's judgment, just as the ability to see through her own eyes the possible viewpoint of a black mother was fundamental for her in formulating a judgment that sought to be impartial.

What appears as the "Introduction" to Arendt's "Reflections" was originally published as a "Reply" to two of her critics. To neither of them did she in fact reply: one, in a brash combination of ignorance and prejudice, placed himself outside the community of judges; the other so thoroughly misunderstood Arendt that, instead of replying, she wrote what really is an introduction to the essay, a summation of its arguments emphasizing their principles. Later, in 1965, Arendt did reply in a letter to Ralph Ellison, admitting that she had overlooked the "ideal of sacrifice" of black parents in introducing their children to the realities of racial experience. That is an element which rightfully claims a place in judgment's quest, not for apodictic certainty but for a consensus reached in the agreement of diverse opinion. Yet it hardly alters Arendt's basic constitutional argument against enforced school desegregation, any more than it accounts for the absence of the black student's father in the photograph. The desegregation of schools has not achieved its intended goals; many of Arendt's warnings have been realized, and the entire question remains open to judgment.*

*A sensitive account of Arendt's judgment in "Reflections on Little Rock" can be found in Kirstie M. McClure, "The Odor of Judgment: Exemplarity, Propriety, and Politics in the Company of Hannah Arendt," in *Hannah Arendt and the Meaning of Politics,* eds. C. Calhoun and J. McGowan (Minneapolis, University of Minnesota Press: 1997), pp. 53–84. See also Learned Hand's Holmes Lectures at Harvard Law School for his opposition to *Brown v. Board of Education.*

"*The Deputy:* Guilt by Silence?" and "Auschwitz on Trial" are both also examples of Arendt's judgment, the first of Pius XII's "guilt," which in her reading of Hochhuth's play was for something left undone, a sin of omission. The pope had not denounced Hitler's destruction of European Jewry, and if he had done so the consequences of his action were unknowable to him or anyone else. Her judgment of the pope raised the further question of why *we* avoid our responsibility to judge the failure of a particular man, who claimed to be Jesus Christ's deputy on earth, to act; and why, rather than exercise judgment, we prefer to throw out two thousand years of Christianity and discharge the very idea of humanity. The second was her judgment of a world turned upside down, a factitious world that had lost all semblance of reality, in which every imaginable horror was possible even when not officially permitted. In the essay on Auschwitz Arendt showed one thing that seemingly was impossible, namely, rendering justice to the only decent man on trial, the physician Franz Lucas, who, unlike Eichmann, apparently *did* think about what he had done and was struck dumb when he realized the full implications of having been a "citizen" of a nakedly criminal state.

Acknowledgments. It would be sheer folly to attempt to acknowledge individually the many scholars whose work on Arendt has influenced and guided me from the beginning. I thank them collectively, and will mention by name only a few friends, including scholars, who in different ways have supported the general project of publishing Arendt's unpublished and uncollected writings, of which this volume forms a part. In alphabetical order they are Dore Ashton, Bethania Assy, Jack Barth, Richard J. Bernstein, John Black, Edna Brocke, Margaret Canovan, Keith David, Bernard Flynn, Antonia Grunenberg, Rochelle Gurstein, Gerard

R. Hoolahan, George Kateb, Lotte Kohler, Mary and Robert Lazarus, Ursula Ludz, Arien Mack, Matti Megged, Gail Persky, Jonathan Schell, Ray Tsao, Dana Villa, Judith Walz, David Wigdor, and Elisabeth Young-Bruehl.

It is an immense satisfaction to be working with Schocken Books, not least because Hannah Arendt was an editor at Schocken from 1946 to 1948, where she brought out, among other works, luminous editions of Kafka. I am grateful to Rahel Lerner for having located the photograph that illustrates the essay on Little Rock. My gratitude to Daniel Frank, not only for his patience but also for his acute editorial judgment, is unbounded. Anyone who has worked with Arendt knows how unusual it is to find, particularly today, a publisher who has deep knowledge or who cares deeply about her thought. To find knowledge and care in the same person, as I have in Dan Frank, is virtually unheard of.

Lastly, thoughtful young men and women in many countries have begun to understand that being at home in the world requires rethinking the past and reconstituting its treasures and disasters as *their* treasures and disasters. They recognize that "thinking without a bannister," in Arendt's phrase, is the condition under which the will to act still makes sense to them. These youths, who turn to "Hannah" (as they call her) as a guide they trust, will find the difficulty and urgency of what faces them nowhere more decisively confirmed than in these writings on responsibility and judgment. This volume, therefore, is dedicated to the "newcomers," as Hannah Arendt called them, on whom the future of the human world, if it is to have one, depends.

RESPONSIBILITY AND JUDGMENT

PROLOGUE*

Ever since I received the rather startling news of your decision to choose me as the recipient of the Sonning Prize in recognition of my contribution to European civilization, I have been trying to figure out what I could possibly say in response. Seen from the perspective of my own life, on the one hand, and of my general attitude to such public events on the other, the simple fact with which I find myself confronted stirred up so many partly conflicting reactions and reflections that it wasn't easy for me to come to terms with it—apart from the fundamental gratitude which leaves us helpless whenever the world offers us a true gift, that is, something which really comes to us gratuitously, when Fortuna smiles, splendidly disregarding whatever we have cherished consciously or half-consciously as our aims, expectations, or goals.

Let me try and sort these things out. I'll start with the purely biographical. It is no small matter to be recognized for a contribution to European civilization for somebody who left Europe thirty-five years ago by no means voluntarily—and then became a citizen of the United States, entirely and consciously voluntarily because the Republic was indeed a government of law and not of men. What I learned in these first crucial years between immigra-

*This speech was delivered by Hannah Arendt upon receiving Denmark's Sonning Prize in 1975. See the introduction for further commentary.

tion and naturalization amounted roughly to a self-taught course in the political philosophy of the Founding Fathers, and what convinced me was the factual existence of a body politic, utterly unlike the European nation-states with their homogeneous populations, their organic sense of history, their more or less decisive division into classes, and their national sovereignty with its notion of *raison d'état*. The idea that when the chips were down diversity must be sacrificed to the *"union sacrée"* of the nation, once the greatest triumph of the assimilatory power of the dominant ethnic group, only now has begun to crumble under the pressure of the threatening transformation of all government—the government of the United states not excluded—into bureaucracies, the rule of neither law nor men but of anonymous offices or computers whose entirely depersonalized domination may turn out to be a greater threat to freedom and to that minimum of civility, without which no communal life is conceivable, than the most outrageous arbitrariness of past tyrannies has ever been. But these dangers of sheer bigness coupled with technocracy whose dominance threatens indeed all forms of government with extinction, with "withering away"—at first still an ideological well-intended pipe dream whose nightmarish properties could be detected only by critical examination—were not yet on the agenda of day-to-day politics, and what influenced me when I came to the United States was precisely the freedom of becoming a citizen without having to pay the price of assimilation.

I am, as you know, a Jew, *feminini generis* as you can see, born and educated in Germany as, no doubt, you can hear, and formed to a certain extent by eight long and rather happy years in France. I don't know what I contributed to European civilization, but I do admit that I clung throughout these years to this European background in all its details with great tenacity occasionally amounting to a slightly polemical stubbornness since I lived of course among people, often among old friends, who tried very hard to do just the opposite: to do their best to behave, to sound, and to feel like "true Americans," following mostly the sheer force of habit, the habit of living in a nation-state in which you must be like a national if you wish to belong. My trouble was that I had never wished to belong, not even in Germany, and that I therefore had difficulty in understanding the great role which homesickness quite naturally plays among all immigrants, especially in the United States where national origin, after it lost its political relevance, became the strongest bond in society and in private life. However, what for those around me was a country, perhaps a landscape, a set of habits and traditions, and, most importantly, a certain mentality, was for me a language. And if I ever did anything consciously for European civilization, it certainly was nothing but the deliberate intent, from the moment I fled Germany, not to exchange my mother tongue against whatever language I was offered or forced to use. It seemed to me that for most people, namely, all those who are not especially gifted for languages, the mother tongue remains the only reliable yardstick for whatever languages later are acquired through learning; and this for the simple reason that the words we use in ordinary speech receive their specific weight, the one that guides our usage and saves it from mindless clichés, through the manifold associations which arise automatically and uniquely out of the treasure of great poetry with which that particular language and no other has been blessed.

The second issue which could not but come up for special consideration from the perspective of my own life concerns the country to which I now owe this recognition. I have always been fascinated by the particular way the Danish people and their government handled and solved the highly explosive problems posed by the Nazi conquest of Europe. I have often thought that this extraordinary story, of which you, of course, know more than I do, should be required reading in all political science courses which deal with the relations between power and violence, whose frequent equation belongs among the elementary fallacies not only of political theory but of actual political practice. This episode of your history offers a highly instructive example of the great power potential inherent in nonviolent action and in resistance to an opponent possessing vastly superior means of violence. And since the most spectacular victory in this battle concerns the defeat of the "Final Solution" and the salvation of nearly all the Jews on Danish territory, regardless of their origin, whether they were Danish citizens or stateless refugees from Germany, it seems indeed only natural that Jews who are survivors of the catastrophe should feel themselves related to this country in a very special way.

There are two things which I found particularly impressive in this story. There is *first* the fact that prior to the war Denmark had treated its refugees by no means nicely; like other nation-states it refused them naturalization and permission to work. Despite the absence of anti-Semitism, Jews as foreigners were not welcome, but the right to asylum, nowhere else respected, apparently was considered sacrosanct. For when the Nazis demanded first only stateless persons for deportation, that is, German refugees whom they had deprived of their nationality, the Danes explained that because these refugees were no longer German citizens the Nazis could not claim them without Danish assent. And *second,* while there were a few countries in Nazi-occupied Europe which succeeded by hook or by crook in saving most of their Jews, I think the Danes were the only ones who dared speak out on the subject to their masters. And the result was that under the pressure of public opinion, and threatened neither by armed resistance nor by guerrilla tactics, the German officials in the country changed their minds; they were no longer reliable, they were overpowered by what they had most disdained, mere words, spoken freely and publicly. This had happened nowhere else.

Let me now come to the other side of these considerations. This ceremony today is no doubt a public event, and the honor which you bestow upon its recipient expresses a public recognition of someone who by this very circumstance is transformed into a public figure. In this respect, I am afraid, your choice is open to doubt. I do not wish to raise here the delicate question of merit; an honor, if I understand it rightly, gives us an impressive lesson in humility, for it implies that it is not for us to judge ourselves, that we are not fit to judge our own accomplishments as we judge those of others. I am quite willing to accept this necessary humility because I have always believed that no one can know himself, for no one *appears* to himself as he appears to others. Only poor Narcissus will let himself be deluded by his own reflected image, pining away from love of a mirage. But while I am willing to yield to humility when confronted with the obvious fact that no one can be a judge in his own case, I am not willing to give up my faculty of judgment altogether, and say, as perhaps a true Christian believer would say, "Who am I to judge?" As a matter of purely personal, individual inclination I would, I think, agree with the poet W. H. Auden:

> Private faces in public places
> Are wiser and nicer
> Than public faces in private places.*

In other words, by personal temperament and inclination— those innate psychic qualities which form not necessarily our final

*From W. H. Auden, "Shorts."—Ed.

judgments but certainly our prejudices and instinctive impulses—
I tend to shy away from the public realm. This may sound false
or inauthentic to those who have read certain of my books and
remember my praise, perhaps even glorification, of the public
realm as offering the proper space of appearances for political
speech and action. In matters of theory and understanding it is
not uncommon for outsiders and mere spectators to gain a sharper
and deeper insight into the actual meaning of what happens to go
on before or around them than would be possible for the actual
actors and participants, who are entirely absorbed, as they must
be, by the events themselves of which they are a part. It is indeed
quite possible to understand and reflect about politics without
being a so-called political animal.

These original impulses, birth defects if you wish, were
strongly supported by two very different trends, both inimical to
everything public, which quite naturally coincided during the
twenties of this century, the period after World War I, which even
then, at least in the opinion of the contemporary younger generation, marked the decline of Europe. My own decision to study
philosophy was quite common then, though perhaps not run-of-
the-mill, and this commitment to a *bios theōrētikos*, to a contem-
plative way of life, already implied, even though I may not have
known it, a noncommitment to the public. Old Epicurus' exhorta-
tion to the philosopher, *lathē biōsas*, "live in hiding," frequently
misunderstood as a counsel of prudence, actually arises quite
naturally out of the way of life of the thinker. For thinking itself,
as distinct from other human activities, not only is an activity that
is invisible—that does not manifest itself outwardly—but also
and in this respect perhaps uniquely, has no *urge* to appear or even
a very restricted impulse to communicate to others. Since Plato,
thinking has been defined as a soundless dialogue between me and
myself; it is the only way in which I can keep myself company and

be content with it. Philosophy is a solitary business, and it seems only natural that the need for it arises in times of transition when men no longer rely on the stability of the world and their role in it, and when the question concerning the general conditions of human life, which as such are properly coeval with the appearance of man on earth, gain an uncommon poignancy. Hegel may have been right: "The owl of Minerva spreads its wings only with the falling of dusk."

This falling of dusk, the darkening of the public scene, however, did not take place in silence by any means. On the contrary, never was the public scene so filled with public announcements, usually quite optimistic, and the noise that moved the air was composed not only of the propaganda slogans of the two antagonistic ideologies, each promising a different wave of the future, but also by the down-to-earth statements of respectable politicians and statements from left-of-center, right-of-center, and center, all of which together had the net effect of desubstantializing every issue they touched, in addition to confusing utterly the minds of their audiences. This almost automatic rejection of everything public was very widespread in the Europe of the twenties with its "lost generations"—as they called themselves—who of course were minorities in all countries, vanguards or elites, depending on how they were evaluated. That they were small in number does not make them any less characteristic of the climate of the times, although it may explain the curious general misrepresentation of the "roaring twenties," their exaltation and the almost total oblivion of the disintegration of all political institutions that preceded the great catastrophes of the thirties. Testimony to this antipublic climate of the times can be found in poetry, in art, and in philosophy; it was the decade when Heidegger discovered *das man,* the "They" as opposed to the "authentic being a self," and when Bergson in France found it necessary "to recover the fundamental self" from the "requirements of social life in general and language in particular." It was of that decade in England that Auden said, in four lines what to many must have sounded almost too commonplace to be said at all:

> All words like Peace and Love,
> All sane affirmative speech,
> Had been soiled, profaned, debased
> To a horrid mechanical screech.*

Such inclinations—idiosyncracies? matters of taste?—which I have tried to date historically and explain factually, if acquired in the formative years of one's life, are liable to extend very far. They can lead to a passion for secrecy and anonymity, as if only that could matter to you personally which could be kept secret— "Never seek to tell thy love / Love that never told can be" or *"Willst du dein Herz mir schenken, / So fang es heimlich an"*—and as though even a name known in public, that is, *fame*, could only taint you with the inauthenticity of Heidegger's "They," with Bergson's "social self," and corrupt your speech with the vulgarity of Auden's "horrid mechanical screech." There existed after World War I a curious social structure which still has escaped the attention of the professional literary critics as well as that of the professional historians or social scientists, and which could best be described as an international "society of celebrities"; even today it would not be too difficult to draw up a list of its members, and one would find among them none of the names of those who in the end turned out to be the most influential authors of the period. It is true that none of those "internationals" of the twenties responded very well to their collective expectation of soli-

---

*From W. H. Auden, "We Too Had Known Golden Hours."—Ed.

darity in the thirties, but it is, I think, also irrefutable that no one of them crumbled faster or threw the rest into greater despair than the entire sudden collapse of this apolitical society whose members, spoilt by the "radiant power of fame," were less able to cope with catastrophe than the nonfamous multitudes who were only deprived of the protective power of their passports. I have drawn from Stefan Zweig's autobiography, *The World of Yesterday*, which he wrote and published shortly before he committed suicide. It is, as far as I know, the only written testimony to this elusive and, to be sure, illusive phenomenon whose mere aura assured those who were permitted to bask in fame's radiance of what today we would call their "identity."

If I were not too old to decently adopt the current speech habits of the young generation, I could truthfully say that the fact of this prize has had its most immediate and, in my case, its most logical consequence in setting off a "crisis of identity." The "society of celebrities," to be sure, is no longer a threat; thank God it no longer exists. Nothing is more transient in our world, less stable and solid, than that form of success which brings fame; nothing comes swifter and more readily than oblivion. It would be more in keeping with my own generation—a generation that is old but not quite dead—to turn away from all these psychological considerations and to accept this felicitous intrusion into my life as just a piece of good luck, but without ever forgetting that the gods, at least the Greek gods, are ironical and also tricky. Somewhat in this vein, Socrates who began to worry and start his own aporetic questioning after the Delphic oracle, known for its cryptic ambiguities, had declared him to be the wisest of all mortals. According to him that was a dangerous hyperbole, perhaps a hint that no man is wise, and that Apollo had meant to tell him how he could actualize this insight by perplexing his fellow citizens. So, what

could the gods have meant by making you select for public honor
somebody like me, who is neither a public figure nor has the ambition to become one?

Since the trouble here obviously has something to do with me
as a person, let me try another approach to this problem of suddenly being changed into a public figure by the undeniable force
not of fame but of public recognition. Let me first remind you of
the etymological origin of the word "person," which has been
adopted almost unchanged from the Latin *persona* by the European languages with the same unanimity as, for instance, the word
"politics" has been derived from the Greek *polis*. It is, of course,
not without significance that such an important word in our contemporary vocabularies, which all over Europe we use to discuss a
great variety of legal, political, and philosophical matters, derives
from an identical source in antiquity. This ancient vocabulary
provides something like the fundamental chord which in many
modulations and variations sounds through the intellectual history of Western mankind.

Persona, at any event, originally referred to the actor's mask
that covered his individual "personal" face and indicated to the
spectator the role and the part of the actor in the play. But in this
mask, which was designed and determined by the play, there
existed a broad opening at the place of the mouth through which
the individual, undisguised voice of the actor could sound. It is
from this sounding through that the word *persona* was derived:
per-sonare, "to sound through," is the verb of which *persona*, the
mask, is the noun. And the Romans themselves were the first to
use the noun in a metaphorical sense; in Roman law *persona* was
somebody who possessed civil rights, in sharp distinction from
the word *homo*, denoting someone who was nothing but a member of the human species, different, to be sure, from an animal but

without any specific qualification or distinction, so that *homo,* like
the Greek *anthropos,* was frequently used contemptuously to designate people not protected by any law.

I found this Latin understanding of what a person is helpful for
my considerations because it invites further metaphorical usage,
metaphors being the daily bread of all conceptual thought. The
Roman mask corresponds with great precision to our own way of
appearing in a society where we are not citizens, that is, not equal-
ized by the public space established and reserved for political
speech and political acts, but where we are accepted as individuals in our own right and yet by no means as human beings as
such. We always appear in a world which is a stage and are recognized according to the roles which our professions assign us, as
physicians or lawyers, as authors or publishers, as teachers or students, and so on. It is through this role, sounding through it, as
it were, that something else manifests itself, something entirely
idiosyncratic and undefinable and still unmistakably identifiable,
so that we are not confused by a sudden change of roles, when for
instance a student arrives at his goal which was to become a
teacher, or when a hostess, whom socially we know as a physician,
serves drinks instead of taking care of her patients. In other
words, the advantage of adopting the notion of *persona* for my
considerations lies in the fact that the masks or roles which the
world assigns us, and which we must accept and even acquire
if we wish to take part in the world's play at all, are exchangeable; they are not inalienable in the sense in which we speak of
"inalienable rights," and they are not a permanent fixture annexed
to our inner self in the sense in which the voice of conscience, as
most people believe, is something the human soul constantly
bears within itself.

It is in this sense that I can come to terms with appearing here as a "public figure" for the purpose of a public event. It means that when the events for which the mask was designed are over, and I have finished using and abusing my individual right to sound through the mask, things will again snap back into place. Then I, greatly honored and deeply thankful for this moment, shall be free not only to exchange the roles and masks that the great play of the world may offer, but free even to move through that play in my naked "thisness," identifiable, I hope, but not definable and not seduced by the great temptation of recognition which, in no matter what form, can only recognize us *as* such and such, that is, as something which we fundamentally are *not*.

Copenhagen
April 18, 1975

❖•❖ I ❖•❖
RESPONSIBILITY

PERSONAL RESPONSIBILITY
UNDER DICTATORSHIP

To begin, I want to comment on the rather furious controversy touched off by my book *Eichmann in Jerusalem*. I deliberately use the words "touched off," rather than the word "caused," for a large part of the controversy was devoted to a book that was never written. My first reaction, therefore, was to dismiss the whole affair with the famous words of an Austrian wit: "There is nothing so entertaining as the discussion of a book nobody has read." As this went on, however, and as, especially in its later stages, there were more and more voices who not only attacked me for what I had never said but, on the contrary, began to defend me for it, it dawned on me that there might be more to this slightly eerie exercise than sensation or entertainment. It seemed to me also that more than "emotions" were involved, that is, more than honest misunderstandings that in some instances caused an authentic breakdown of communication between author and reader—and more too than the distortions and falsifications of interest groups, which were much less afraid of my book than that it might initiate an impartial and detailed further examination of the period in question.

The controversy invariably raised all kinds of strictly moral issues, many of which had never occurred to me, whereas others had been mentioned by me only in passing. I had given a factual account of the trial, and even the book's subtitle, *A Report on the Banality of Evil*, seemed to me so glaringly borne out by the facts of the case that I felt it needed no further explanation. I had pointed to a fact which I felt was shocking because it contradicts our theories concerning evil, hence to something true but not plausible.

I had somehow taken it for granted that we all still believe with Socrates that it is better to suffer than to do wrong. This belief turned out to be a mistake. There was a widespread conviction that it is impossible to withstand temptation of any kind, that none of us could be trusted or even be expected to be trustworthy when the chips are down, that to be tempted and to be forced are almost the same, whereas in the words of Mary McCarthy, who first spotted this fallacy: "If somebody points a gun at you and says, 'Kill your friend or I will kill you,' he is *tempting* you, that is all." And while a temptation where one's life is at stake may be a legal excuse for a crime, it certainly is not a moral justification. Finally, and in a way most surprisingly, since after all we dealt with a trial whose result invariably was the passing of judgment, I was told that judging itself is wrong: no one can judge who had not been there. This, incidentally, was Eichmann's own argument against the district court's judgment. When told that there had been alternatives and that he could have escaped his murderous duties, he insisted that these were postwar legends born of hindsight and supported by people who did not know or had forgotten how things had actually been.

There are a number of reasons why the discussion of the right or the ability to judge touches on the most important moral issue. Two things are involved here: First, how can I tell right from wrong, if the majority or my whole environment has prejudged the issue? *Who am I to judge?* And second, to what extent, if at all, can we judge past events or occurrences at which we were not present? As to the latter, it seems glaringly obvious that no historiography and no courtroom procedure would be possible at all if we denied ourselves this capability. One might go a step further and maintain that there are very few instances in which, in using our capacity to judge, we do not judge by hindsight, and again this is equally true of the historiographer as it is of the trial judge, who may have good reasons to mistrust eyewitness accounts or the judgment of those who were present. Moreover, since this question of judging without being present is usually coupled with the accusation of arrogance, who has ever maintained that by judging a wrong I presuppose that I myself would be incapable of committing it? Even the judge who condemns a man for murder may still say, and there but for the grace of God go I!

Thus, prima facie, all this looks like elaborate nonsense, but when many people, without having been manipulated, begin to talk nonsense, and if intelligent people are among them, there is usually more involved than just nonsense. There exists in our society a widespread fear of judging that has nothing whatever to do with the biblical "Judge not, that ye be not judged," and if this fear speaks in terms of "casting the first stone," it takes this word in vain. For behind the unwillingness to judge lurks the suspicion that no one is a free agent, and hence the doubt that anyone is responsible or could be expected to answer for what he has done. The moment moral issues are raised, even in passing, he who raises them will be confronted with this frightful lack of self-confidence and hence of pride, and also with a kind of mock-modesty that in saying, Who am I to judge? actually means We're all alike, equally bad, and those who try, or pretend that they try, to remain halfway decent are either saints or hypocrites, and in either case should leave us alone. Hence the huge outcry the moment anyone fixes specific blame on some particular person instead of blaming all deeds or events on historical trends and dialectical movements, in short on some mysterious necessity that works behind the backs of men and bestows upon everything they do some kind of deeper meaning. As long as one traces the roots of what Hitler did back to Plato or Gioacchino da Fiore or Hegel or Nietzsche, or to modern science and technology, or to nihilism or the French Revolution, everything is all right. But the moment one calls Hitler a mass murderer—conceding, of course, that this particular mass murderer was politically very gifted and also that the whole phenomenon of the Third Reich cannot be explained solely on the grounds of who Hitler was and how he influenced people—there is general agreement that such judgment of the person is vulgar, lacks sophistication, and should not be permitted to interfere with the interpretation of History. Thus, to give you another example from a contemporary controversy, the argument of Rolf Hochhuth's play *The Deputy*, in which Pope Pius XII stands accused of his singular silence at the time of the great massacres of Jews in the East, was immediately countered, and not only by outcries from the Catholic hierarchy, which after all is understandable. It was also countered by the falsifications of the born image makers: Hochhuth, it has been said, accused the pope as the chief culprit in order to exculpate Hitler and the German people, which is a simple untruth. More significant in our context has been the reproach that it is "of course" superficial to accuse the pope, all of Christianity stands accused; or even more to the point: "No doubt, there is ground for serious accusation, but the defendant is the whole human race."* The point I wish to

*Robert Weltsch, "Ein Deutscher klagt den Papst an" in *Summa iniuria oder Durfte der Papst schweigen? Hochhuths "Stellvertreter" in der öffentlichen Kritik*, Edit. F. J. Raddatz (Rowohlt: 1963) 156.—Ed.

raise here goes beyond the well-known fallacy of the concept of collective guilt as first applied to the German people and its collective past—all of Germany stands accused and the whole of German history from Luther to Hitler—which in practice turned into a highly effective whitewash of all those who had actually done something, for where all are guilty, no one is. You have only to put Christianity or the whole human race into the place originally reserved for Germany to see, or so it would seem, the absurdity of the concept, for now not even the Germans are guilty any longer: no one at all is for whom we have so much as a name instead of the concept of collective guilt. What I wish to point out, in addition to these considerations, is how deep-seated the fear of passing judgment, of naming names, and of fixing blame—especially, alas, upon people in power and high position, dead or alive—must be if such desperate intellectual maneuvers are being called upon for help. For is it not obvious that Christianity has survived rather handsomely many popes who were worse than Pius XII, precisely because it was never all of Christianity that stood accused? And what shall one say of those who would rather throw all mankind out of the window, as it were, in order to save one man in high position, and to save him from the accusation not even of having committed a crime, but merely of an admittedly grave sin of omission?

It is fortunate and wise that no law exists for sins of omission and no human court is called upon to sit in judgment over them. But it is equally fortunate that there exists still one institution in society in which it is well-nigh impossible to evade issues of personal responsibility, where all justifications of a nonspecific, abstract nature—from the Zeitgeist down to the Oedipus complex—break down, where not systems or trends or original sin are judged, but men of flesh and blood like you and me, whose deeds are of course still human deeds but who appear before a tribunal because they have broken some law whose maintenance we regard as essential for the integrity of our common humanity. Legal and moral issues are by no means the same, but they have a certain affinity with each other because they both presuppose the power of judgment. No courtroom reporter, if he knows what he is doing, can avoid becoming involved in these questions. How can we tell right from wrong, independent of knowledge of the law? And how can we judge without having been in the same situation?

It is at this point that I think it would be proper to make my second personal remark. If the heat caused by my "sitting in judgment" has proved, as I think it has, how uncomfortable most of us are when confronted with moral issues, I better admit that not the least uncomfortable one is myself. My early intellectual formation occurred in an atmosphere where nobody paid much attention to moral questions; we were brought up under the assumption: *Das Moralische versteht sich von selbst*, moral conduct is a matter of course. I still remember quite well my own youthful opinion of the moral rectitude we usually call character; all insistence on such virtue would have appeared to me as Philistine, because this, too, we thought was a matter of course and hence of no great importance—not a decisive quality, for instance, in the evaluation of a given person. To be sure, every once in a while we were confronted with moral weakness, with lack of steadfastness or loyalty, with this curious, almost automatic yielding under pressure, especially of public opinion, which is so symptomatic of the educated strata of certain societies, but we had no idea how serious such things were and least of all where they could lead. We did not know much about the nature of these phenomena, and I am afraid we cared even less. Well, it turned out that we would be given ample opportunity to learn. For my generation and people of my origin, the lesson began in 1933 and it ended not when just German Jews but the whole world had been given notice of monstrosities no one believed possible at the beginning. What we have learned since, and it is by no means unimportant, can be counted as additions and ramifications of the knowledge acquired during those first twelve years, from 1933 to 1945. Many of us have needed the last twenty years in order to come to terms with what happened, not in 1933, but in 1941 and 1942 and 1943, up to the bitter end. And by this, I do not mean personal grief and sorrow, but the horror itself to which, as we can see now, none of the concerned parties has as yet been able to reconcile itself. The Germans have coined for this whole complex the highly questionable term of their "unmastered past." Well, it looks as though today, after so many years, this German past has turned out to remain somehow unmanageable for a good part of the civilized world. At the time the horror itself, in its naked monstrosity, seemed not only to me but to many others to transcend all moral categories and to explode all standards of jurisdiction; it was something men could neither punish adequately nor forgive. And in this speechless horror, I fear, we all tended to forget the strictly moral and manageable lessons we had been taught before, and would be taught again, in innumerable discussions, both inside and outside of courtrooms.

In order to clarify the distinction between the speechless horror, in which one learns nothing, and the not at all horrible but frequently disgusting experiences where people's conduct is open to normal judgments, let me first mention a fact which is obvious and yet rarely mentioned. What mattered in our early, nontheoretical education in morality was never the conduct of the true culprit of whom even then no one in his right mind could expect other than the worst. Thus we were outraged, but not morally disturbed, by the bestial behavior of the storm troopers in the concentration camps and the torture cellars of the secret police, and it would have been strange indeed to grow morally indignant over the speeches of the Nazi bigwigs in power, whose opinions had been common knowledge for years. The new regime posed to us then nothing more than a very complex political problem, one aspect of which was the intrusion of criminality into the public realm. I think we were also prepared for the consequences of ruthless terror and we would gladly have admitted that this kind of fear is likely to make cowards of most men. All this was terrible and dangerous, but it posed no moral problems. The moral issue arose only with the phenomenon of "coordination," that is, not with fear-inspired hypocrisy, but with this very early eagerness not to miss the train of History, with this, as it were, honest overnight change of opinion that befell a great majority of public figures in all walks of life and all ramifications of culture, accompanied, as it was, by an incredible ease with which lifelong friendships were broken and discarded. In brief, what disturbed us was the behavior not of our enemies but of our friends, who had done nothing to bring this situation about. They were not responsible for the Nazis, they were only impressed by the Nazi success and unable to pit their own judgment against the verdict of History, as they read it. Without taking into account the almost universal breakdown, not of personal responsibility, but of personal *judgment* in the early stages of the Nazi regime, it is impossible to understand what actually happened. It is true that many of these people were quickly disenchanted, and it is well known that most of the men of July 20, 1944, who paid with their lives for their conspiracy against Hitler, had been connected with the regime at some time or other. Still, I think this early moral disintegration in

German society, hardly perceptible to the outsider, was like a kind of dress rehearsal for its total breakdown, which was to occur during the war years.

I brought these personal matters to your attention in order to lay myself open, not to the accusation of arrogance, which I think is beside the point, but to the more justifiable doubt whether people with so little mental or conceptual preparation for moral issues are at all qualified to discuss them. We had to learn everything from scratch, in the raw, as it were—that is, without the help of categories and general rules under which to subsume our experiences. There stand, however, on the other side of the fence, all those who were fully qualified in matters of morality and held them in the highest esteem. These people proved not only to be incapable of learning anything; but worse, yielding easily to temptation, they most convincingly demonstrated through their application of traditional concepts and yardsticks during and after the fact, how inadequate these had become, how little, as we shall see, they had been framed or intended to be applied to conditions as they actually arose. The more these things are discussed, the clearer it becomes, I think, that we actually find ourselves here in a position between the devil and the deep sea.

To give at this point but one particular instance of our bedevilment in all these matters, consider the question of legal punishment, punishment that is usually justified on one of the following grounds: the need of society to be protected against crime, the improvement of the criminal, the deterring force of the warning example for potential criminals, and, finally, retributive justice. A moment of reflection will convince you that none of these grounds is valid for the punishment of the so-called war criminals: these people were not ordinary criminals and hardly any one of them can reasonably be expected to commit further crimes;

society is in no need of being protected from them. That they can be improved through prison sentences is even less likely than in the case of ordinary criminals, and as to the possibility of deterring such criminals in the future, the chances again are dismally small in view of the extraordinary circumstances under which these crimes were committed or might be committed in the future. Even the notion of retribution, the only nonutilitarian reason given for legal punishment and hence somehow out of tune with current legal thought, is hardly applicable in view of the magnitude of the crime. And yet, though none of the reasons for punishment which we usually invoke is valid, our sense of justice would find it intolerable to forego punishment and let those who murdered thousands and hundreds of thousands and millions go scot-free. If this were nothing but a desire for revenge, it would be ridiculous, quite apart from the fact that the law and the punishment it metes out appeared on earth in order to break the unending vicious circle of vengeance. Thus, here we are, demanding and meting out punishment in accordance with our sense of justice, while, on the other hand, this same sense of justice informs us that all our previous notions about punishment and its justifications have failed us.

To return to my personal reflections on who should be qualified to discuss such matters: is it those who have standards and norms which do not fit the experience, or those who have nothing to fall back upon but their experience, an experience, moreover, unpatterned by preconceived concepts? How can you think, and even more important in our context, how can you judge without holding on to preconceived standards, norms, and general rules under which the particular cases and instances can be subsumed? Or to put it differently, what happens to the human faculty of judgment when it is faced with occurrences that spell the breakdown of all customary standards and hence are unprecedented in the sense that they are not foreseen in the general rules, not even as exceptions from such rules? A valid answer to these questions would have to start with an analysis of the still very mysterious nature of human judgment, of what it can and what it cannot achieve. For only if we assume that there exists a human faculty which enables us to judge rationally without being carried away by either emotion or self-interest, and which at the same time functions spontaneously, that is to say, is not bound by standards and rules under which particular cases are simply subsumed, but on the contrary, produces its own principles by virtue of the judging activity itself; only under this assumption can we risk ourselves on this very slippery moral ground with some hope of finding a firm footing.

Luckily for me, our topic tonight does not require that I offer you a philosophy of judgment. But even a restricted approach to the problem of morality and its foundations demands the clarification of one general question as well as a few distinctions which, I fear, are not generally accepted. The general question concerns the first part of my title: "Personal Responsibility." This term must be understood in contrast to political responsibility which every government assumes for the deeds and misdeeds of its predecessor and every nation for the deeds and misdeeds of the past. When Napoleon, seizing power in France after the revolution, said: I shall assume the responsibility for everything France ever did from Louis the Saint to the Committee of Public Safety, he only stated a little emphatically one of the basic facts of all political life. And as for the nation, it is obvious that every generation, by virtue of being born into a historical continuum, is burdened by the sins of the fathers as it is blessed with the deeds of the ancestors. Whoever takes upon himself political responsibility will always come to the point where he says with Hamlet:

The time is out of joint: O cursed spite
That ever I was born to set it right!

To set the time aright means to renew the world, and this we can do because we all arrived at one time or another as newcomers in a world which was there before us and will still be there when we are gone, when we shall have left its burden to our successors. But this is not the kind of responsibility I am talking about here; it is not personal, strictly speaking, and it is only in a metaphorical sense that we can say we *feel* guilty for the sins of our fathers or our people or of mankind, in short for deeds we have *not* done. Morally speaking, it is as wrong to feel guilty without having done anything specific as it is to feel free of all guilt if one actually is guilty of something. I have always regarded it as the quintessence of moral confusion that during the postwar period in Germany those who personally were completely innocent assured each other and the world at large how guilty they felt, while very few of the criminals were prepared to admit even the slightest remorse. The result of this spontaneous admission of collective guilt was of course a very effective, though unintended, whitewash of those who *had* done something: as we have already seen, where all are guilty, no one is. And when we heard, in the recent discussion in Germany about an extension of the statute of limitations for the Nazi murderers, how the minister of justice countered any such extension with the argument that further zeal in looking for what the Germans call "the murderers among us" would only result in moral complacency among the Germans who are not murderers (*Der Spiegel*, no. 5, 1963, p. 23), that is, in those who are innocent, we see at once how dangerous this moral confusion can become. The argument is not new. A few years back, the execution of the death sentence for Eichmann aroused widespread opposition, on the grounds that it might ease the conscience of ordinary Germans and "serve to expiate the guilt felt by many young persons in Germany," as Martin Buber put it. Well, if young people in Germany, too young to have done anything at all, *feel* guilty, they are either wrong, confused, or they are playing intellectual games. There is no such thing as collective guilt or collective innocence; guilt and innocence make sense only if applied to individuals.

Recently, during the discussion of the Eichmann trial, these comparatively simple matters have been complicated through what I'll call the cog-theory. When we describe a political system—how it works, the relations between the various branches of government, how the huge bureaucratic machineries function of which the channels of command are part, and how the civilian and the military and the police forces are interconnected, to mention only outstanding characteristics—it is inevitable that we speak of all persons used by the system in terms of cogs and wheels that keep the administration running. Each cog, that is, each person, must be expendable without changing the system, an assumption underlying all bureaucracies, all civil services, and all functions properly speaking. This viewpoint is the viewpoint of political science, and if we accuse or rather evaluate in its frame of reference, we speak of good and bad systems and our criteria are the freedom or the happiness or the degree of participation of the citizens, but the question of the personal responsibility of those who run the whole affair is a marginal issue. Here it is indeed true what all the defendants in the postwar trials said to excuse themselves: if I had not done it, somebody else could and would have.

For in any dictatorship, let alone a totalitarian dictatorship, even the comparatively small number of decision makers who can still be named in normal government has shrunk to the figure of

One, while all institutions and bodies that initiate control over or ratify executive decision have been abolished. In the Third Reich, at any rate, there was only one man who did and could make decisions and hence was politically fully responsible. That was Hitler himself who, therefore, not in a fit of megalomania but quite correctly once described himself as the only man in all Germany who was irreplaceable. Everybody else from high to low who had anything to do with public affairs was in fact a cog, whether he knew it or not. Does this mean that nobody else could be held personally responsible?

When I went to Jerusalem to attend the Eichmann trial, I felt that it was the great advantage of courtroom procedure that this whole cog-business makes no sense in its setting, and therefore forces us to look at all these questions from a different point of view. To be sure, that the defense would try to plead that Eichmann was but a small cog was predictable; that the defendant himself would think in these terms was probable, and he did so up to a point; whereas the attempt of the prosecution to make of him the biggest cog ever—worse and more important than Hitler— was an unexpected curiosity. The judges did what was right and proper, they discarded the whole notion, and so, incidentally, did I, all blame and praise to the contrary notwithstanding. For, as the judges took great pains to point out explicitly, in a courtroom there is no system on trial, no History or historical trend, no ism, anti-Semitism for instance, but a person, and if the defendant happens to be a functionary, he stands accused precisely because even a functionary is still a human being, and it is in this capacity that he stands trial. Obviously, in most criminal organizations the small cogs are actually committing the big crimes, and one could even argue that one of the characteristics of the organized criminality of the Third Reich was that it demanded tangible proof of criminal implication of all its servants, and not only of the lower echelons. Hence, the question addressed by the court to the defendant is, Did you, such and such, an individual with a name, a date, and place of birth, identifiable and by that token not expendable, commit the crime you stand accused of, and Why did you do it? If the defendant answers: "It was not I as a person who did it, I had neither the will nor the power to do anything out of my own initiative; I was a mere cog, expendable, everybody in my place would have done it; that I stand before this tribunal is an accident"—this answer will be ruled out as immaterial. If the defendant were permitted to plead either guilty or not guilty as representing a system, he would indeed become a *scapegoat*. (Eichmann himself wished to become a scapegoat—he proposed to hang himself publicly and to take all "sins" upon himself. The court denied him this last occasion for elating sentiments.) In every bureaucratic system the shifting of responsibilities is a matter of daily routine, and if one wishes to define bureaucracy in terms of political science, that is, as a form of government—the rule of offices, as contrasted to the rule of men, of one man, or of the few, or of the many—bureaucracy unhappily is the rule of nobody and for this very reason perhaps the least human and most cruel form of rulership. But in the courtroom, these definitions are of no avail. For to the answer: "Not I but the system did it in which I was a cog," the court immediately raises the next question: "And why, if you please, did you become a cog or continue to be a cog under such circumstances?" If the accused wishes to shift responsibilities, he must again implicate other persons, he must name names, and these persons appear then as possible codefendants, they do not appear as the embodiment of bureaucratic or any other necessity. The Eichmann trial, like all such trials, would have been devoid of all interest if it had not transformed the cog or "referent" of Section IV B4 in the Reich Security Head Office into a man. Only because this operation was achieved even before the trial started could the question of personal responsibility, and hence of legal guilt, arise at all. And even this transformation of a cog into a man does not imply that something like cog-ness, the fact that systems tranform men into cogs, and totalitarian systems more totally than others, was on trial. This interpretation would be but another escape from the strict limitations of courtroom procedure.

Still, while courtroom procedure or the question of personal responsibility under dictatorship cannot permit the shifting of responsibility from man to system, the system cannot be left out of account altogether. It appears in the form of circumstances, from the legal as well as the moral point of view, much in the same sense in which we take into account the conditions of underprivileged persons as mitigating circumstances, but not as excuses, in the case of crimes committed in the milieu of poverty. And it is for this reason that, coming to the second part of my title, "Dictatorship," I must now bother you with a few distinctions which will help us to understand these circumstances. Totalitarian forms of government and dictatorships in the usual sense are not the same, and most of what I have to say applies to totalitarianism. Dictatorship in the old Roman sense of the word was devised and has remained an emergency measure of constitutional, lawful government, strictly limited in time and power; we still know it well enough as the state of emergency or of martial law proclaimed in disaster areas or in time of war. We furthermore know modern dictatorships as new forms of government, where either the military seize power, abolish civilian government, and deprive the citizens of their political rights and liberties, or where one party seizes the state apparatus at the expense of all other parties and hence of all organized political opposition. Both types spell the end of political freedom, but private life and nonpolitical activity are not necessarily touched. It is true that these regimes usually persecute political opponents with great ruthlessness and they certainly are very far from being constitutional forms of government in the sense we have come to understand them—no constitutional government is possible without provisions being made for the rights of an opposition—but they are not criminal in the common sense of the word either. If they commit crimes these are directed against outspoken foes of the regime in power. But the crimes of totalitarian governments concerned people who were "innocent" even from the viewpoint of the party in power. It was for this reason of common criminality that most countries signed an agreement after the war not to bestow the status of political refugee upon those culprits who escaped from Nazi Germany.

Moreover, total domination reaches out into all, not only the political, spheres of life. Totalitarian society, as distinguished from totalitarian government, is indeed monolithic; all public manifestations, cultural, artistic, or learned, and all organizations, welfare and social services, even sports and entertainment, are "coordinated." There is no office and indeed no job of any public significance, from advertising agencies to the judiciary, from play-acting to sports journalism, from primary and secondary schooling to the universities and learned societies, in which an unequivocal acceptance of the ruling principles is not demanded. Whoever participates in public life at all, regardless of party membership or membership in the elite formations of the regime, is implicated in one way or another in the deeds of the regime as a whole. What the courts demand in all these postwar trials is that the defendants should not have participated in crimes legalized by that government, and this nonparticipation taken as a legal standard for right and wrong poses considerable problems precisely with respect to the question of responsibility. For the simple truth of the matter is that only those who withdrew from public life altogether, who refused political responsibility of any sort, could avoid becoming implicated in crimes, that is, could avoid legal and moral responsibility. In the tumultuous discussion of moral issues which has been going on ever since the defeat of Nazi Germany, and the disclosure of the total complicity in crimes of all ranks of official society, that is, of the total collapse of normal moral standards, the following argument has been raised in endless variations: We who appear guilty today are in fact those who stayed on the job in order to prevent worse things from happening; only those who remained inside had a chance to mitigate things and to help at least some people; we gave the devil his due without selling our soul to him, whereas those who did nothing shirked all responsibilities and thought only of themselves, of the salvation of their precious souls. Politically speaking, this argument might have made sense if an overthrow of the Hitler regime had been achieved, or even attempted, in the very early stages. For it is true that a totalitarian system can be overthrown only from within— not through revolution, but through a coup d'etat—unless, of course, it is defeated in war. (We may perhaps assume that something of this sort occurred in the Soviet Union, either before or immediately after Stalin's death; the turning point from an outright totalitarian system to a one-party dictatorship or tyranny probably came with the liquidation of Beria, the head of the secret police.) But the people who speak in this manner were by no means the conspirators—successful or not. They are as a rule those civil servants without whose expert knowledge neither the Hitler regime nor the Adenauer administration that succeeded it would have been able to survive. Hitler had inherited civil servants from the Weimar Republic, which had inherited them from Imperial Germany, just as Adenauer was to inherit them from the Nazis, without much difficulty.

I must here remind you that the personal or moral issue, as distinct from legal accountability, hardly arises with those who were convinced adherents of the regime: that they could not feel guilty but only defeated was almost a matter of course, unless they changed their minds and repented. And yet, even this simple issue has become confused because when the day of reckoning finally came it turned out that there had been no convinced adherents, at least not of the criminal program for which they stood trial. And the trouble is that, though this was a lie, it is not a simple or total lie. For what had started in the initial stages with politically neutral people who were not Nazis but cooperated with them, happened in the last stages with the party members and even with the elite formations of the SS: there were very few people even in the Third Reich who wholeheartedly agreed with the late crimes of the regime and a great number who were perfectly willing to commit them nevertheless. And now every single one of them, wherever he stood and whatever he did, claims that those who, under one pretext or another, had retired into private life had chosen the easy, the irresponsible way out. Unless, of course, they had used their private station as a cover for active opposition—a choice which can be easily dismissed since it is obviously not everybody's business to be a saint or a hero. But personal or moral responsibility is everybody's business and there, it is argued, it was more "responsible" to stay on the job no matter under what conditions or with what consequences.

In their moral justification, the argument of the lesser evil has played a prominent role. If you are confronted with two evils, thus the argument runs, it is your duty to opt for the lesser one, whereas it is irresponsible to refuse to choose altogether. Those who denounce the moral fallacy of this argument are usually accused of a germ-proof moralism which is alien to political circumstances, of being unwilling to dirty their hands; and it must be admitted that it is not so much political or moral philosophy (with the sole exception of Kant, who for this very reason frequently stands accused of moralistic rigorism) but religious thought that most unequivocally has rejected all compromises with lesser evils. Thus the Talmud holds, as I was told during a recent discussion of these matters: if they ask you to sacrifice one man for the security of the community, don't surrender him; if they ask you to give one woman to be ravished for the sake of all women, don't let her be ravished. And it is in the same vein, and clearly remembering Vatican policy during the last war, that Pope John XXIII wrote about the political behavior of Pope and Bishop, which is called the "practice of prudence": they "must beware of . . . in any way conniving with evil in the hope that by doing so they may be useful to someone."

Politically, the weakness of the argument has always been that those who choose the lesser evil forget very quickly that they chose evil. Since the evil of the Third Reich finally was so monstrous that by no stretch of the imagination could it be called a "lesser evil," one might have assumed that this time the argument would have collapsed once and for all, which surprisingly is not the case. Moreover, if we look at the techniques of totalitarian government, it is obvious that the argument of "the lesser evil"— far from being raised only from the outside by those who do not belong to the ruling elite—is one of the mechanisms built into the machinery of terror and criminality. Acceptance of lesser evils is consciously used in conditioning the government officials as well as the population at large to the acceptance of evil as such. To give but one among many examples: the extermination of Jews was preceded by a very gradual sequence of anti-Jewish measures, each of which was accepted with the argument that refusal to cooperate would make things worse—until a stage was reached where nothing worse could possibly have happened. The fact that in this last stage the argument was not abandoned and survives even today when its fallacy has become so glaringly obvious—in the discussion of the Hochhuth play we heard again that a protest from the Vatican in whatever form would only have made things worse!—is surprising enough. We see here how unwilling the human mind is to face realities which in one way or another contradict totally its framework of reference. Unfortunately, it seems to be much easier to condition human behavior and to make people conduct themselves in the most unexpected and outrageous manner, than it is to persuade anybody to learn from experience, as the saying goes; that is, to start thinking and judging instead of applying categories and formulas which are deeply ingrained in our mind, but whose basis of experience has long been forgotten and whose plausibility resides in their intellectual consistency rather than in their adequacy to actual events.

To clarify this predicament of judging without being able to fall back upon the application of generally accepted rules, I'll switch from moral to legal standards because the latter are generally better defined. You may know that in the trials of war criminals and the discussion of personal responsibility, the defendants and their lawyers appealed either to the argument that these crimes were "acts of state," or that they were committed upon "superior orders." These two categories should not be confused. Superior orders are legally within the realm of jurisdiction, even though the defendant may find himself in the classically "difficult position" of the soldier "liable to be shot by a court martial if he disobeys an order, and to be hanged by a judge and jury if he obeys it" (as Dicey puts it in his *Law of the Constitution*). Acts of state, however, are altogether outside the legal framework; they are presumably sovereign acts over which no court has jurisdiction. Now, the theory behind the formula of acts of state claims that sovereign governments may under extraordinary circumstances be forced to use criminal means because their very existence or the maintenance of their power depends on it; the reason-of-state, thus the argument runs, cannot be bound by legal limitations or moral considerations, which are valid for private citizens who live within its boundaries, because the state as a whole, and hence the existence of everything that goes on inside it, is at stake. In this theory, the act of state is tacitly likened to the "crime" an individual may be forced to commit in self-defense, that is, to an act which also is permitted to go unpunished because of extraordinary circumstances, where survival as such is threatened. What makes this argument inapplicable to the crimes committed by totalitarian governments and their servants is not only that these crimes were in no way prompted by necessity of one form or another; on the contrary, one could argue with considerable force that, for instance, the Nazi government would have been able to survive, even perhaps to win the war, if it had not committed its well-known crimes. It may be of even greater importance, theoretically, that the reason-of-state argument, which underlies the whole discussion of acts of state, presupposes that such a crime is committed within a context of legality which it serves to maintain together with the political existence of the nation. The law to be enforced stands in need of political power, hence an element of power politics is always involved in the maintenance of legal order. (I am, of course, talking here not about acts committed against other nations, nor am I concerned here with the question of whether war itself can be defined as a "crime against peace"—to use the language of the Nuremberg trials.) What neither the political reason-of-state theory nor the legal concept of acts of state foresaw was the complete reversal of legality; in the case of the Hitler regime, the whole state machinery enforced what normally are considered criminal activities, to put it mildly: there was hardly an act of state which according to normal standards was not criminal. Hence, it was no longer the criminal act which, as an exception to the rule, supposedly served to maintain the rule of the party in power—as for instance in the case of such famous crimes as the murder of Matteoti in Mussolini's Italy, or the assassination of the duc d'Enghien by Napoleon—but on the contrary, occasional noncriminal acts— such as Himmler's order to stop the extermination program— were exceptions to the "law" of Nazi Germany, concessions made to dire necessity. To revert for a moment to the distinction between totalitarian government and other dictatorships, it is precisely the relative rarity of outright crimes that distinguishes fascist dictatorships from fully developed totalitarian ones, although it is of course true that there are more crimes committed by fascist or military dictatorships than would even be conceivable under constitutional government. What matters in our context is only that they are still clearly recognizable as exceptions and that the regime does not openly acknowledge them.

In a similar way the argument of "superior orders," or the judges' counterargument that the fact of superior orders is no excuse for the commission of crimes, is inadequate. Here, too, the presupposition is that orders normally are not criminal and that for this very reason the receiver of orders can be expected to recognize the criminal nature of a particular order—as in the case of an officer gone mad who orders the shooting of other officers or in the case of maltreatment or killing of prisoners of war. In juridical terms, the orders to be disobeyed must be "manifestly unlawful"; unlawfulness "should fly like a black flag as a warning reading Prohibited." In other words, as far as the man is concerned who has to decide whether to obey or disobey, the order must be clearly marked off as an exception, and the trouble is that in totalitarian regimes, and especially in the last years of the Hitler regime, this mark clearly belonged to noncriminal orders. Thus for Eichmann, who had decided to be and remain a law-abiding citizen of the Third Reich, the black flag of manifest unlawfulness flew above those late orders given by Himmler in the fall of 1944, according to which deportations were to be stopped and the installations of the death factories dismantled. The text from which I just quoted is contained in the judgment of an Israeli Military Court, which, more than most other courts in the world, was aware of the difficulties inherent in the word "lawfulness," in view of the outright and, as it were, legally criminal nature of Hitler's Germany. It therefore went beyond the usual phraseology that a "feeling of lawfulness . . . lies deep within every human conscience, also of those who are not conversant with books of laws," and spoke of "an unlawfulness glaring to the eye and repulsive to the heart, provided the eye is not blind and the heart is not stony and corrupt"—which is all very fine, but will, I am afraid, be found wanting when the chips are down. For in these cases, the men who did wrong were very well acquainted with the letter and the spirit of the law of the country they lived in, and today, when they are held responsible, what we actually require of them is a "feeling of lawfulness" deep within themselves to *contradict* the law of the land and their knowledge of it. Under such circumstances there may be considerably more required than an eye not blind and a heart not stony and corrupt in order to spot "unlawfulness." They acted under conditions in which every moral act was illegal and every legal act was a crime.

Hence, the rather optimistic view of human nature, which speaks so clearly from the verdict not only of the judges in the Jerusalem trial but of all postwar trials, presupposes an independent human faculty, unsupported by law and public opinion, that judges in full spontaneity every deed and intent anew whenever the occasion arises. Perhaps we do possess such a faculty and are lawgivers, every single one of us, whenever we act: but this was not the opinion of the judges. Despite all the rhetoric, they meant hardly more than that a *feeling* for such things has been inbred in us for so many centuries that it could not suddenly have been lost. And this, I think, is very doubtful in view of the evidence we possess, and also in view of the fact that year in, year out, one "unlawful" order followed the other, all of them not haphazardly demanding just any crimes that were unconnected with each other, but building up with utter consistency and care the so-called new order. This "new order" was exactly what it said it was—not only gruesomely novel, but also and above all, an *order*.

The widespread notion that we deal here with nothing more than a gang of criminals who in conspiracy will commit just any crimes is grievously misleading. True, there was a fluctuating number of criminals in the elite formations of the movement and a greater number of men guilty of atrocities. Only in the beginning of the regime, however, in the concentration camps under the authority of the storm troopers, did these atrocities have a clear political object: to spread fear and to flood in a wave of unspeakable terror all attempts at organized opposition. But these atrocities were not typical and what is more important, although there was a great permissiveness about them, they were not actu-

ally permitted. Just as stealing was not permitted or the acceptance of bribes. On the contrary, as Eichmann was to insist time
and again, the directives said: "unnecessary hardships are to be
avoided," and when during the police interrogation it was suggested to him that these words sounded a bit ironical when dealing
with people who were being sent to their certain deaths, he did not
even understand what the examining police officer was talking
about. Eichmann's conscience rebelled at the idea of cruelty, not
that of murder. Equally misleading is the common notion that we
deal here with an outbreak of modern nihilism, if we understand
the nihilistic credo in the sense of the nineteenth century: "all is
permitted." The ease with which consciences could be dulled was
partly the direct consequence of the fact that by no means all was
permitted.

For the moral point of this matter is never reached by calling
what happened by the name of "genocide" or by counting the
many millions of victims: extermination of whole peoples had
happened before in antiquity, as well as in modern colonization. It
is reached only when we realize that this happened within the
frame of a legal order and that the cornerstone of this "new law"
consisted of the command "Thou shalt kill," not thy enemy but
innocent people who were not even potentially dangerous, and
not for any reason of necessity but, on the contrary, even against
all military and other utilitarian considerations. The killing program was not meant to come to an end with the last Jew to be
found on earth, and it had nothing to do with the war except
that Hitler believed he needed a war as a smoke screen for his
nonmilitary killing operations; those operations themselves were
intended to continue on an even more grandiose scale in time
of peace. And these deeds were not committed by outlaws, monsters, or raving sadists, but by the most respected members of

respectable society. Finally, it must be realized that although these mass murderers acted consistently with a racist or anti-Semitic, or at any rate a demographic ideology, the murderers and their direct accomplices more often than not did not believe in these ideological justifications; for them, it was enough that everything happened according to the "will of the Führer," which was the law of the land, and in accordance with the "words of the Führer," which had the force of law.

The best proof, if proof were still needed, of the extent to which the whole people, regardless of party affiliation and direct implication, believed in the "new order" for no other reason than that that was the way things were, was perhaps the incredible remark Eichmann's lawyer, who had never belonged to the Nazi Party, made twice during the trial in Jerusalem, to the effect that what had happened in Auschwitz and the other extermination camps had been "a medical matter." It was as though morality, at the very moment of its total collapse within an old and highly civilized nation, stood revealed in the original meaning of the word, as a set of *mores,* of customs and manners, which could be exchanged for another set with no more trouble than it would take to change the table manners of a whole people.*

I have dwelt at some length upon this overall situation because no discussion of personal responsibility would make much sense without some precise knowledge of the factual background. Let me now raise two questions: First, in what way were those few different who in all walks of life did not collaborate and refused to participate in public life, though they could not and did not rise in rebellion? And second, if we agree that those who did serve on whatever level and in whatever capacity were not simply mon-

*Editor's note: Arendt was fond of drawing an analogy between customs and table manners and used this analogy in a number of other discussions.

sters, what was it that made them behave as they did? On what moral, as distinguished from legal, grounds did they justify their conduct after the defeat of the regime and the breakdown of the "new order" with its new set of values? The answer to the first question is relatively simple: the nonparticipants, called irresponsible by the majority, were the only ones who dared judge by themselves, and they were capable of doing so not because they disposed of a better system of values or because the old standards of right and wrong were still firmly planted in their mind and conscience. On the contrary, all our experiences tell us that it was precisely the members of *respectable* society, who had not been touched by the intellectual and moral upheaval in the early stages of the Nazi period, who were the first to yield. They simply exchanged one system of values against another. I therefore would suggest that the nonparticipants were those whose consciences did not function in this, as it were, automatic way—as though we dispose of a set of learned or innate rules which we then apply to the particular case as it arises, so that every new experience or situation is already prejudged and we need only act out whatever we learned or possessed beforehand. Their criterion, I think, was a different one: they asked themselves to what extent they would still be able to live in peace with themselves after having committed certain deeds; and they decided that it would be better to do nothing, not because the world would then be changed for the better, but simply because only on this condition could they go on living with themselves at all. Hence, they also chose to die when they were forced to participate. To put it crudely, they refused to murder, not so much because they still held fast to the command "Thou shalt not kill," but because they were unwilling to live together with a murderer—themselves.

The precondition for this kind of judging is not a highly developed intelligence or sophistication in moral matters, but rather the disposition to live together explicitly with oneself, to have intercourse with oneself, that is, to be engaged in that silent dialogue between me and myself which, since Socrates and Plato, we usually call thinking. This kind of thinking, though at the root of all philosophical thought, is not technical and does not concern theoretical problems. The dividing line between those who want to think and therefore have to judge by themselves, and those who do not, strikes across all social and cultural or educational differences. In this respect, the total moral collapse of respectable society during the Hitler regime may teach us that under such circumstances those who cherish values and hold fast to moral norms and standards are not reliable: we now know that moral norms and standards can be changed overnight, and that all that then will be left is the mere habit of holding fast to something. Much more reliable will be the doubters and skeptics, not because skepticism is good or doubting wholesome, but because they are used to examine things and to make up their own minds. Best of all will be those who know only one thing for certain: that whatever else happens, as long as we live we shall have to live together with ourselves.

But how is it with the reproach of irresponsibility leveled against these few who washed their hands of what was going on all around them? I think we shall have to admit that there exist extreme situations in which responsibility for the world, which is primarily political, cannot be assumed because political responsibility always presupposes at least a minimum of political power. Impotence or complete powerlessnes is, I think, a valid excuse. Its validity is all the stronger as it seems to require a certain moral quality even to recognize powerlessness, the good will and good faith to face realities and not to live in illusions. Moreover, it is precisely in this admission of one's own impotence that a last remnant of strength and even power can still be preserved even under desperate conditions.

This last point may become a bit clearer when we now turn our attention to my second question, to those who not only participated willy-nilly as it were but who thought it their duty to do whatever was demanded. Their argument was different from those of the mere participants who invoked the lesser evil, or the Zeitgeist, thereby implicitly denying the human faculty of judgment, or in surprisingly rare cases the fear which in totalitarian governments is all pervasive. The argument from the Nuremberg trials to the Eichmann trial and the more recent trials in Germany has always been the same: every organization demands obedience to superiors as well as obedience to the laws of the land. Obedience is a political virtue of the first order, and without it no body politic could survive. Unrestricted freedom of conscience exists nowhere, for it would spell the doom of every organized community. All this sounds so plausible that it takes some effort to detect the fallacy. Its plausibility rests on the truth that "all governments," in the words of Madison, even the most autocratic ones, even tyrannies, "rest on *consent*," and the fallacy lies in the equation of consent with obedience. An adult consents where a child obeys; if an adult is said to obey, he actually *supports* the organization or the authority or the law that claims "obedience." The fallacy is all the more pernicious as it can claim a very old tradition. Our use of the word "obedience" for all these strictly political situations goes back to the age-old notion of political science which, since Plato and Aristotle, tells us that every body politic is constituted of rulers and ruled, and that the former give commands and the latter obey orders.

Of course, I cannot here go into the reasons why these concepts have crept into our tradition of political thought, but I should like to point out that they supplanted earlier and, I think, more accurate notions of the relations between men in the sphere of concerted action. According to these earlier notions every action, accomplished by a plurality of men, can be divided into two stages: the beginning, which is initiated by a "leader," and the accomplishment, in which many join to see through what then becomes a common enterprise. In our context, all that matters is the insight that no man, however strong, can ever accomplish anything, good or bad, without the help of others. What you have here is the notion of an equality which accounts for a "leader" who is never more than *primus inter pares*, the first among his peers. Those who seem to obey him actually support him and his enterprise; without such "obedience" he would be helpless, whereas in the nursery or under conditions of slavery—the two spheres in which the notion of obedience made sense and from which it was then transposed into political matters—it is the child or the slave who becomes helpless if he refuses to "cooperate." Even in a strictly bureaucratic organization, with its fixed hierarchical order, it would make much more sense to look upon the functioning of the "cogs" and wheels in terms of overall support for a common enterprise than in our usual terms of obedience to superiors. If I obey the laws of the land, I actually support its constitution, as becomes glaringly obvious in the case of revolutionists and rebels who disobey because they have withdrawn this tacit consent.

In these terms, the nonparticipators in public life under a dictatorship are those who have refused their support by shunning those places of "responsibility" where such support, under the name of obedience, is required. And we have only for a moment to imagine what would happen to any of these forms of government if enough people would act "irresponsibly" and refuse support, even without active resistance and rebellion, to see how effective a weapon this could be. It is in fact one of the many variations of nonviolent action and resistance—for instance the power that is potential in civil *dis*obedience—which are being discovered in our century. The reason, however, that we can hold these new criminals, who never committed a crime out of their own initiative, nevertheless responsible for what they did is that there is no such thing as obedience in political and moral matters. The only domain where the word could possibly apply to adults who are not slaves is the domain of religion, in which people say that they *obey* the word or the command of God because the relationship between God and man can rightly be seen in terms similar to the relation between adult and child.

Hence the question addressed to those who participated and obeyed orders should never be, "Why did you obey?" but "Why did you *support?*" This change of words is no semantic irrelevancy for those who know the strange and powerful influence mere "words" have over the minds of men who, first of all, are speaking animals. Much would be gained if we could eliminate this pernicious word "obedience" from our vocabulary of moral and political thought. If we think these matters through, we might regain some measure of self-confidence and even pride, that is, regain what former times called the dignity or the honor of man: not perhaps of mankind but of the status of being human.

1964

SOME QUESTIONS OF
MORAL PHILOSOPHY

I

The thoughts of many of us, I suppose, have wandered back during the last weeks to Winston Spencer Churchill, the greatest statesman thus far of our century, who just died after an incredibly long life, the summit of which was reached at the threshold of old age. This happenstance, if such it was, like almost everything he stood for in his convictions, in his writings, in the grand but not grandiose manner of his speeches, stood in conspicuous contrast to whatever we may think the Zeitgeist of this age to be. It is perhaps this contrast that touches us most when we consider his greatness. He has been called a figure of the eighteenth century driven into the twentieth as though the virtues of the past had taken over our destinies in their most desperate crisis, and this, I think, is true as far as it goes. But perhaps there is more to it. It is as though, in this shifting of centuries, some permanent eminence of the human spirit flashed up for an historically brief moment to show that whatever makes for greatness—nobility, dignity, steadfastness, and a kind of laughing courage—remains essentially the same throughout the centuries.

Still Churchill, so old-fashioned or, as I have suggested, beyond the fashions of the times, was by no means unaware of the decisive currents or undercurrents of the age in which he lived. He wrote the following words in the nineteen-thirties when the true monstrosities of the century were yet unknown: "Scarcely anything, material or established, which I was brought up to believe was permanent and vital, has lasted. Everything I was sure, or was taught to be sure, was impossible, has happened." I wanted to mention these succinct words which, alas, became fully true only some years after they were uttered, in order to introduce the basic experiences which invariably lie behind or beneath them. Among the many things which were still thought to be "permanent and vital" at the beginning of the century and yet have not lasted, I chose to turn our attention to the moral issues, those which concern individual conduct and behavior, the few rules and standards according to which men used to tell right from wrong, and which were invoked to judge or justify others and themselves, and whose validity were supposed to be self-evident to every sane person either as a part of divine or of natural law. Until, that is, without much notice, all this collapsed almost overnight, and then it was as though morality suddenly stood revealed in the original meaning of the word, as a set of *mores*, customs and manners, which could be exchanged for another set with hardly more trouble than it would take to change the table manners of an individual or a people. How strange and how frightening it suddenly appeared that the very terms we use to designate these things—"morality," with its Latin origin, and "ethics," with its Greek origin—should never have meant more than usages and habits. And also that two thousand five hundred years of thought, in literature, philosophy, and religion, should not have brought forth another word, notwithstanding all the highflown phrases, all assertions and preachings about the existence of a conscience which speaks with an identical voice to all men. What had happened? Did we finally awake from a dream?

To be sure, a few had known before that there was something wrong with this assumption of self-evidence for moral commandments as though the "Thou shalt not bear false testimony" could ever have the same validity as the statement: two and two equal four. Nietzsche's quest for "new values" certainly was a clear indication of the devaluation of what his time called "values" and what former times more correctly had called virtues. The only standard Nietzsche came up with was Life itself, and his criticism of the traditional and essentially Christian virtues was guided by the much more general insight that not only all Christian but also all Platonic ethics use yardsticks and measurements which are not derived from this world but from something beyond it—be it the sky of ideas stretching over the dark cave of strictly human affairs or the truly transcendent beyond of a divinely ordained afterlife. Nietzsche called himself a moralist, and no doubt he was; but to establish life as the highest good is actually, so far as ethics are concerned, question-begging, since all ethics, Christian or non-Christian, presuppose that life is *not* the highest good for mortal men and that there is always more at stake in life than the sustenance and procreation of individual living organisms. That which is at stake may be very different; it may be greatness and fame as in pre-Socratic Greece; it may be the permanence of the city as in Roman virtue; it may be the health of the soul in this life or the salvation of the soul in the hereafter; it may be freedom or justice, or many more such things.

Were these things or principles, from which all virtues are ultimately derived, mere values which could be exchanged against other values whenever people changed their minds about them? And would they, as Nietzsche seems to indicate, all go overboard before the overriding claim of Life itself? To be sure, he could not have known that the existence of mankind as a whole could ever be put into jeopardy by human conduct, and in this marginal event one could indeed argue that Life, the survival of the world and the human species, are the highest good. But this would mean no more than that any ethics or morality would simply cease to exist. And in principle this thought was anticipated by the old Latin question: *Fiat justitia, pereat mundus* (Should the world perish that justice be done?), and the question was answered by Kant: "If justice perishes, human life on earth has lost its meaning." *("Wenn die Gerechtigkeit untergeht, hat es keinen Wert mehr, dass Menschen auf Erden leben.")* Hence, the only new moral principle, proclaimed in modern times, turns out to be not the assertion of "new values" but the negation of morality as such, although Nietzsche, of course, did not know this. And it is his abiding greatness that he dared to demonstrate how shabby and meaningless morality had become.

Churchill's words were uttered in the form of a statement, but we, with the wisdom of hindsight, shall be tempted to read them also as premonition. And if it were just a question of premonitions I could indeed add an astounding number of quotations which would go back at least to the first third of the eighteenth century. The point of the matter for us, however, is that we deal no longer with premonitions, but with facts.

We—at least the older ones among us—have witnessed the total collapse of all established moral standards in public and private life during the nineteen-thirties and -forties, not only (as is now usually assumed) in Hitler's Germany but also in Stalin's Russia. Still, the differences between the two are significant enough to be mentioned. It has often been noted that the Russian Revolution caused social upheaval and social remolding of the entire nation unparalleled even in the wake of Nazi Germany's radical fascist dictatorship, which, it is true, left the property relation almost intact and did not eliminate the dominant groups in society. From this, it usually is concluded that what happened in the Third Reich was by nature and not only by historical accident less permanent and less extreme. This may or may not be true with respect to strictly political developments, but it certainly is a fallacy if we regard the issue of morality. Seen from a strictly moral viewpoint, Stalin's crimes were, so to speak, old fashioned; like an ordinary criminal, he never admitted them but kept them surrounded in a cloud of hypocrisy and doubletalk while his followers justified them as temporary means in the pursuit of the "good" cause, or, if they happened to be a bit more sophisticated, by the laws of history to which the revolutionary has to submit and sacrifice himself if need be. Nothing in Marxism, moreover, despite all the talk about "bourgeois morality" announces a new set of moral values. If anything is characteristic of Lenin or Trotsky as the representatives of the professional revolutionary, it is the naïve belief that once the social circumstances are changed through revolution, mankind will follow automatically the few moral precepts that have been known and repeated since the dawn of history.

In this respect, the German developments are much more extreme and perhaps also more revealing. There is not only the gruesome fact of elaborately established death factories and the utter absence of hypocrisy in those very substantial numbers who were involved in the extermination program. Equally important, but perhaps more frightening, was the matter-of-course collaboration from all strata of German society, including the older elites which the Nazis left untouched, and who never identified themselves with the party in power. I think it is justifiable on factual grounds to maintain that morally, though not socially, the Nazi regime was much more extreme than the Stalin regime at its worst. It did indeed announce a new set of values and introduced a legal system designed in accordance with them. It proved more-over that no one had to be a convinced Nazi to conform, and to forget overnight, as it were, not his social status, but the moral convictions which once went with it.

In the discussion of these matters, and especially in the general moral denunciation of the Nazi crimes, it is almost always over-looked that the true moral issue did not arise with the behavior of the Nazis but of those who only "coordinated" themselves and did not act out of conviction. It is not too difficult to see and even to understand how someone may decide "to prove a villain" and, given the opportunity, to try out a reversal of the decalogue, start-ing with the command "Thou shalt kill," and ending with a pre-cept "Thou shalt lie." A number of criminals, as we know only too well, are present in every community, and while most of them suffer from a rather limited imagination, it may be conceded that a few of them probably are no less gifted than Hitler and some of his henchmen. What these people did was horrible and the way they organized first Germany and then Nazi-occupied Europe is of great interest for political science and the study of forms of government; but neither the one nor the other poses any moral problems. Morality collapsed into a mere set of mores—manners, customs, conventions to be changed at will—not with criminals, but with ordinary people, who, as long as moral standards were socially accepted, never dreamt of doubting what they had been taught to believe in. And this matter, that is, the problem it raises is not resolved if we admit, as we must, that the Nazi doctrine did not remain with the German people, that Hitler's criminal morality was changed back again at a moment's notice, at the moment "history" had given the notice of defeat. Hence we must say that we witnessed the total collapse of a "moral" order not once but twice, and this sudden return to "normality," contrary to what is often complacently assumed, can only reinforce our doubts.

When I think back to the last two decades since the end of the last war, I have the feeling that this moral issue has lain dormant because it was concealed by something about which it is indeed much more difficult to speak and with which it is almost impossible to come to terms—the horror itself in its naked monstrosity. When we were first confronted with it, it seemed, not only to me but to many others, to transcend all moral categories as it certainly exploded all juridical standards. You could express this in various ways. I used to say, this is something which should never have happened for men will be unable either to punish it or forgive it. We shall not be able to become reconciled to it, to come to terms with it, as we must with everything that is past—either because it was bad and we need to overcome it or because it was good and we cannot bear to let it go. It is a past which has grown worse as the years have gone by, and this is partly because the Germans for such a long time refused to prosecute even the murderers among themselves, but partly also because this past could not be "mastered" by anybody. Even the famous healing power of time has somehow failed us. On the contrary, this past has managed to grow worse as the years have gone by so that we are sometimes tempted to think, this will never be over as long as we are not all dead. No doubt, this is partly due to the complacency of the Adenauer regime which for such a long time did absolutely nothing about the famous "murderers within our midst" and did not regard participation in the Hitler regime, unless it bordered on criminality, as a reason to disqualify anybody for public office. But these are, I think, only partial explanations: the fact is also that this past has turned out to be "unmastered" by everybody, not only by the German nation. And the inability of civilized courtroom procedure to come to terms with it in juridical form, its insistence on pretending that these new-fangled murderers are in no way different from ordinary ones and acted out of the same motives, is only one, though perhaps in the long run the most fateful, consequence of this state of affairs. I will not speak about this here where we deal with moral, not legal issues. What I wanted to indicate is that the same speechless horror, this refusal to think the unthinkable, has perhaps prevented a very necessary reappraisal of legal categories as it has made us forget the strictly moral, and, one hopes, more manageable, lessons which are closely connected with the whole story but which look like harmless side issues if compared with the horror.

Unfortunately, there is one more aspect to be reckoned with as an obstacle in our enterprise. Since people find it difficult, and rightly so, to live with something that takes their breath away and renders them speechless, they have all too frequently yielded to the obvious temptation to translate their speechlessness into whatever expressions for emotions were close at hand, all of them inadequate. As a result, today the whole story is usually told in terms of sentiments which need not even be cheap in themselves to sentimentalize and cheapen the story. There are very few examples for which this is not true, and these are mostly unrecognized or unknown. The whole atmosphere in which things are discussed today is overcharged with emotions, often of a not very high caliber, and whoever raises these questions must expect to be dragged down, if at all possible, to a level on which nothing serious can be discussed at all. However that may be, let us keep in mind this distinction between the speechless horror, in which one learns nothing other than what can be directly communicated, and the not horrible but often disgusting experiences where people's conduct is open to normal judgment and where the question of morals and ethics arises.

I said that the moral issue lay dormant for a considerable time, implying that it has come to life during the last few years. What has made it come to life? There are, as I see it, several inter-connected matters which tend to be cumulative. There was first and most importantly, the effect of the postwar trials of the so-called war criminals. What was decisive here was the simple fact of courtroom procedure that forced everybody, even political scientists, to look at these matters from a moral viewpoint. It is, I think, well-known that there exists hardly a walk of life in which you'll find people as wary and suspicious of moral standards, even of the standard of justice, as in the legal professions. The modern social and psychological sciences have, of course, also contributed to this general skepticism. And yet, the simple fact of courtroom procedure in criminal cases, the sequence of accusation-defense-judgment that persists in all the varieties of legal systems and is as old as recorded history, defies all scruples and doubts—not, to be sure, in the sense that it can put them to rest, but in the sense that this particular institution rests on the assumption of personal responsibility and guilt, on the one hand, and on a belief in the functioning of conscience, on the other. Legal and moral issues are by no means the same, but they have in common that they deal with persons, and not with systems or organizations.

It is the undeniable greatness of the judiciary that it must focus its attention on the individual person, and that even in the age of mass society where everybody is tempted to regard himself as a mere cog in some kind of machinery—be it the well-oiled machinery of some huge bureaucratic enterprise, social, political, or professional, or the chaotic, ill-adjusted chance pattern of circumstances under which we all somehow spend our lives. The almost automatic shifting of responsibility that habitually takes place in modern society comes to a sudden halt the moment you enter a courtroom. All justifications of a nonspecific abstract nature—everything from the Zeitgeist down to the Oedipus complex that indicates that you are not a man but a function of something and hence yourself an exchangeable thing rather than a somebody—break down. No matter what the scientific fashions of the time may say, no matter how much they may have penetrated public opinion and hence also influenced the practitioners of the law, the institution itself defies, and must defy, them all or pass out of existence. And the moment you come to the individual person, the question to be raised is no longer, How did this system function? but, Why did the defendant become a functionary in this organization?[1]

This, of course, is not to deny that it is important to the political and social sciences to understand the functioning of totalitarian governments, to probe into the essence of bureaucracy and its inevitable tendency to make functionaries of men, mere cogs in the administrative machinery, and thus to dehumanize them. The point is that the administration of justice can consider these factors only to the extent that they are circumstances, perhaps mitigating ones, of whatever a man of flesh and blood did. In a perfect bureaucracy—which in terms of rulership is the rule by nobody—courtroom procedure would be superfluous, one would simply have to exchange unfit cogs against fitter ones. When Hitler said that he hoped for the day when it would be considered a disgrace in Germany to be a jurist he spoke with great consistency of his dream of a perfect bureaucracy.

The speechless horror, which I mentioned before as an adequate reaction to the system as a whole, dissolves in the courtroom where we deal with persons in the ordered discourse of accusation, defense, and judgment. The reason these courtroom procedures could bring to life specifically moral questions—which is not the case in the trials of ordinary criminals—is obvious; these people were not ordinary criminals but rather very ordinary people who had committed crimes with more or less enthusiasm, simply because they did what they had been told to do. Among them, there were also ordinary criminals who could do with impunity under the Nazi system what they had always wanted to do; but much as the sadists and perverts stood in the limelight in the publicity of these trials, in our context they are of less interest.

I think it can be shown that these trials led to a more general probing into the specific share of guilt of those who did not belong to any of the criminal categories but who played their role in the regime nevertheless, or of whoever only kept silent and tolerated things as they were when they were in a position to speak out. You remember the outcry that greeted Hochhuth's accusation of Pope Pius XII and also my own book on the Eichmann trial. If we disregard the voices of directly interested parties—the Vatican or Jewish organizations—the outstanding characteristic in these "controversies" was the overwhelming interest in strictly moral issues. Even more striking than this interest was perhaps the incredible moral confusion these debates have revealed, together with an odd tendency to take the side of the culprit whoever he might be at the moment. There was a whole chorus of voices that assured me that "there sits an Eichmann in every one of us" just as there was a whole chorus that told Hochhuth that not Pope Pius XII—after all only one man and one pope—was guilty but all of Christianity and even the whole human race. The only true culprits, it frequently was felt and even said, were people like Hochhuth and myself who dared to sit in judgment; for no one can judge who had not been in the same circumstances under which, presumably, one would have behaved like all others. This position, incidentally, coincided oddly with Eichmann's view on these matters.

In other words, while the moral issues were hotly debated they were at the same time sidestepped and evaded with equal eagerness. And this was not due to the specific issues under discussion but seems to happen whenever moral topics are discussed, not in general but in a particular case. Thus I am reminded of an incident a few years ago in connection with the famous quiz show cheating on television. An article by Hans Morgenthau in the *New York Times Magazine* ("Reaction to the Van Doren Reaction," November 22, 1959) pointed out the obvious—that it was wrong to cheat for money, doubly wrong in intellectual matters, and triply wrong for a teacher. The response was heated outrage: such judgment was against Christian charity and no man, except a saint, could be expected to resist the temptation of so much money. And this was not said in a cynical mood to make fun of philistine respectability, and it was not meant as a nihilistic argument. No one said—as would invariably have happened thirty or forty years ago, at least in Europe—that cheating is fun, that virtue is boring and moral people are tiresome. Nor did anybody say that the television quiz program was wrong, that anything like a $64,000 question was almost an invitation for fraudulent behavior, nor stand up for the dignity of learning and criticize the university for not preventing one of its members from indulging in what obviously is unprofessional conduct, even if no cheating were to take place. From the numerous letters written in response to the article, it became quite clear that the public at large, including many students, thought that only one person was to be blamed unequivocally: the man who judged, and not the man who had done wrong, not an institution, not society in general or the mass media in particular.

Now let me enumerate briefly the general questions which this factual situation, as I see it, has put on the agenda. The first conclusion I think is that no one in his right mind can any longer claim that moral conduct is a matter of course—*das Moralische versteht sich von selbst,* an assumption under which the generation I belong to was still brought up. This assumption included a sharp distinction between legality and morality, and while there existed a vague, inarticulate consensus that by and large the law of the land spells out whatever the moral law may demand, there was not much doubt that in case of conflict the moral law was the higher law and had to be obeyed first. This claim in turn could make sense only if we took for granted all those phenomena which we usually have in mind when we speak of human conscience. Whatever the source of moral knowledge might be— divine commandments or human reason—every sane man, it was assumed, carried within himself a voice that tells him what is right and what is wrong, and this regardless of the law of the land and regardless of the voices of his fellowmen. Kant once mentioned that there might be a difficulty: "No one," he said, "who spent his life among rascals without knowing anybody else could have a concept of virtue." *("Den Begriff der Tugend würde kein Mensch haben, wenn er immer unter lauter Spitzbuben wäre.")* But he meant no more by this than that the human mind is guided by examples in these matters. Not for a moment would he have doubted that, confronted with the example of virtue, human reason knows what is right and that its opposite is wrong. To be sure, Kant believed he had articulated the formula which the human mind applies whenever it has to tell right from wrong. He called this formula the categorical imperative; but he was under no illusion that he had made a discovery in moral philosophy which would have implied that no one before him knew what is right and wrong— obviously an absurd notion. He compares his formula (about which we shall have more to say in the coming lectures) to a "compass" with which men will find it easy "to distinguish what is good, what is bad . . . Without in the least teaching common reason anything new, we need only to draw its attention to its own principle, in the manner of Socrates, thus showing that neither science nor philosophy is needed in order to know what one has to do in order to be honest and good. . . . [Indeed,] the knowledge of what everyone is obliged to do, and thus also to know, [is] within the reach of everyone, even the most ordinary man."[2] And if someone had asked Kant where this knowledge within reach of everybody is located, he would have replied in the rational structure of the human mind, whereas, of course, others had located the same knowledge in the human heart. What Kant would not have taken for granted is that man will also act according to his judgment. Man is not only a rational being, he also belongs to the world of the senses which will tempt him to yield to his inclinations instead of following his reason or his heart. Hence moral conduct is not a matter of course, but moral knowledge, the knowledge of right and wrong, is. Because inclinations and temptation are rooted in human nature, though not in human reason, Kant called the fact that man is tempted to do wrong by following his inclinations "radical evil." Neither he nor any other moral philosopher actually believed that man could will evil for its own sake; all transgressions are explained by Kant as exceptions that a man is tempted to make from a law which he otherwise recognizes as being valid—thus the thief recognizes the laws of property, even wishes to be protected by them, and only makes a temporary exception from them in his own favor.

No one wants to be wicked, and those who nevertheless act wickedly fall into an *absurdum morale*—into moral absurdity. He who does this is actually in contradiction with himself, his own reason, and therefore, in Kant's own words, he must despise himself. That this fear of self-contempt could not possibly be enough to guarantee legality is obvious; but as long as you moved in a society of law-abiding citizens you somehow assumed that self-contempt would work. Kant of course knew that self-contempt, or rather the fear of having to despise yourself, very often did not work, and his explanation of this was that man can lie to himself. He therefore repeatedly declared that the really "sore or foul spot" in human nature is mendacity, the faculty of lying.[3] At first glance this statement seems very surprising because none of our ethical or religious codes (with the exception of that of Zoroaster) ever contained a commandment "Thou shalt not lie"— quite apart from the consideration that not only we but all codes of civilized nations have put murder at the top of the list of human crimes. Oddly enough, Dostoevsky seems to have shared— without knowing it of course—Kant's opinion. In *The Brothers Karamazov*, Dmitri K. asks the Starov, "What must I do to win salvation?" and the Starov replies, "Above all else, never lie to yourself."

I have left out of this very schematic and preliminary account all specifically religious moral precepts and beliefs, not because I think them unimportant (quite the contrary is the case), but because at the moment morality collapsed they played hardly any role. Clearly no one was any longer afraid of an avenging God or, more concretely speaking, of possible punishments in a hereafter. As Nietzsche once remarked: *"Naivität, als ob Moral übrigbliebe, wenn der sanktionierende* Gott *fehlt! Das 'Jenseits' absolut notwendig, wenn der Glaube an Moral aufrechterhalten werden soll."*[4] Nor did the churches think of so threatening their believers once the crimes turned out to be demanded by the authority of the state. And those few who in all churches and all walks of life refused to participate in crimes did not plead religious beliefs or fears, even if they happened to be believers, but simply stated, like others, that they could not themselves bear responsibility for such deeds. This sounds rather strange and certainly is at odds with the innumerable pious pronunciations of the churches after the war, especially the repeated admonitions from all sides that nothing will save us except a return to religion. But it is a fact and it shows to what an extent religion, if it is more than a social business, has indeed become the most private of private affairs. For, of course, we don't know what went on in the hearts of these men, whether or not they were afraid of hell and eternal damnation. All we know is that hardly anyone thought these oldest beliefs fit for public justification.

There is however another reason why I left religion out of account and began by indicating the great importance of Kant in these matters. Moral philosophy has no place wherever religion, and especially revealed religion in the Hebrew-Christian sense, is the valid standard for human behavior and the valid criterion for judging it. This of course does not mean that certain teachings which we know only in a religious context are not of the greatest relevance for moral philosophy. If you look back to traditional, premodern philosophy, as it developed within the framework of the Christian religion, you will at once discover that there existed no moral subdivision within philosophy. Medieval philosophy was divided into cosmology, ontology, psychology, and rational theology—that is, into a doctrine about nature and the universe, about Being, about the nature of the human mind and soul, and, finally, about the rational proofs of the existence of God. Insofar as "ethical" questions were discussed at all, especially in Thomas Aquinas, this was done in the fashion of antiquity, where ethics was part and parcel of political philosophy—defining the conduct of man insofar as he was a citizen. Thus, you have in Aristotle two treatises which together contain what he himself calls philosophy of things human: his *Nicomachean Ethics* and his *Politics*. The former deals with the citizen, the latter with civil institutions; the former precedes the latter because the "good life" of the citizen is the raison d'être of the polis, the institution of the city. The goal is to find out which is the best constitution, and the treatise on the good life, the *Ethics*, ends with an outline of the program for the treatise on politics. Aquinas, both the faithful disciple of Aristotle and a Christian, always must come to the point where he has to differ with the master, and nowhere is the difference more glaring than when he holds that every fault or sin is a violation of the laws prescribed to nature by divine reason. To be sure, Aristotle too knows of the divine, which to him is the imperishable and the immortal, and he too thinks that man's highest virtue, precisely because he is mortal, consists in dwelling as much as possible in the neighborhood of the divine. But there is no prescription, no command, to this effect that could be obeyed or disobeyed. The whole question turns around the "good life," which way of life is best for man, something obviously up to man to find out and to judge.

In late antiquity, after the decline of the polis, the various philosophy schools, especially the Stoics and the Epicureans, not only developed a kind of moral philosophy, they had a tendency, at least in their late Roman versions, to transform all philosophy into moral teachings. The quest for the good life remained the same: How can I attain maximum happiness here on earth? only this question was now separated from all political implications, and raised by men in their private capacity. This whole literature is full of wise recommendations, but you won't find in it, any more than in Aristotle, a real command which ultimately is beyond argument, as you must in all religious teachings. Even Aquinas, the greatest rationalizer of Christianity, had to admit that the ultimate reason why a particular prescription is right and a particular command has to be obeyed lies in its divine origin. God said so.

This can be a conclusive answer only within the framework of *revealed* religion; outside this framework, we cannot but raise the question which, as far as I know, Socrates was the first to raise, in Plato's *Euthyphro* where he wishes to know, "Do the gods love piety because it is pious, or is it pious because they love it?" Or to put it in another way, Do the gods love goodness because it is good or do we call it good because the gods love it? Socrates leaves us with the question, and a believer, no doubt, is bound to say that it is their divine origin that distinguishes good principles from evil—they are in accordance with a law given by God to nature and to man, the summit of his creation. Insofar as man is God's creation, the same things, to be sure, which God "loves" must also appear good to him, and in this sense Aquinas once indeed remarked, as though in answer to Socrates' question, that God commands the good because it is good—as opposed to Duns Scotus, who held the good is good because God commands it. But even in this most rationalized form, the *obligatory* character of the good for man lies in God's command. From this follows the all-important principle that in religion, but not in morality, sin is primarily understood as disobedience. Nowhere in the strictly religious tradition will you find the unequivocal and indeed radical answer Kant gave to the Socratic question: "We shall not look upon actions as obligatory because they are the commands of God, but shall regard them as divine commands because we have an inward obligation to them."[5] Only where this emancipation from religious commands has been achieved, where in Kant's own words in *Lectures on Ethics:* "We ourselves are judges of the revelation. . . . ," hence where morality is a strictly human affair, can we speak of moral philosophy.[6] And the same Kant, who in his theoretical philosophy was so concerned with keeping the door open to religion, even after having shown that we can have no knowledge in these matters, was equally careful to block all passages which may have led back to religion in his practical or moral philosophy. Just as "God is in no sense the author of the fact that the triangle has three angles," so "not even God can be the author of [the laws of] morality" (*Lectures on Ethics* 52). In this unequivocal sense, until Kant, moral philosophy had ceased to exist after antiquity. Probably you will think here of Spinoza who called his chief work *Ethics,* but Spinoza begins his work with a section entitled "Of God," and from this first part everything that follows is derived. Whether or not moral philosophy has existed since Kant is at least an open question.

Moral conduct, from what we have heard so far, seems to depend primarily upon the intercourse of man with himself. He must not contradict himself by making an exception in his own favor, he must not place himself in a position in which he would have to despise himself. Morally speaking, this should be enough not only to enable him to tell right from wrong but also to do right and avoid wrong. Kant, with the consistency of thought which is the mark of the great philosopher, therefore puts the duties man has to himself ahead of the duties to others—something which certainly is very surprising, standing in curious contradiction to what we usually understand by moral behavior. It certainly is not a matter of concern with the other but with the self, not of meekness but of human dignity and even human pride. The standard is neither the love of some neighbor nor self-love, but self-respect.

This comes out most clearly and most beautifully in a famous passage of Kant's *Critique of Practical Reason:* "Two things fill the mind with ever new and increasing admiration and awe, the oftener and more steadily we reflect on them: the starry heaven above me and the moral law within me." One might conclude that these "two things" are on the same level and affect the human mind in the same way. Well, the opposite is the case. Kant continues by saying: "The former view of a countless multitude of worlds annihilates, as it were, my importance as an animal creature. . . . The latter, on the contrary, infinitely raises my worth as that of an intelligence by my personality, in which the moral law reveals a life independent of all animality and even of the whole world of sense."[7] Hence, what saves me from annihilation, from being "a mere speck" in the infinity of the universe, is precisely this "invisible self" that can pit itself against it. I underline this element of pride not only because it goes against the grain of Christian ethics, but also because the loss of a feeling for it seems to me most manifest in those who discuss these matters today, mostly without even knowing how to appeal to the Christian virtue of humility. This, however, is not to deny that there exists a crucial problem in this moral concern with the self. How difficult this problem may be is gauged by the fact that religious commands were likewise unable to formulate their general moral prescriptions without turning to the self as the ultimate standard—"Love thy neighbor as thyself," or "Don't do unto others what you don't want done to yourself."

Secondly, moral conduct has nothing to do with obedience to any law that is given from the outside—be it the law of God or the laws of men. In Kant's terminology, this is the distinction between legality and morality. Legality is morally neutral: it has its place in institutionalized religion and in politics, but not in morality. The political order does not require moral integrity but only law-abiding citizens, and the Church is always a church of sinners. These orders of a given community must be distinguished from the moral order binding for all men, even all rational beings. In Kant's own words: "The problem of organizing a state, however hard as it may seem, can be solved even for a race of devils, if only they are intelligent."[8] In a similar spirit, it has been said that the devil makes a good theologian. In the political order, as in the religious framework, obedience may have its place, and just as this obedience is enforced in institutionalized religion by the threat of future punishments, so the legal order exists only to the extent of the existence of sanctions. What cannot be punished is permitted. If, however, I can be said at all to obey the categorical imperative, it means that I am obeying my own reason, and the law which I give myself is valid for all rational creatures, all intelligible beings no matter where they may have their dwelling place. For if I don't want to contradict myself, I act in such a manner that the maxim of my act can become a universal law. I am the legislator, sin or crime can no longer be defined as disobedience to somebody else's law, but on the contrary as refusal to act my part as legislator of the world.

This rebellious aspect of Kant's teachings is frequently overlooked because he put his general formula—that a moral act is an act which lays down a universally valid law—into the form of an imperative instead of defining it in a proposition. The chief reason for this self-misunderstanding in Kant is the highly equivocal meaning of the word "law" in the Western tradition of thought. When Kant spoke of the moral law, he used the word in accordance with political usage in which the law of the land is considered obligatory for all inhabitants in the sense that they have to obey it. That obedience is singled out as my attitude toward the law of the land is in turn due to the transformation the term had undergone through religious usage where the Law of God can indeed address man only in the form of a Command, "Thou shalt"—the obligation, as we saw, being not the content of the law nor the possible consent of man to it, but the fact that God had told us so. Here nothing counts but obedience.

To these two interconnected meanings of the word we must now add the very important and quite different usage made by combining the concept of law with nature. Laws of nature are also, so to speak, obligatory: I follow a law of nature when I die, but it cannot be said, except metaphorically, that I obey it. Kant therefore distinguished between "laws of nature" and the moral "laws of freedom," which carry no necessity, only an obligation. But if we understand by law either commands which I must obey or the necessity of nature to which I am subject anyhow, then the term "law of freedom" is a contradiction in terms. The reason why we are not aware of the contradiction is that even in our usage there are still present much older connotations from Greek and especially Roman antiquity, connotations which, whatever else they may signify, have nothing to do with commandments and obedience or necessity.

Kant defined the categorical imperative by contrasting it with the hypothetical imperative. The latter tells us what we ought to do if we wish to attain a certain goal; it indicates a means to an end. It is actually no imperative in the moral sense at all. The categorical imperative tells us what to do without reference to another end. This distinction is not at all derived from moral phenomena but taken from Kant's analysis of certain propositions in the *Critique of Pure Reason* where you find categorical and hypothetical (as well as disjunctive) propositions in the table of judgments. A categorical proposition could be, for example: this body is heavy; to which could correspond a hypothetical proposition: if I support this body I stagger under its weight. In his *Critique of Practical Reason*, Kant transformed these propositions into imperatives to give them an obligatory character. Although the content is derived from reason—and while reason may compel, it never compels in the form of an imperative (no one would tell anybody: "Thou shalt say, 'two and two make four' ")— the imperative form is felt to be necessary because here the reasonable proposition addresses itself to the Will. In Kant's own words: "The conception of an objective principle, so far as it constrains a will, is a command (of reason), and the formula of this command is called an *imperative*" (*Foundations of the Metaphysics of Morals* 30).

Does reason then command the will? In that case the will would no longer be free but would stand under the dictate of reason. Reason can only tell the will: this is good, in accordance with reason; if you wish to attain it you ought to act accordingly. Which in Kant's terminology would be a kind of hypothetical imperative, or no imperative at all. And this perplexity does not grow less when we hear that "the will is nothing else than practical reason" and that "reason infallibly determines the will," so that we must either conclude that reason determines itself or, as with Kant, that "the will is a faculty of choosing only that which reason . . . recognizes as . . . good" (*Foundations* 29). It would then follow that the will is nothing but an executive organ for reason, the execution branch of the human faculties, a conclusion that stands in the most flagrant contradiction to the famous first sentence of the work from which I have quoted, *Foundations of the Metaphysics of Morals:* "Nothing in the world—indeed nothing even beyond the world—can possibly be conceived which could be called good without qualification except a *good will*" (*Foundations* 9).

Some of the perplexities into which I have led you here arise out of the perplexities inherent in the human faculty of willing itself, a faculty of which ancient philosophy knew nothing and which was not discovered in its awesome complexities before Paul and Augustine. I will return to this subject later, but here I merely wish to draw your attention to the need Kant felt to give his rational proposition an obligatory character, for, in distinction to the perplexities of the will, the problem of making moral propositions obligatory has plagued moral philosophy since its beginning with Socrates. When Socrates said it is better to suffer wrong than to do wrong, he made a statement which according to him was a statement of reason, and the trouble with this statement ever since has been that it cannot be proved. Its validity cannot be demonstrated without stepping outside the discourse of rational argument. In Kant, as in all philosophy after antiquity, you have the additional difficulty of how to persuade the will to accept the dictate of reason. If we leave the contradictions aside and address ourselves only to what Kant meant to say, then he obviously thought of the Good Will as the will that when told "Thou shalt" will answer, "Yes, I will." And in order to describe this relationship between two human faculties which clearly are not the same and where clearly one does not automatically determine the other, he introduced the form of the imperative and brought back the concept of obedience, through a back door as it were.[9]

There is, finally, the most shocking perplexity which I merely indicated before: the evasion, the sidestepping, or the explaining away of human wickedness. If the tradition of moral philosophy (as distinguished from the tradition of religious thought) is agreed on one point from Socrates to Kant and, as we shall see, to the present, then that is that it is impossible for man to do wicked things deliberately, to want evil for evil's sake. To be sure, the catalogue of human vices is old and rich, and in an enumeration where neither gluttony nor sloth (minor matters after all) are missing, sadism, the sheer pleasure in causing and contemplating pain and suffering, is curiously missing; that is, the one vice which we have reason to call the vice of all vices, that for untold centuries has been known only in pornographic literature and paintings of the perverse. It may always have been common enough but was usually restricted to the bedroom and only seldom dragged into the courtroom. Even the Bible, where all other human shortcomings occur somewhere, is silent on it as far as I know; and this may be the reason why Tertullian and also Thomas Aquinas in all innocence, as it were, counted the contemplation of the sufferings in hell among the pleasures to be expected in Paradise. The first to be really scandalized by this was Nietzsche (*Genealogy of Morals* 1.15). Aquinas, incidentally, qualified the future joys: not the sufferings as such, but as proof of divine justice, are pleasing to the saints.

But these are only vices, and religious, in contrast to philosophic, thought tells about original sin and the corruption of human nature. But not even there do we hear of deliberate wrongdoing: Cain did not want to become Cain when he went and slew Abel, and even Judas Iscariot, the greatest example of mortal sin, went and hanged himself. Religiously (not morally) speaking, it seems that they must all be forgiven because they did not know what they were doing. There is one exception to this rule and it occurs in the teaching of Jesus of Nazareth, the same who had preached forgiveness for all those sins which in one way or another can be explained by human weakness, that is, dogmatically speaking, by the corruption of human nature through the original fall. And yet this great lover of sinners, of those who trespassed, once mentions in the same context that there are others who cause *skandala*, disgraceful offenses, for which "it were better that a millstone were hanged about his neck, and he cast into the sea." It were better that he had never been born. But Jesus does not tell us what the nature is of these scandalous offenses: we feel the truth of his words but cannot pin it down.

We might be a bit better off if we would permit ourselves to turn to literature, to Shakespeare or Melville or Dostoevsky, where we find the great villains. They also may not be able to tell us anything specific about the nature of evil, but at least they don't dodge it. We know, and we can almost see, how it haunted their minds constantly, and how well aware they were of the possibilities of human wickedness. And yet, I wonder if it would help us much. In the depths of the greatest villains—Iago (not Macbeth or Richard III), Claggart in Melville's *Billy Budd,* and everywhere in Dostoevsky—there is always despair and the envy which goes with despair. That all radical evil comes from the depths of despair we have been told explicitly by Kierkegaard— and we could have learned it from Milton's Satan and many others. It sounds so very convincing and plausible because we have also been told and taught that the devil is not only *diabolos,* the slanderer who bears false testimony, or Satan, the adversary who tempts men, but that he is also Lucifer the light-bearer, a Fallen Angel. In other words, we did not need Hegel and the power of negation in order to combine the best and the worst. There has always been some kind of nobility about the real evildoer, though of course not about the little scoundrel who lies and cheats at games. Claggart and Iago act out of envy of those they know are better than themselves; it is the simple God-given nobility of the Moor that is envied, or the even simpler purity and innocence of a lowly shipmate whose social and professional better Claggart clearly is. I don't doubt the psychological insight of either Kierkegaard or the literature which is on his side. But is it not obvious that there is still some nobility even in this despair-born envy, which we know to be utterly absent from the real thing? According to Nietzsche, the man who despises himself respects at least the one in him who despises! But the real evil is what causes us speechless horror, when all we can say is: This should never have happened.

II

The very words we use for the matters under discussion, "ethics" and "morals," mean much more than their etymological origin indicates. We do not deal with customs or manners or habits, nor even with virtues strictly speaking, since virtues are the result of some training or teaching. We deal, rather, with the assertion, upheld by all philosophers who ever touched the matter, that, first, there is a distinction between right and wrong, and that it is an absolute distinction, unlike distinctions between large and small, heavy and light, which are relative; and that, second, every sane human being is able to make this distinction. It would seem to follow from these assumptions that there can be no new discoveries in moral philosophy—that what is right and what is wrong has always been known. We were surprised that this whole division of philosophy has never received another name indicating its true nature, for we agreed that the basic assumption of all moral philosophy, that it is better to suffer wrong than to do wrong, plus the conviction that this statement is self-evident to every sane person, has not stood the test of time. On the contrary, our own experiences seem to affirm that the original names of these matters *(mores* and *ethos)*, which imply that they are but manners, customs, and habits, may in a sense be more adequate than philosophers have thought. Still, we were not ready to throw moral philosophy out of the window for this reason. For we took the agreement of philosophic and religious thought in this matter to weigh as heavily as the etymological origin of the words we use and the experiences we have had ourselves.

The very few moral propositions which supposedly sum up all special precepts and commands, such as "Love thy neighbor as *thyself*," "Don't do unto others what you don't want to be done to *yourself*," and, finally, Kant's famous formula: "Act in such a way that the maxim of your action can become a general law for all intelligible beings," all take as their standard the Self and hence the intercourse of man with himself. In our context it does not matter whether the standard is self-love, as in the Hebrew-Christian precepts, or the fear of self-contempt as in Kant. We were surprised at this because morality, after all, is supposed to rule man's conduct toward others, and if we speak of goodness or think of those persons in history who were good—Jesus of Nazareth, St. Francis of Assisi, and so forth—we are likely to praise them for their selflessness, just as we usually equate human wickedness with some kind of selfishness, egoism, and the like.

And here again, language is on the side of the Self, as it was on the side of those who believe all questions of morals are merely matters of customs and manners. Conscience in all languages means originally not a faculty of knowing and judging right and wrong but what we now call consciousness, that is, the faculty by which we know, are aware of, ourselves. In Latin as in Greek, the word for consciousness was taken over to indicate conscience as well; in French the same word *conscience* is still used for both, the cognitive and the moral meaning; and in English, the word "conscience" has only recently acquired its special moral meaning. We are reminded of the old Delphic *gnothi sauton*, know thyself, inscribed on the temple of Apollo, which together with *meden agan,* nothing too much, can and have been taken as the first prephilosophic general moral precepts.

Moral propositions, like all propositions claiming to be true, must be either self-evident or sustained by proofs or demonstrations. If they are self-evident, they are of a coercive nature; the human mind cannot help accepting them, it bows to the dictate of reason. The evidence is compelling and no argument to sustain them is needed, no discourse except elucidation and clarification. To be sure, what is presupposed here is "right reason" and you may object that not all men are equally endowed with it. In the case of moral, as distinguished from scientific, truth, however, it is assumed that the commonest man and the most sophisticated one are equally open to compelling evidence—that every human being is in possession of this kind of rationality, of the moral law within me, as Kant used to say. Moral propositions have always been held to be self-evident and it was very early discovered that they can't be proved, that they are axiomatic. From this it would follow that an obligation—the "Thou shalt" or "Shalt not," the imperative—is unnecessary and I tried to show the historical reasons for Kant's categorical imperative, which might just as well have been a categorical statement—like Socrates' statement: it is better to suffer wrong than to do wrong, and not: Thou shalt suffer wrong rather than do it. Socrates still believed that with sufficient reasons before you, you cannot fail to act accordingly, whereas Kant, knowing that the will—this faculty unknown to antiquity—can say no to reason, felt it necessary to introduce an obligation. The obligation, however, is by no means self-evident, and it has never been proved without stepping outside the range of rational discourse. Behind the "thou shalt," "thou shalt not," stands an "or else," the threat of a sanction enforced by an avenging God or by the consent of the community, or by conscience, which is the threat of the self-punishment which we commonly call repentance. In the case of Kant, conscience threatens you with self-contempt; in the case of Socrates, as we shall see, with self-contradiction. And those who fear self-contempt or self-contradiction are again those who live with themselves; they find moral propositions self-evident, they don't need the obligation.

An example from our recent experiences illustrates this point. If you examine the few, the very few, who in the moral collapse of Nazi Germany remained completely intact and free of all guilt, you will discover that they never went through anything like a great moral conflict or a crisis of conscience. They did not ponder the various issues—the issue of the lesser evil or of loyalty to their country or to their oath, or whatever else there might have been at stake. Nothing of the sort. They might have debated the pros and cons of action and there were always many reasons that spoke against the chances of any success in this direction; also they might have been afraid, and there was much to fear. But they never doubted that crimes remained crimes even if legalized by the government, and that it was better not to participate in these crimes under any circumstances. In other words, they did not feel an obligation but acted according to something which was self-evident to them even though it was no longer self-evident to those around them. Hence their conscience, if that is what it was, had no obligatory character, it said, "This I *can't* do," rather than, "This I *ought* not to do."

The positive side of this "I can't" is that it corresponds to the self-evidence of the moral proposition; it means: I can't murder innocent people just as I can't say, "two and two equal five." You can always counter the "thou shalt" or the "you ought" by talking back: I will not or I cannot for whatever reasons. Morally the only reliable people when the chips are down are those who say "I can't."[10] The disadvantage of this complete adequacy of the alleged self-evidence or moral truth is that it must remain entirely negative. It has nothing whatsoever to do with action, it says no more than "I'd rather suffer than do." Politically speaking—that is, from the viewpoint of the community or of the world we live in—it is irresponsible; its standard is the self and not the world, neither its improvement nor change. These people are neither heroes nor saints, and if they become martyrs, which of course may happen, it happens against their will. In the world, moreover, where power counts, they are impotent. We might call them moral personalities, but we shall see later that this is almost a redundancy; the quality of being a person, as distinguished from merely being human, is not among the individual properties, gifts, talents, or shortcomings, with which men are born, and which they may use or abuse. An individual's personal quality is precisely his "moral" quality, if we take the word neither in its etymological nor in its conventional sense but in the sense of moral philosophy.

There is finally the perplexity that philosophic as well as religious thought somehow evades the problem of evil. According to our tradition, all human wickedness is accounted for by either human blindness and ignorance or human weakness, the inclination to yield to temptation. Man—so the implied argument runs—is able neither to do good automatically nor to do evil deliberately. He is *tempted* to do evil and he needs an *effort* to do good. So deeply rooted has this notion become—not through the teachings of Jesus of Nazareth, but through the doctrines of Christian moral philosophy —that people commonly regard as right what they don't like to do and as wrong whatever tempts them. The most famous and also the most influential philosophic statement of this age-old prejudice you will find in Kant, to whom all inclination is temptation by definition, the mere inclination to do good as well as the temptation to do wrong. This is best illustrated in a little-known anecdote that tells of Kant taking his proverbial daily walk through the streets of Königsberg at exactly the same hour every day and of his having yielded to the habit of giving alms to the beggars he encountered. For this purpose he brought new coins with him, so as not to insult the beggars by giving them shabby, worn-out pieces of money. He also used to give about three times as much as was common, with the result, of course, that he was beleaguered by beggars. He finally had to change the hour of his daily walk but was too ashamed of himself to tell the truth and invented some butcher's apprentice who, he said, had assaulted him. For his real reason for changing his promenade was of course that this habit of giving could in no way be reconciled with his moral formula, the categorical imperative. Which general law, indeed, valid for all possible worlds or intelligible beings, could be derived from the maxim "Give to everybody who asks of you"?

I tell you this story also to indicate an insight into human nature which only very seldom we find expressed theoretically in the history of moral thought. It is, I think, a simple fact that people are at least as often *tempted* to do good and need an *effort* to do evil as vice versa. Machiavelli knew this quite well when he said in *The Prince* that rulers must be taught "how *not* to be good," and he did not mean that they ought to be taught how to be evil and wicked, but simply how to avoid both inclinations, and to act according to political, as distinguished from moral and religious, as well as from criminal principles. For Machiavelli, the standard by which you judge is the world and not the self—the standard is exclusively political—and that is what makes him so important for moral philosophy. He is more interested in Florence than in the salvation of his soul, and he thinks that people who are more concerned with the salvation of souls than with the world should keep out of politics. On a much lower level of thought, though much more influential, we find Rousseau's assertion that man is good and becomes wicked in and through society. But Rousseau means no more than that society makes men indifferent to the sufferings of their fellow men, whereas man by nature has an "innate repugnance to see others suffer"—hence, he speaks of certain natural, almost physical properties which we might well share with other animal species of which the opposite is perversion, no less physical and no less part of our animal nature, but not evil and deliberate wickedness.

But let us come back for a moment to this issue of inclination and temptation, and the question of why Kant tended to equate them, of why he saw in every inclination a temptation to lead one astray. Every inclination turns outward, it leans out of the self in the direction of whatever may affect me from the outside world. It is precisely through inclination, through leaning out of myself as I may lean out of the window to look into the street, that I establish contact with the world. Under no circumstances can my inclination be determined by my intercourse with myself; if I bring myself into play, if I reflect upon myself, I lose, as it were, the object of my inclination. The old and yet strange notion that I can love myself presupposes that I can incline towards myself as I incline out of myself toward others, be they objects or people. In Kant's language, inclination means to be *affected* by things outside myself, things which I may desire or for which I may feel a natural affinity; and this being-affected by something that does not rise out of myself, my reason or my will, is for Kant inconsistent with human freedom. I am attracted or repelled by something and am therefore no longer a free agent. The moral law, on the contrary, valid as you will remember for all intelligible beings, including the possible inhabitants of another planet or angels, is free from being affected by anything but itself. And since freedom is defined as *not* being determined by external causes, only a will free from inclination can be called good and free. We found the evasion of evil in this philosophy to reside in the assumption that the will cannot be free and wicked at the same time. Wickedness in Kant's term is an *absurdum morale,* a moral absurdity.[11]

In the *Gorgias,* Socrates proposes three highly paradoxical statements: (1) It is better to suffer wrong than to do wrong; (2) It is better for the doer to be punished than to go unpunished; and (3) The tyrant who can do with impunity whatever he pleases is an unhappy man. We shall not be concerned with the last of these statements, and only touch upon the second. We have lost the ear for the paradoxical nature of such statements. It is pointed out to Socrates by Polus, one of his interlocutors, that he "says such things as no human being would utter" (*Gorgias* 473e) and Socrates does not deny this. On the contrary, he is convinced that all Athenians will agree with Polus, and that he is "left alone, unable to agree" with them (472b); and yet he believes every man actually does agree with him—without knowing it—just as the Great King and the bad tyrant never discovered they were the most miserable of all men. Throughout the dialogue runs the conviction of all concerned that every man wishes and does what he thinks is best for himself; it is taken for granted that what is best for the individual is also good for the commonwealth and the question of what to do in case of a conflict is nowhere explicitly raised. Those engaged in the dialogue are to decide what constitutes happiness and what misery, and to call upon the opinions of the many, of numbers, is like letting children form a tribunal about matters of health and dieting, when the physician is in the dock and the cook draws up the indictment. Nothing that Socrates says in support of his paradoxes convinces his adversaries even for a moment, and the whole enterprise ends like the much greater enterprise of the *Republic,* with Socrates telling a "myth" which he believes is a "logos," that is, a reasoned argument, and which he tells Callicles as if it were the truth (*Georgias* 523a–527b). And then you read the tale, perhaps an old wives' tale, about life after death: death is the separation of body and soul, when the soul, stripped of its body, appears naked before an equally bodiless judge, "soul itself piercing very soul" (523e). After this comes the parting of the ways, one to the Island of the Blessed, and the other to Tartarus and the punishment of crooked, ugly souls, stained with the scars of crimes. Some of these will be improved by the punishment while the worst are made examples to be beheld by others, presumably in a sort of Purgatory, "that they may see what they suffer and fear and become better" (525b). And it is clear that Tartarus will be well-populated and the Blessed Island almost a desert, most likely inhabited by a few "philosophers who did not engage in many activities during their lifetimes, and were not busybodies, but concerned themselves only with what regarded them" (526c).

The two statements which are at stake: that it is better for a wrongdoer to be punished than to go unpunished, and that it is better to suffer wrong than to do wrong, do not at all belong in the same category, and the myth, strictly speaking, refers only to the paradox about punishment. It spins out a metaphor introduced earlier in the dialogue, the metaphor of a healthy and a diseased or crooked soul taken over from the state of the body, which permits Plato to liken punishment to the taking of medicine. It is unlikely that this metaphorical way of speaking about the soul is Socratic. It was Plato who first developed a doctrine of the soul;

and it is equally unlikely that Socrates, who in distinction to Plato was certainly not a poet, ever told such pretty tales. For our purposes, we shall retain only the following points of the myth: first, that these myths always occur after it has become quite obvious that all attempts to convince have failed, and hence as a kind of alternative to reasoned argument; second, that their underlying tenor invariably says that if you cannot be convinced by what I say, it would be better for you to believe in the following tale; and, third, that of all people it is the philosopher who arrives at the Island of the Blessed.

Let us now turn our attention to this inability to convince, on one side, and to the unshaken conviction of Socrates that he is right even though he admits that the whole world stands against him, on the other. Quite at the end of the dialogue he admits even a bit more: he concedes stupidity and ignorance *(apaideusia)* (527d–e), and by no means ironically. We talk about these matters, he says, like children who can never hold the same opinion on the same issue for any length of time, but change their minds constantly. ("For it seems to me shameful that, being what apparently at this moment we are, we should consider ourselves to be fine fellows, when we can never hold to the same views about the same questions—and those too the most vital of all—so deplorably uneducated are we!" [527d]) But the matters at stake here are not child's play; on the contrary, they are "the greatest" matters. This admission that we change our minds about moral matters is very serious. Socrates seems to agree here with his opponents who hold that only the might-is-right doctrine is "natural," that everything else, and especially all laws, are by convention only, and that conventions change from place to place and from time to time. So that "what is right *(ta dikaia)* has no natural existence at all, that men are perpetually disputing about rights

and altering them, and whatever alteration they make at any time
is at that time authoritative, owing its existence to artifice and legislation, and not in any way to nature" (*Laws* 889e–890a).

I have quoted to you from Plato's last work, in which Socrates
does not appear, but which makes clear allusion to the *Gorgias.*
Here Plato has abandoned both the Socratic belief in the wholesome effect of discourse and his own earlier conviction that one
must invent, as it were, a myth with which to threaten the multitude. Persuasion, he says, will not be possible, because these
things seem hard to understand, "not to mention that it would
require a dismal length of time." He therefore proposes that the
"laws be written down" because then they will be "always at rest."
The laws, of course, will again be man-made and not "natural,"
but they will conform to what Plato called Ideas; and while wise
men will know that the laws are not "natural" and everlasting—
only a human imitation—the multitude will end by believing that
they are, because they are "at rest" and do not change. These laws
are not the truth, but they are not mere conventions either. Conventions are arrived at by consent, the consensus of the people,
and you will remember that in the *Gorgias* Socrates' opponents
are described as "lovers of the *demos,* the people," true democ-
rats, we may say, against whom Socrates describes himself as the
lover of philosophy, which does not say one thing today and
another tomorrow, but always the same thing. But it is philosophy, not Socrates, that is unchanging and always the same, and
though Socrates confesses to being in love with wisdom, he most
emphatically denies that he is wise: his wisdom consists merely in
knowing that no mortal can be wise.

It is precisely on this point that Plato parted company with
Socrates. In the doctrine of Ideas, which is exclusively Platonic
and not Socratic, and which for these purposes you find best

expounded in the *Republic,* Plato taught the separate existence of a realm of Ideas, or Forms, in which such things as Justice, Goodness, etc. "exist by nature with a being of their own." Not through discourse, but by looking toward these Forms, visible to the eyes of the mind, the philosopher is informed by Truth, and through his soul, which is invisible and imperishable—as contrasted with the body which is both visible and perishable, and subject to constant change—he partakes of the invisible, imperishable, unchangeable Truth. He partakes of it, that is, through seeing and beholding it, not through reasoning and argument. When I told you of the self-evidence of general moral statements, of their compelling nature for those who perceive them and of the impossibility of proving their axiomatic verity to those who do not perceive them, I was talking in Platonic rather than Socratic terms. Socrates believed in the spoken word, that is, in the argument which can be arrived at by reasoning, and such reasoning can proceed only in a sequence of spoken statements. These statements must follow each other logically, they must not contradict each other. The aim, as he says in the *Gorgias,* is "to fix and bind them . . . in words which are like bonds of iron and adamant so that neither you nor anybody else will be able to break them." Everybody who can speak and is aware of the rules of contradiction should then be bound by the final conclusion. The early Platonic dialogues could easily be read as a great series of refutations of this belief; the trouble is precisely that words and arguments cannot be "fixed with iron bonds." This is not possible because they "move around" *(Euthyphro),* because the reasoning process itself is without end. Within the realm of words, and all thinking as a process is a process of speaking, we shall never find an iron rule by which to determine what is right and what is wrong with the same certainty with which we determine—to use again

Socratic or Platonic examples—what is small and big through number, what is heavy and light through weight, where the standard or measurement is always the same. Plato's doctrine of Ideas introduced such standards and measurements into philosophy, and the whole problem of how to tell right from wrong now boiled down to whether or not I am in possession of the standard or the "idea" which I must apply in each particular case. Hence, for Plato, the whole question of who will and who won't behave according to moral precepts ultimately is decided by the kind of "soul" a man possesses, and this soul allegedly can be made better through punishment.

You find this point made very explicitly in the *Republic*, where Socrates encounters in Thrasymachus the same difficulties he encounters in Callicles in the *Gorgias*. Thrasymachus holds that that which is in the interest of the ruler is called "just"; "just" is nothing but the name given by those holding power to any action they enjoin by law upon their subjects. Callicles, on the contrary, had explained that laws, mere conventions, are made by the weak majority to protect them against the few who are strong. The two theories are only seemingly in opposition: the question of right and wrong in both instances is a question of power, and we can switch without difficulties from the *Gorgias* to the *Republic* in this respect (although by no means in others). In the *Republic*, there are two disciples of Socrates present at the dialogue between Socrates and Thrasymachus, Glaucon and Adeimantus, and they are no more convinced by Socrates' arguments than Thrasymachus himself. Hence they plead Thrasymachus' cause. Socrates, after hearing them, exclaims, "There must indeed be some divine quality in your nature [*physis*, see *Republic* 367e], if you can plead the cause of injustice so eloquently and still not be convinced yourselves that it is better than justice." Socrates, having failed to con-

vince his own disciples, is at a loss what to do next. And he turns
from his strictly moral quest (as we now would say) to the political question of which is the best form of government, giving as
his excuse that it is easier to read large letters than small ones, and
assuming that he will find in an examination of the state the same
traits he wanted to analyze in persons—since the state is only the
man writ large. In our context, it is decisive that it is clearly their
own nature that has convinced Glaucon and Adeimantus of the
truth that justice is better than injustice; but when it comes to
arguing about the matter, they are not convinced by Socrates'
arguments and show that they can argue very well and very convincingly against what they know to be true. It is not the *logos*
that convinces them, but what they see with the eyes of the mind,
and the Parable of the Cave is also in part a tale of the impossibility of translating convincingly such seen evidence into words
and arguments.

If you think these matters through, you will easily arrive at
the Platonic solution: those few whose nature, the nature of their
souls, lets them see the truth, don't need any obligation, any "Thou
Shalt—or else," because what matters is self-evident. And since
those who don't see the truth can't be convinced by arguments,
some means has to be found to make them behave, to force them
to act, without being convinced—as though they, too, had "seen."
These means are of course those myths of a hereafter, which
Plato used to conclude many of the dialogues that treat of moral
and political matters—stories which he introduces in the beginning rather diffidently, perhaps only as old wives' tales, and finally
in his last work (the *Laws*) abandons altogether.

I have dwelt on the Platonic teaching to show you how matters
stand—or shall we say stood?—if you don't put your trust in
conscience. Its etymological origin notwithstanding (that is, its

original identity with consciousness), conscience acquired its specific moral character only when it was understood as an organ through which man hears the word of God rather than his own words. Hence, if we wish to talk about these matters in secular terms, we have very little to fall back on other than ancient, pre-Christian philosophy. And isn't it striking that you find here, in the midst of philosophic thought which is in no way bound by any religious dogma, a doctrine of hell, purgatory, and paradise, complete with a Last Judgment, rewards and punishments, the distinction between venial and mortal sins, and the rest of it? The only thing which you will look for in vain is the notion that sins can be forgiven.

However we wish to interpret this astounding fact, let us be clear about one thing: that ours is the first generation since the rise of Christianity in the West in which the masses, and not only a small elite, no longer believe in "future states" (as the Founding Fathers still put it) and who therefore are committed (it would seem) to think of conscience as an organ that will react without hope for rewards and without fear of punishment. Whether people still believe that this conscience is informed by some divine voice is, to say the very least, open to doubt. The fact that all our legal institutions, insofar as they are concerned with criminal acts, still rely on such an organ to inform every man of right and wrong, even though he may not be conversant with books of law, is no argument for its existence. Institutions frequently long survive the basic principles on which they are founded.

But let us return to Socrates, who knew nothing of Plato's doctrine of Ideas, and hence nothing of the axiomatic, nondiscursive self-evidence of things seen with the eyes of the mind. In the *Gorgias* Socrates, confronted with the paradoxical nature of his statement and his inability to convince, makes the following reply: he first says that Callicles will "not be in agreement with himself but that throughout his life he will contradict himself." And then he adds that as far as he himself is concerned he believes that "it would be better for me that my lyre or a chorus I direct were out of tune and loud with discord, and that most men should not agree with me and contradict me, rather than that I, being one, should be out of tune with myself and contradict myself" (482b–c). The key notion in this sentence is *"I who am one,"* which is unfortunately left out in many English translations. The meaning is clear: even though I am one, I am not simply one, I have a self and I am related to this self as my own self. This self is by no means an illusion; it makes itself heard by talking to me—I talk to myself, I am not only aware of myself—and in this sense, though I am one, I am two-in-one and there can be harmony or disharmony with the self. If I disagree with other people, I can walk away; but I cannot walk away from myself, and therefore I better first try to be in agreement with myself before I take all others into consideration. This same sentence also spells out the actual reason it is better to suffer wrong than to do wrong: if I do wrong I am condemned to live together with a wrongdoer in an unbearable intimacy; I can never get rid of him. Hence the crime that remains hidden from the eyes of gods and men, a crime that does not appear at all because there is no one to whom it appears and which you'll find mentioned in Plato time and again, actually does not exist: as I am my own partner when I am thinking, I am my own witness when I am acting. I know the agent and am condemned to live together with him. He is not silent. This is the only reason Socrates ever gives, and the question is both why this reason does not convince his opponent and why it is a sufficient reason for those people whom Plato in the *Republic* calls men endowed with a noble nature. But please be aware that Socrates here talks about something else altogether: it is not a question of seeing something imperishable and divine outside yourself, for whose apperception you need a special organ, just as you need eyesight for perceiving the visible world around you. With Socrates, no special organ is needed because you remain within yourself and no transcendent standard, as we would say, or nothing outside yourself, received with the eyes of the mind, informs you of right and wrong. To be sure, it is difficult if not impossible to convince others in discourse of the truth of the statement, but you yourself have arrived at it for the sake of this living with yourself that becomes manifest in discourse between you and yourself. If you are at odds with your self it is as though you were forced to live and have daily intercourse with your own enemy. No one can want that. If you do wrong you live together with a wrongdoer, and while many prefer to do wrong for their own benefit rather than suffer wrong, no one will prefer to live together with a thief or a murderer or a liar. This is what people forget who praise the tyrant who has come into power through murder and fraud.

In the *Gorgias*, there exists only one short reference to what this relationship between the I and the Self, between me and myself, consists of. And I therefore turn to another dialogue, the *Theaetetus,* the dialogue on knowledge, where Socrates gives a clear account of it. He wishes to explain what he understands by *dianoeisthai,* to think a matter through, and he says: "I call it a discourse that the mind carries on with itself about any subject it is considering. And I'll explain it to you though I am not too sure about it myself. It looks to me as though this is nothing else but *dialegesthai,* talking something through, only that the mind asks itself questions and answers them, saying yes or no to itself. Then it arrives at the limit where things must be decided, when the two say the same and are no longer uncertain, which we then set down as the mind's opinion. Making up one's mind and forming an opinion I thus call discourse, and the opinion itself I call a spoken statement, pronounced not to someone else and aloud but silently to oneself." And you find the same description in almost identical words in the *Sophist:* thought and spoken statement are the same, except that the thought is a dialogue carried on by the mind with itself without sound, and opinion is the end of this dialogue. That a wrongdoer will not be a very good partner for this silent dialogue seems rather obvious.[12]

From what we know of the historical Socrates it seems likely that he who spent his days in the marketplace—the same marketplace which Plato's philosopher shuns explicitly *(Theaetetus)*—must have believed that all men do not have an innate voice of conscience, but feel the need to talk matters through; that all men talk to themselves. Or, to put it more technically, that all men are two-in-one, not only in the sense of consciousness and self-consciousness (that whatever I do I am at the same time somehow aware of doing it), but in the very specific and active sense of this silent dialogue, of having constant intercourse, of being on speaking terms with themselves. If they only knew what they were doing, so Socrates must have thought, they would understand how important it was for them to do nothing that could spoil it. If the faculty of speech distinguishes man from other animal species—and this is what the Greeks actually believed and what Aristotle later said in his famous definition of man—then it is this silent dialogue of myself with myself in which my specifically human quality is proved. In other words, Socrates believed that men are not merely rational animals but thinking beings, and that they would rather give up all other ambitions and even suffer injury and insult than to forfeit this faculty.

The first to differ was Plato, as we saw, who expected to see only philosophers—who made thinking their special business—

on the Island of the Blessed. And since it is impossible to deny that no other human activity demands so peremptorily and inevitably the intercourse of myself with myself than the silent dialogue of thought, and since, after all, thinking does not belong among the most frequent and most common occupations of men, we have a natural tendency to agree with him. Except we forget that we, who no longer believe in thinking as a common human habit, still uphold that even the most common men should be aware of what is right and what is wrong, and should agree with Socrates that it is better to suffer than to do wrong. The political concern is not whether the act of striking somebody unjustly or of being struck unjustly is more disgraceful. The concern is exclusively with having a world in which such acts do not occur (*Gorgias* 508).

Let me indicate some of the directions into which these considerations may lead us with respect to the perplexities I stated at the beginning.

The reason moral philosophy, though dealing with the "greatest matters," never found a name adequate to its high purpose may reside in the fact that the philosophers could not think of it as a separate section of philosophy, like logic, cosmology, ontology, etc. If the moral precept rises out of the thinking activity itself, if it is the implied condition of the silent dialogue between me and myself, on whatever issue, then it is rather the prephilosophical condition of philosophy itself, and a condition therefore which philosophic thought shares with all other, nontechnical ways of thinking. For the objects of this activity are of course by no means restricted to specifically philosophic or, for that matter, scientific topics. Thinking as an activity can arise out of every occurrence; it is present when I, having watched an incident in the street or having become implicated in some occurrence, now start considering what has happened, telling it to myself as a kind of story, preparing it in this way for its subsequent communication to others, and so forth. The same is of course even truer if the topic of my silent consideration happens to be something I have done myself. To do wrong means to spoil this ability; the safest way for the criminal never to be detected and to escape punishment is to forget what he did, and not to think about it any more. By the same token, we may say that repentance first of all consists in not forgetting what one did, in "returning to it," as the Hebrew verb *shuv* indicates. This connection of thinking and remembering is especially important in our context. No one can remember what he has not thought through in talking about it with himself.

However, while thinking in this nontechnical sense is certainly no prerogative of any special kind of men, philosophers or scientists, etc.—you find it present in all walks of life and may find it entirely absent in what we call intellectuals—it cannot be denied that it certainly is much less frequent than Socrates supposed, although one hopes a bit more frequent than Plato feared. No doubt I can refuse to think and to remember and still remain quite normally human. The danger, however, not only for myself, whose speech, having forfeited the highest actualization of the human capacity for speech, will therefore become meaningless, but also for others who are forced to live with a possibly highly intelligent and still entirely thoughtless creature, is very great. If I refuse to remember, I am actually ready to do anything—just as my courage would be absolutely reckless if pain, for instance, were an experience immediately forgotten.

This question of remembrance brings us at least one small step nearer to the bothersome question of the nature of evil. Philosophy (and also great literature, as I mentioned before) knows the villain only as somebody who is in despair and whose despair sheds a certain nobility about him. I am not going to deny that this type of evildoer exists, but I am certain that the greatest evils we know of are not due to him who has to face himself again and whose curse is that he cannot forget. The greatest evildoers are those who don't remember because they have never given thought to the matter, and, without remembrance, nothing can hold them back. For human beings, thinking of past matters means moving in the dimension of depth, striking roots and thus stabilizing themselves, so as not to be swept away by whatever may occur—the Zeitgeist or History or simple temptation. The greatest evil is not radical, it has no roots, and because it has no roots it has no limitations, it can go to unthinkable extremes and sweep over the whole world.

I mentioned the quality of being a person as distinguished from being merely human (as the Greeks distinguished themselves as *logon echon* from the barbarians), and I said that to speak about a moral personality is almost a redundancy. Taking our cue from Socrates' justification of his moral proposition, we may now say that in this process of thought in which I actualize the specifically human difference of speech, I explicitly constitute myself a person, and I shall remain one to the extent that I am capable of such constitution ever again and anew. If this is what we commonly call personality, and it has nothing to do with gifts and intelligence, it is the simple, almost automatic result of thoughtfulness. To put it another way, in granting pardon, it is the person and not the crime that is forgiven; in rootless evil there is no person left whom one could ever forgive.

It is in this connection that the curious insistence of all moral and religious thought on the importance of self-attachment may perhaps be a bit better understood. It is not a question of loving myself as I may love others, but of being more dependent on this silent partner I carry with myself, more at his mercy, as it were, than is perhaps the case with anybody else. The fear of losing oneself is legitimate, for it is the fear of no longer being able to talk with oneself. And not only grief and sorrow but also joy and happiness and all the other emotions would be altogether unbearable if they had to remain mute, inarticulate.

But there is still another side to this matter. The Socratic-Platonic description of the process of thinking seems to me so important because it implies, albeit only in passing, the fact that men exist in the plural and not in the singular, that men and not Man inhabit the earth. Even if we are by ourselves, when we articulate or actualize this being-alone we find that we are in company, in the company of ourselves. Loneliness, that nightmare which, as we all know, can very well overcome us in the midst of a crowd, is precisely this being deserted by oneself, the temporary inability to become two-in-one, as it were, while in a situation where there is no one else to keep us company. Seen from this viewpoint, it is indeed true that my conduct toward others will depend on my conduct toward myself. Only no specific content, no special duties and obligations are involved, nothing indeed but the sheer capacity of thought and remembrance, or its loss.

Let me finally remind you of those murderers in the Third Reich who led not only an impeccable family life but liked to spend their leisure time reading Hölderlin and listening to Bach, proving (as though proof in this matter had been lacking before) that intellectuals can as easily be led into crime as anybody else. But aren't sensitivity, and a feeling for the so-called higher things in life, mental capacities? They certainly are, but this capacity for appreciation has nothing whatever to do with thought, which, as we must remember, is an *activity* and not the passive enjoyment of something. Insofar as thinking is an activity, it can be translated into products, into such things as poems or music or paintings. All things of this kind are actually thought-things just as furniture and the objects of our daily use are rightly called use-objects: the ones are inspired by thought and the others are inspired by usage, by some human need and want. The point about these highly cultivated murderers is that there has been not a single one of them who wrote a poem worth remembering or a piece of music worth listening to or painted a picture that anybody would care to hang on his walls. More than thoughtfulness is needed to write a good poem or piece of music, or to paint a picture—you need special gifts. But no gifts will withstand the loss of integrity which you lose when you have lost this most common capacity for thought and remembrance.

III

Morality concerns the individual in his singularity. The criterion of right and wrong, the answer to the question, what ought I to do? depends in the last analysis neither on habits and customs, which I share with those around me, nor on a command of either divine or human origin, but on what I decide with regard to myself. In other words, I cannot do certain things, because having done them I shall no longer be able to live with myself. This living-with-myself is more than consciousness, more than the self-awareness that accompanies me in whatever I do and in whichever state I am. To be with myself and to judge by myself is articulated and actualized in the processes of thought, and every thought process is an activity in which I speak with myself about whatever happens to concern me. The mode of existence present in this silent dialogue of myself with myself, I now shall call *solitude*. Hence, solitude is more than, and different from, other modes of being alone, particularly and most importantly loneliness and isolation.

Solitude means that though alone, I am together with somebody (myself, that is). It means that I am two-in-one, whereas loneliness as well as isolation do not know this kind of schism, this inner dichotomy in which I can ask questions of myself and receive answers. Solitude and its corresponding activity, which is thinking, can be interrupted either by somebody else addressing me or, like every other activity, by doing something else, or by sheer exhaustion. In any of these cases, the two that I was in thought become *one* again. If somebody addresses me, I must now talk to him, and not to myself, and in talking to him, I change. I become one, possessing of course self-awareness, that is, consciousness, but no longer fully and articulately in possession of myself. If I am addressed by one person only and if, as sometimes happens, we begin to talk in the form of dialogue about the very same things either one of us has been concerned about while still in solitude, then it is as if I now address another self. And this other self, *allos authos*, was rightly defined by Aristotle as the friend. If, on the other hand, my thought process in solitude stops for some reason, I also become one again. Because this one who I now am is without company, I may reach out for the company of others—people, books, music—and if they fail me or if I am unable to establish contact with them, I am overcome by boredom and loneliness. For this I do not have to be alone: I can be very bored and very lonely in the midst of a crowd, but not in actual solitude, that is, in my own company, or together with a friend, in the sense of another self. This is why it is much harder to bear being alone in a crowd than in solitude—as Meister Eckhart once remarked.

The last mode of being alone, which I call isolation, occurs when I am neither together with myself nor in the company of others but concerned with the things of the world. Isolation can be the natural condition for all kinds of work where I am so concentrated on what I am doing that the presence of others, including myself, can only disturb me. Such work may be productive, the actual fabrication of some new object, but need not be so: learning, even the mere reading of a book requires some degree of isolation, of being protected against the presence of others. Isolation can also occur as a negative phenomenon: others with whom I share a certain concern for the world may desert me. This happens frequently in political life—it is the enforced leisure of the politician, or rather of the man who is himself a citizen but has lost contact with his fellow citizens. Isolation in this second negative sense can be borne only if it is transformed into solitude, and every one who is acquainted with Latin literature will know how the Romans, in contrast to the Greeks, discovered solitude and with it philosophy as a way of life in the enforced leisure which accompanies removal from public affairs. When you discover solitude from the standpoint of an active life spent in the company of your peers, you will come to the point at which Cato said, "Never am I more active than when I do nothing, never am I less alone than when I am by myself." You can still hear in these words, I think, the surprise of an active man, originally not alone and far from doing nothing, in the delights of solitude and the two-in-one activity of thought.

If, on the other hand, you come to discover solitude out of the nightmare of loneliness, you will understand why a philosopher, Nietzsche, presented his thoughts on this matter in a poem ("Aus

Hohen Bergen," at the end of *Beyond Good and Evil*), celebrating the Noontime of Life, when the desperate yearnings of loneliness for friends and company have come to an end because *"Um Mittag war's da wurde Eins zu Zwei"*—one became two. (There exists a much earlier aphorism on presenting thoughts in a poem in which Nietzsche remarks: "The poet presents his thoughts on the carriage of rhythm: usually because they could not walk" [*Human, All-Too-Human* 189]. What has happened, one would like to ask politely, when a philosopher does likewise?)

I mention these various forms of being alone, or the various ways in which human singularity articulates and actualizes itself, because it is so very easy to confuse them, not only because we tend to be sloppy and unconcerned with distinctions, but also because they invariably and almost unnoticeably change into one another. The concern with the self as the ultimate standard of moral conduct exists of course only in solitude. Its demonstrable validity is found in the general formula "It is better to suffer wrong than to do wrong," which, as we saw, rests on the insight that it is better to be at odds with the whole world than, being one, to be at odds with myself. This validity can therefore be maintained only for man insofar as he is a thinking being, needing himself for company for the sake of the thought process. Nothing of what we said is valid for loneliness and isolation.

Thinking and remembering, we said, is the human way of striking roots, of taking one's place in the world into which we all arrive as strangers. What we usually call a person or a personality, as distinguished from a mere human being or a nobody, actually grows out of this root-striking process of thinking. In this sense, I said it is almost a redundancy to speak of a moral personality; a person, to be sure, can still be good-natured or ill-natured, his inclinations can be generous or stingy, he may be aggressive or compliant, open or secretive; he may be given to all sorts of vices just as he may be born intelligent or stupid, beautiful or ugly, friendly or rather unkind. All this has little to do with the matters which concern us here. If he is a thinking being, rooted in his thoughts and remembrances, and hence knowing that he has to live with himself, there will be limits to what he can permit himself to do, and these limits will not be imposed on him from the outside, but will be self-set. These limits can change considerably and uncomfortably from person to person, from country to country, from century to century; but limitless, extreme evil is possible only where these self-grown roots, which automatically limit the possibilities, are entirely absent. They are absent where men skid only over the surface of events, where they permit themselves to be carried away without ever penetrating into whatever depth they may be capable of. This depth, of course, changes again from person to person, from century to century, in its specific quality as well as its dimensions. Socrates believed that by teaching people *how* to think, how to talk with themselves, as distinguished from the orator's art of how to persuade and from the wise man's ambition of teaching *what* to think and how to learn, he would improve his fellow citizens; but if we accept this assumption and then ask him what the sanctions would be for that famous crime hidden from the eyes of gods and men, he could have answered only by saying: the loss of this capacity, the loss of solitude, and, as I tried to illustrate, with it the loss of creativity— in other words, the loss of the self that constitutes the person.

Since moral philosophy was, after all, the product of philosophy, and since philosophers could not have survived the loss of the self and the loss of solitude, we may no longer be so surprised that the ultimate standard for conduct toward others has always been the self, not only in strictly philosophic but also in religious thought. Thus we find a rather typical mixture of pre-Christian and Christian thought in Nicholas of Cusa, who (in his *Vision of God* 7) lets God address man almost in the same words as the "Know Thyself" of Delphi: *Sis tu tuus et ego ero tuus* ("If Thou art Thine, I [namely God] will be Thine"). The basis of all conduct, he says, is "that I choose to be myself" *(ut ego eligam mei ipsis esse)*, and man is free because God has left him free to be himself if he so wills *(ut sim, si volam, mei ipsius)*. To this we must now add that this standard, though it can be verified in the experiences and the essential conditions of thought, does not lend itself to being spelled out in specific precepts and laws of behavior. Hence, the almost unanimous assumption of moral philosophy throughout the centuries stands in curious contradiction to our current belief that the law of the land spells out the essential moral rules upon which all men agree, either because God told them so or because they can be derived from the nature of man.

Since Socrates believed that what we now call morality, which indeed concerns man in his singularity, also improves man as a citizen, it is only fair to take into account the political objections which were raised then and which can still be raised today. Against Socrates' claim of improving the citizens, the city claimed that he corrupted the youth of Athens and that he undermined the traditional beliefs on which moral conduct rested. Let me spell out the objections, citing or paraphrasing what you'll find chiefly in the *Apology*. Socrates, spending his life in examining himself and others, instructing them and himself in thinking, cannot but question all existing standards and measurements. Far from making others more "moral," he undermines morality and shatters unquestioning belief and unquestioning obedience. Perhaps he was falsely accused of wanting to introduce new gods, but then only because he did worse: he "never either taught or professed to teach any knowledge whatever." Furthermore, as he himself admits, his calling had led him into *(idioteuein alla me demosieuein)* a life of privacy in which he has shunned life with the people at large, which is public life. That is, he has almost proved how right public opinion in Athens was when it said that philosophy was only for the young who are not yet admitted to citizenship, and that even then, while necessary for education, it should be practiced with caution because it induced *malakia,* softness of spirit. Finally, to top it all, and again upon Socrates' own admission, all he could show for himself when it came to actual conduct was a "voice" speaking from within himself that would turn him back from something he intended to do but that never urged him to act.

None of these objections can be dismissed out of hand. To think means to examine and to question; it always involves that shattering of idols of which Nietzsche was so fond. When Socrates was through with questioning, nothing was left to hold on to—neither the accepted standards of the common people, nor the accepted counterstandards of the Sophists. The dialogue with myself in solitude or with another self, even when conducted in the marketplace shuns the multitude. And when Socrates said that in his opinion no greater good ever befell Athens than his arousing the city as a gadfly arouses a large, well-bred but rather sluggish horse, then he could have meant only that nothing better can ever befall a multitude than to be broken up into single men again who can be appealed to in their singularity. If this were possible, if every man could be made to think and judge by himself, then indeed it might also be possible to do without fixed standards and rules. If this possibility is denied, and it has been denied by almost everyone after Socrates, then it is easily understood why the polis considered him a dangerous man. Anyone who only listened to the Socratic examination without thinking, without entering the thought process itself, could very well be corrupted; that is, deprived of the standards which he held unthinkingly. In other words, every one who was corruptible was now in grave danger of being corrupted. This ambiguity, that the same act will make good men better and bad men worse, was once alluded to by Nietzsche who complained of having been misunderstood by a woman: "She told me that she had no morality—and I thought that she had, like myself, a more severe morality."[13] The misunderstanding is common although the reproach in this particular case (Lou Andreas Salome) was far off the mark. All this is true enough as long as we admit that conventions, the rules and standards by which we usually live, don't show up too well under examination and that it would be foolhardy to place any reliance upon them in times of emergency. From which it follows that Socratic morality is politically relevant only in times of crisis and that the self as the ultimate criterion of moral conduct is politically a kind of emergency measure. And this implies that the invocation of allegedly moral principles for matters of everyday conduct is usually a fraud; we hardly need experience to tell us that the narrow moralists who constantly appeal to high moral principles and fixed standards are usually the first to adhere to whatever fixed standards they are offered and that respectable society, what the French call *les bien-pensants,* is more liable to become very nonrespectable and even criminal than most bohemians and beatniks. All the things we have been talking about here are important only in exceptional circumstances; and countries in which such exceptional circumstances became the rule of the land and the question of how to behave in such circumstances became the most burning issue of the day, stand, by this very fact, accused of bad government, to put it mildly. But those who under perfectly normal conditions appeal to high-flung moral standards are very much like those who take God's name in vain.

This quality of the moral issue, that it is politically a borderline phenomenon, becomes manifest when we consider that the only recommendation we are entitled to expect from the "It is better to be at odds with the whole world than being one to be at odds with myself," will always remain entirely negative. It will never tell you what to do, only prevent you from doing certain things, even though they are done by everybody around you. It should not be forgotten that the thinking process itself is incompatible with any other activity. The idiomatic *"stop* and think" is indeed entirely right. Whenever we think, we stop whatever else we may have been doing, and as long as we are two-in-one, we are unable to do anything but think.

Hence, there is more than a mere distinction between thinking and acting. There exists an inherent tension between these two kinds of activity; and Plato's scorn of the busybodies, those who keep going and never stop, is a mood that in one form or another will appear in every true philosopher. This tension, however, has been glossed over through a notion which also has been dear to all philosophers, the idea that to think is also a form of acting; that thinking, as is sometimes said, is a kind of "inner action." There are many reasons for this confusion—irrelevant reasons when the philosopher speaks in self-defense against reproaches that come from the side of acting men and of citizens, and relevant reasons which originate in the nature of thought. And thought, in con- tradistinction to contemplation with which it is all too frequently equated, is indeed an *activity,* and moreover, an activity that has certain moral results, namely that he who thinks constitutes him- self into somebody, a person or a personality. But activity and action are not the same, and the result of the thinking activity is a kind of by-product with regard to the activity itself. It is not the same as the goal which an act aims at and consciously intends. The distinction between thought and action is often expressed in the contrast of Spirit and Power, whereby Spirit and Impotence are automatically equated, and there is indeed more than a grain of truth in these expressions.

The main distinction, politically speaking, between Thought and Action lies in that I am only with my own self or the self of another while I am thinking, whereas I am in the company of the many the moment I start to act. Power for human beings who are not omnipotent can only reside in one of the many forms of human plurality, whereas every mode of human singularity is impotent by definition. It is true, however, that even in the singularity or duality of thinking processes, plurality is somehow germinally present insofar as I can think only by splitting up into two although I am one. But this two-in-one, looked upon from the standpoint of human plurality, is like the last trace of company— even when being *one* by myself, I am or can become two—which becomes so very important only because we discover plurality where we would least expect it. But insofar as being with others is concerned, it still must be regarded as a marginal phenomenon.

These considerations perhaps may explain why Socratic morality, with its negative, marginal qualities, has revealed itself as the only working morality in borderline situations, that is, in times of crisis and emergency. When standards are no longer valid anyhow—as in Athens in the last third of the fifth century and in the fourth century, or in Europe in the last third of the nineteenth century and in the twentieth century—nothing is left but the example of Socrates, who may not have been the greatest philosopher but who still is the philosopher par excellence. Whereby we must not forget that for the philosopher, who not only thinks but is extraordinarily and, in the opinion of many of his fellow citizens, inordinately fond of thinking, the moral by-product of thought is in itself of secondary importance. He does not examine things to improve either himself or others. If his fellow citizens, who are inclined to suspect him anyhow, should tell him: "We will let you go, on the condition that you give up this investigation of yours, and philosophy," the answer will always be the Socratic answer: "I hold you in the highest regard and affection but . . . as long as I have breath and strength I will not give up philosophy . . . [and] I shall not change my way of life."

Let me come back once more to the problem of conscience, whose very existence has become questionable through our more recent experiences. Conscience supposedly is a way of *feeling* beyond reason and argument and of knowing through sentiment what is right and wrong. What has been revealed beyond doubt, I think, is the fact that such feelings indeed exist, that people *feel* guilty or feel innocent, but that alas, these feelings are no reliable indications, are in fact no indications at all, of right and wrong. Guilt-feelings can, for instance, be aroused through a conflict between old habits and new commands—the old habit not to kill and the new command to kill—but they can just as well be aroused by the opposite: once killing or whatever the "new morality" demands has become a habit and is accepted by everyone, the same man will feel guilty if he does not conform. In other words, these feelings indicate conformity and nonconformity, they don't indicate morality. Antiquity, as I said before, did not yet know the phenomenon of conscience; it was discovered as the organ in man which hears the voice of God and later taken up by secular philosophy where it is of doubtful legitimacy. Within the realm of religious experience, there can't be a conflict of conscience. The voice of God speaks clearly and the question is only if I will obey it or not. Conflicts of conscience in secular terms, on the other hand, are actually nothing but deliberations between me and myself; they are not resolved through feeling but through thinking. Insofar, however, as conscience means no more than this being at peace with myself which is the condition sine qua non of thinking, it is indeed a reality; but this, as we know now, will only say, I can't and I won't. Since it is related to one's own self, no impulse to act can be expected from it.[14]

Finally, let us remember the few indications I gave of how the problem of evil looks from the standpoint of this strictly philosophic kind of morality. Evil, as defined with respect to the self and the thinking intercourse between me and myself, remains as formal, empty of content, as Kant's categorical imperative whose formalism has so often outraged his critics. If Kant said every maxim is wrong which cannot become a universally valid law, it is as if Socrates had said every act is wrong with whose agent I cannot go on living together. In comparison, Kant's formula appears less formal and much stricter; theft and murder, forgery and bearing false witness are prohibited with equal force. The question of whether I would not prefer to live with a thief rather than a murderer, that maybe I would mind a forger considerably less than somebody who has borne false witness, etc., is not even posed. The reason for this difference is also that Kant actually, despite many affirmations to the contrary, never quite distinguished between legality and morality, and that he wanted morality to become, without any intermediaries, the source of law, so that man, wherever he went and whatever he did, was his own lawgiver, an entirely autonomous person. In Kant's formula, it is the same evil that makes man either a thief or a murderer, the same fatal weakness in human nature. Another, and of course very weighty, example of an enumeration of transgressions which are not gradated according to seriousness is the decalogue, which also was supposed to be the foundation of the law of the land.

Now it is true that if you take only one of the three Socratic formulas, "It is better to suffer wrong than to do wrong," you find the same curious indifference to possible degrees of evil; but this disappears if you add the second criterion of having to live with yourself as we did here. For this is a purely moral principle, as distinguished from a legal one. As far as the agent is concerned, all he can say is "This I can't do" or, in case he has committed his act, "This I should never have done," implying that he might have done wrong before but without fatal consequences. At this point, there appears a distinction between transgressions, such as those we are confronted with daily and with which we know how to come to terms or how to get rid of either through punishment or through forgiveness, and those offenses where all we can say is "This should never have happened." From that statement it is but one step to conclude that whoever did it should never have been born. Obviously this distinction is very similar to the distinction of Jesus of Nazareth between the transgressions which I am supposed to forgive "seven times a day" and those offenses where "it were better for him that a millstone were hanged about his neck and he cast into the sea."

In our context there are two things especially suggestive in this saying. First, the word used here for offense is *skandalon*, which originally meant a trap laid for one's enemies and which here is used as the equivalent for the Hebrew word *mikhshol* or *ʒur mikhshol* which means "stumbling block." This distinction between mere transgressions and these deadly stumbling blocks seems to indicate more than the current distinction between venial and mortal sins; it indicates that these stumbling blocks cannot be removed from our path as can mere transgressions. Second, and only seemingly inconsistent with this reading of the text, please note that it were better *for him* had he never been born, for this phrase makes the remark read as though the agent of this offense, the nature of which is only indicated as an unsurmountable obstacle, had extinguished himself.

But no matter how far we may spin out the inherent consequences of the few statements which in one way or another are still the only insights we can fall back upon in our search for the nature of evil, one thing is undeniable, and that is the intensely personal and, if you will, even subjective quality of all the criteria which were proposed to you here. This is probably the most objectionable aspect of my considerations, and I shall come back to it in the next lecture when I discuss the nature of judgment. Today let me only mention to you, as it were in self-defense, two statements which essentially express the same thought, even though they originate from entirely disparate sources and types of men; they may give you perhaps an indication of what I am driving at. The first of my statements comes from Cicero and the second from Meister Eckhart, the great mystic of the fourteenth century. In the *Tusculan Disputations,* Cicero discusses the conflicting opinions of philosophers on certain issues, which are of no interest in our context. And when he comes to deciding which of them is right and which is wrong, he suddenly and quite unexpectedly introduces an altogether different criterion. He dismisses the question of objective truth and says that given the choice between the opinions of the Pythagoreans and of Plato, "By God I'd much rather go astray with Plato than hold true views with these people." And he lets his partner in the dialogue once more emphasize the point: he too would not mind at all going astray and erring with such a man. Even more surprising than this statement, which is only polemical, is the statement by Eckhart which is

frankly heretical. In one of the so-called sayings that are preserved (and which actually are anecdotes), Eckhart is supposed to
have met the happiest man, who turns out to be a beggar. The
argument goes back and forth until finally the beggar is asked if he
would still think himself happy if he should find himself in hell.
And the beggar who has based his arguments on his love of God
and the assumption that I have present with me whatever I love,
answers, Oh, yes, "I'd much rather be in hell with God than in
heaven without Him." The point is that both Cicero and Eckhart
agree that there comes a point where all objective standards—
truth, rewards and punishments in a hereafter, etc.—yield precedence to the "subjective" criterion of the kind of person I wish to
be and live together with.

If you apply these sayings to the question of the nature of evil,
the result would be a definition of the agent, and how he did it
rather than of the act itself or of its final result. And you will find
this shift from the objective *what* somebody did to the subjective
who of the agent as a marginal datum even in our legal system.
For if it is true that we indict somebody for what he did, it is
equally true that when a murderer is pardoned, one no longer
takes this deed into consideration. It is not murder which is forgiven but the killer, his person as it appears in circumstances and
intentions. The trouble with the Nazi criminals was precisely that
they renounced voluntarily all personal qualities, as if nobody
were left to be either punished or forgiven. They protested time
and again that they had never done anything out of their own initiative, that they had no intentions whatsoever, good or bad, and
that they only obeyed orders.

To put it another way: the greatest evil perpetrated is the evil
committed by nobodies, that is, by human beings who refuse to be
persons. Within the conceptual framework of these considera-

tions we could say that wrongdoers who refuse to think by themselves what they are doing and who also refuse in retrospect to think about it, that is, go back and remember what they did (which is *teshuvah* or repentance), have actually failed to constitute themselves into somebodies. By stubbornly remaining nobodies they prove themselves unfit for intercourse with others who, good, bad, or indifferent, are at the very least persons.

Everything we have discovered until now is negative. We have dealt with an activity and not with action, and the ultimate standard has been the relation toward our own self, not the relation toward others. We shall now turn our attention to action as distinguished from activity and to conduct toward others as distinguished from intercourse with oneself. In both instances we shall remain restricted to moral issues; we shall stick to men in their singularity and leave out of account all political issues such as the constitution of communities and government as well as the citizen's support of the laws of his country or his action in concert with his fellow citizens in support of a common enterprise. Hence, I shall talk about nonpolitical action, which does not take place in public, and about nonpolitical relations to others which are neither relations to other selves, i.e., friends, nor predetermined by some common worldly interest. The two phenomena that will chiefly claim our attention are actually interconnected. The first is the phenomenon of the *will*, which, according to our tradition, stirs me into action, and the second is the question of the nature of the good in an entirely positive sense, rather than the negative question of how to prevent evil.

I mentioned previously that the phenomenon of the will was unknown to antiquity. But before trying to determine its historical origin, which is of considerable interest, I'll try very briefly to give you a short analysis of its function with regard to the other human faculties. Let us suppose that we have before us a dish of strawberries and that I *desire* to eat them. This desire was of course very well known to ancient philosophy; desire has always meant to be attracted by something outside myself. This was natural and not of a very high order, belonging roughly speaking to the animal in man. The question of whether or not I shall yield to this desire was, according to the ancients, decided by reason. If, for instance, I am subject to a certain type of allergy, reason tells me not to reach out to my strawberries. Whether I shall eat them nevertheless, depends on the force of my desires on the one hand, and on the force which reason has over them, on the other. I'll eat my strawberries either because I lack reason altogether or because my reason is weaker than my desire. The well-known opposition of reason and the passions, plus the old question of whether reason is the slave of the passions or, on the contrary, the passions should and could be brought under the control of reason, hearkens back to the old schematic notions about the hierarchy of the human faculties.[15]

It is into this dichotomy that the faculty of will is inserted. The insertion means that neither desire nor reason are abolished or even pushed into an inferior rank; they both still hold their own. But the new discovery is that there is something in man that can say yes or no to the precepts of reason, hence that my yielding to desire is prompted neither by ignorance nor by weakness, but by my will, a third faculty. Reason is not enough and desire is not enough. For—and this is the new discovery in a nutshell—"the mind is not moved until it wills to be moved" (Augustine, *De libero arbitrio voluntatus* 3.1.2). I can decide against the deliberate advice of reason as I can decide against the mere attraction of objects of my appetite, and it is will rather than reason or appetite that decides the issue of what I am going to do. Hence I can will what I do not desire and I can nill, consciously stand against, what reason tells me is right, and in every act this I-will or I-will-not are the decisive factors. The will is the arbiter between reason and desire, and as such the will alone is free. Moreover, while reason reveals what is common to all men, and desire what is common to all living organisms, only the will is entirely my own.[16]

Even from this brief analysis it will be obvious that the discovery of the will must have coincided with the discovery of freedom as a philosophical issue, as distinguished from a political fact. It certainly is quite strange for us to notice that the question of freedom, particularly freedom of the will, that plays such an enormous role in all post-Christian philosophical and religious thought, should never have appeared in ancient philosophy.[17] This strangeness, however, dissolves the moment that we understand that no element of freedom can possibly reside in either reason or desire. Whatever reason on the one hand tells me may be persuasive or compelling, my appetites on the other hand are understood as the desiring reaction to whatever affects me from the outside.

Freedom, according to ancient philosophy, was altogether bound up with the I-can; "free" meant being capable of doing what one wanted to do. To say, for example, that a paralyzed man who lost his freedom of movement or a slave who stood under the command of his master, were nevertheless free insofar as they too had willpower, would have sounded like a contradiction in terms. And if you look into the philosophy of the late Stoics, especially of the slave philosopher Epictetus (whose writings are contemporaneous with those of Paul, the first Christian writer), where the question of inner freedom regardless of external, political circumstances, is raised time and again, you will immediately see that this by no means signifies a shift from desire to will, or from the I-can to the I-will, but only a shift in the objects of my desires.

In order to remain free even though I am a slave, I must so train my appetites that they will desire only what I can obtain, what depends only upon myself, and thus is actually in my power. The paralyzed man, in this interpretation, would be free, just as free as anybody else, if he only would stop wanting to use his limbs.[18]

I brought up the example of Epictetus to avoid misunderstandings. This kind of internalization, of restriction of the I-can from reality to the realms of an interior life that is limitless in its possibilities precisely because it is unreal, has little in common with our question. Much of what Nietzsche had to say in criticism of Christianity is actually applicable only to these last stages of ancient philosophy. Epictetus can indeed be understood as an example of that resentful slave mentality that, when told by his master, "you are not free because you can't do this and that," will reply, "I don't even want to do it, hence I am free."

It has been said, I think by Eric Voegelin, that whatever we understand by the word "soul" was quite unknown before Plato. In the same sense I would like to maintain that the phenomenon of the will in all its complicated intricacies was unknown before Paul, and that Paul's discovery was made in the closest possible connection with the teachings of Jesus of Nazareth. I mentioned before the "Love thy neighbor as thyself." You know that this phrase in the Gospels is actually a quotation from the Old Testament; it is Hebrew, not Christian, in origin. I mentioned it because we found that there too the self is the ultimate standard of what I should and should not do. You also remember that Jesus put against this rule: "But I say unto you love your enemies, bless them that curse you, do good to them that hate you," etc. (Matt. 5.44). This occurs when Jesus radicalizes all the old precepts and commands, as when he says, "Ye have heard that it was said by them of old time, 'Thou shalt not commit adultery'; But I say unto you, That whosoever looketh on a woman to lust after her hath committed adultery with her already in his heart" (Matt. 5.27–28), and more of the like, none of which is alien to Hebrew preaching—it is only very much intensified. The same is true to an extent for the command to "love thy enemy," for we find something of a similar tone already in Proverbs (25.21) where it is said, "If thine enemy be hungry, give him bread to eat; and if he be thirsty, give him water to drink," except that Jesus does not add, "For thou shalt heap coals of fire upon his head and the Lord will reward you" (as Paul does, in Rom. 12, still quoting textually from Proverbs). Jesus only adds, "That ye may be the children of your Father which is in Heaven." In this form, "love thy enemy" is more than a mere intensification of the Hebrew precept. This becomes quite manifest when you remember a few other words spoken in the same context—such as "give to every man that asks of thee" and "him that taketh away thy coat forbid not take thy cloak also" (Matt. 5.40). Nothing indeed is more manifest, I think, than that in these counsels of conduct, the self and the intercourse between me and myself are no longer the ultimate criteria of conduct. The aim here is by no means to suffer rather than to do wrong, but something altogether different, namely to do good to others, and the only criterion is indeed the other.

This curious selflessness, the deliberate attempt at self-extinction for the sake of God or the sake of my neighbor, is indeed the very quintessence of all Christian ethics that deserves this name. And our current equations of goodness with selfless-ness (from which we have concluded, a bit unthinkingly I am afraid, that wickedness and selfishness are the same) are a far echo of the authentic experiences of someone who loved doing good in the way in which Socrates loved the activity of thinking. And just as Socrates knew very well that his love of wisdom rested solidly on the fact that no man can *be* wise, so we find in Jesus the solid conviction that his love for goodness rested on the fact that no man can *be* good: "Why callest thou me good? None is good, save one, that is our Father which is in Heaven." And just as no thinking process is even conceivable without this two-in-one, this splitting up in which the self is actualized and articulated, so on the contrary no doing good is possible if while doing so I am even aware of it. Here nothing counts but "Let not thy left hand know what thy right hand does," and not even "Take heed that ye do not do your alms before man to be seen of them" (Matt. 6.2) is enough; I must be, as it were, absent from myself and not be seen by me. In this sense and in the sense of which we spoke before about solitude, the man who has fallen in love with doing good has embarked upon the most lonely career there can be for man, except if he happens to believe in God, to have God for company and testimony. So strong is this element of real loneliness in every positive attempt at doing good and not being content with shunning evil, that even Kant, who otherwise was so careful to eliminate God and all religious precepts from his moral philosophy, appeals to God as bearing witness to the otherwise unexplorable and undetectable existence of good will.

I discussed briefly the extraordinarily paradoxical nature of Socrates' statement and how we, through habit and tradition, have lost the ear for it. The same can be said with even greater emphasis for the radicalization of old Hebrew commands in Jesus' teachings. The strain he put on his followers must have been beyond bearing, and the only reason we don't feel this anymore is that we hardly take them seriously. The strain of these teachings was felt perhaps by no one more strongly than by Paul after his sudden conversion.

It has often been said that not Jesus of Nazareth but Paul of Tarsus was the founder of Christianity; he certainly was the founder of Christian philosophy with its unique emphasis on the issue of freedom and the problem of free will. The decisive passage, which for a long time, practically throughout the Middle Ages, remained in the center of discussion, occurs in the letter to the Romans. It is the famous chapter 7 which begins with the discussion of the law and ends with man's need to be saved through divine grace. The introduction of the law presupposes the will. Every "Thou Shalt" is answered by an "I will." The law, you will remember, makes it possible for men to distinguish right from wrong "for where no law is, there is no transgression" (Rom. 4.15), hence, "by the law is the knowledge of sin" (Rom. 3.20). Still, and this is the presupposition of what follows, the law that tells clearly what is right and wrong has by no means achieved its purpose; on the contrary, Paul, quoting from the Psalms, says, "There is none that understandeth, there is none that seeketh after God. . . . there is none that doeth good, no, not one" (Rom. 3.11–12). How is this possible? Paul explains it by taking himself as an example: what happens is that he *knows*, that "he consents *(synphemi)* unto the law that it is good," and what is more, he desires to act accordingly, and still "I do that which I would not." "What I would, that I do not; but what I hate, that I do." Hence, "the good that I would I do not; but the evil which I would not, that I do" (Rom. 7.19). From which he can only conclude: "for to will is present with me; but *how* to perform that which is good [and which I will, we may add] I find not." Since Paul believes that the reason why he cannot perform what he wills is the dichotomy of carnal and spiritual man, that there is "another law in my members, warring against the law of my mind," he still can believe that "with the mind I myself serve the law of God; but with the flesh the law of sin."

If we take this passage as seriously as I think we must, it is quite clear that the will, this supposedly mighty instrument that gives all the impulses to act, was discovered in its impotence, in the experience that even if I know *and* withhold consent to my desires, I still am in a position in which I must say, "I cannot." Hence the first thing we learn about the will is an "I-will-but-cannot." The I-will, however, is by no means overwhelmed by the experience of I-cannot, but goes on willing, as it were, and the more it wills, the clearer appears its insufficiency. The will appears here as a kind of *arbiter—liberum arbitrium*—between the mind that knows and the flesh that desires. In this role of arbiter, the will is free; that is, it decides out of its own spontaneity. In the words of Duns Scotus, the thirteenth-century philosopher who, against Aquinas, insisted on the primacy of the will with respect to all other human faculties: "The will alone is the total cause of volition in the will" *(nihil aliud a voluntate est causa totalis volitionis in voluntate)*. But while the will is free, carnal man, though he possesses this faculty of freedom, is altogether not free. He is not strong enough to do what he wills; all his sins and transgressions can be understood as weaknesses, as venial or pardonable sins, except the mortal sin of assenting which becomes the sin against the spirit. To this Scotus adds, rejecting the philosophers: spiritual man is not free either. If the I-can alone is free, both are unfree. If carnal man's cannot is forced by desire, the intellect cannot do wrong because forced by truth. Here, every I-can presupposes an I-must-not.

We shall retain from this first acquaintance with the phenomenon of will the I-will-and-cannot, and notice that this *first split* which the will causes in myself is utterly different from the split that occurs in thought. This split in the will is far from being peaceful—it announces not a dialogue between me and myself but a merciless struggle which lasts unto death. We also will note *the will's impotence* and perhaps get here a first hint of why the will, which among all other human faculties got so power hungry, could be equated in the last and perhaps greatest exponent of this whole trend, namely in Nietzsche, with the will-to-power. We may conclude this stage of the problem with two quotations from Augustine; one from the *Confessions,* the other from one of his letters. What Paul has clearly shown is, first, that "To will and to be able are not the same" *(non hoc est velle quod posse) (Confessions* 8.8); and, second, "If there were no will, the law could not give commands; if the will were sufficient, grace would not help" *(nec lex iuberet, nisi esset voluntas, nec gratia iuvaret, si sat esset voluntas) (Epistolae* 177.5).

The second stage of our problem is developed in the philosophy of Augustine. The decisive step he took beyond the formulations in Paul is the insight that the trap in which the will is caught does not arise out of the dual nature of man, who is both carnal and spiritual. The will itself is a mental faculty and as far as the body is concerned, it has absolute power: "The mind commands the body, and the body obeys instantly; the mind commands itself, and is resisted." Hence, precisely with respect to those carnal phenomena about which Paul despaired, Augustine is quite sure of the power of the will: "You could not imagine anything so much in our power as that when we will to act, we act. Accordingly, there is nothing so much in our power as will itself" *(Retvactationes* 1.8.3 and *De libero arbitoro* 3.2.7). However, because of this resistance of the will to itself, Paul knew what he was talking about. It is in the very nature of the will "partly to will and partly to nill," for if the will were not resisted by itself, it would not have to utter commands and demand obedience. But "it wills not entirely; therefore it commands not entirely. So far forth it commands, as it wills; and so far forth is the thing commanded not done, as it wills not. . . . For were it entire, it would not even command it to be, because it would already be. It is therefore no monstrous thing partly to will partly to be unwilling. . . . [for] there are two wills" (*Confessions* 8.9). In other words, the will itself is split into two, and not only in the sense that I partly will the good and partly the evil, as though there were a contest of two opposing principles within me, and I the scene of the battlefield. The very same thing occurs "when both wills are bad," as, for instance, in the case of the man who partly wills to go to the theater, partly to the circus, and thirdly wants to rob another man's house, and fourthly to commit adultery, for which activities he only now has the opportunity. In the last instance, you will have noted, Augustine has introduced four wills operating at the same time, and we shall be quick to point out that this example and many more come very close to deliberation, and to deliberate and to will are not the same. If, however, you look upon all mental faculties from the assumption of the primacy of the will, as Augustine does in book 8 of the *Confessions,* then deliberation will appear as a form of willing: "Where any one deliberates, there is one soul fluctuating between conflicting wills." Clearly, in these fluctuations, the will itself is now divided into three, four, and more parts, and becomes paralyzed.[19]

We shall pursue this matter further in the next lecture but, for the moment, let us only retain the following: we discovered another human faculty that is split into two, not because it is opposed by an altogether different part of human nature, but because its very essence is to exist only as two-in-one. This split within the will itself, however, is a contest and not a dialogue. For if, on the contrary, the will were one, it would be superfluous, which means that it would have no one to command. Hence the most important manifestation of the will is to give orders. But it now turns out that to be obeyed, the will must at the same time consent or will obedience, so that the split is not between two equals, partners as in a dialogue, but between one who commands and one who obeys. Since no one likes to obey, and since the will, split only within itself, wields no power outside or above itself to enforce its commands, it seems only natural that it will always be resisted to the utmost. Finally, while the mind splits into two in the thinking activity, for which the form of dialogue seems most adequate, it is altogether different with the will. The will is supposed to move us into acting, and for this purpose we must emphatically be One. In other words, a will divided against itself is less adequate for the task of acting, whereas a mind divided within itself is more adequate for the task of deliberation. If that is the way the will is, what good can the will do? And yet without willing, how could I ever be moved to act?

IV

Our discussion of Socratic morality has yielded only negative results and told us no more than the condition under which we would be prevented from doing wrong: the condition of not being at odds with ourselves even though this might mean to be at odds with the whole world. The Socratic formula was based on reason; that is, on a reason that is neither sheer intellect to be applied to whatever might be at hand, nor contemplation, the faculty of seeing with the eyes of the mind some disclosed or revealed truth, but on reason as an activity of thinking. And nothing in this activity indicated that an impulse for doing could arise out of it. From this we concluded that the importance of this formula, which we never doubted, its validity and practical significance, was clearly manifest in emergency situations, in times of crises when, so to speak, we find ourselves with our back against the wall. We spoke of a marginal phenomenon or a borderline precept not because we believed that thinking itself is anything of this sort, but because we held that the moral aspects of thinking were of secondary importance for the thinking process itself, and that it could not yield positive indications for our conduct among others because it was performed in solitude.

We therefore turned to another faculty, the will, which since its discovery in a religious context has claimed the honor of harboring all seeds of action and of having the power to decide what to do, not merely what not to do. And we noticed that while Socratic morality based on the activity of thinking was chiefly concerned with avoiding evil, Christian ethics, based on the faculty of the will, puts the accent entirely on performing, on doing good. We also noticed that the ultimate criterion for Socratic morality in refraining from doing wrong was the self and the intercourse between me and myself—in other words the same axiom of non-contradiction upon which our logic is based and which still plays an eminent role in the foundation of a non-Christian, secular morality in Kant. The ultimate criterion for positively doing good, on the other hand, we found to be selflessness, the losing of interest in yourself. We found that one of the reasons for this surprising shift might be not merely the loving inclination toward your neighbor even if he is your enemy, but the simple fact that no one can do good and know what he is doing. "Thy left hand must not know what thy right hand does." Hence, the split into two, the two-in-one present in the thinking activity is not permitted here. To put it a bit extremely: If I wish to do good I must not think about what I am doing. And in order to take this issue out of the religious context within which it was first formulated, let me quote to you an especially beautiful and very typical passage in Nietzsche which sounds like a late echo of these words. Nietzsche says (*Beyond Good and Evil*, no. 40):

There are acts of such a delicate nature that you better destroy them through some rudeness to make them unrecognizable; there are deeds of love and of an extravagant generosity after which nothing is more advisable than to take a stick and beat up all eye witnesses: just to black out their memory. There are people who know how to black out their own memory, they mistreat it so as to take their revenge on the only witness of their deeds. Shame is ingenious. And it is not of our worst acts that we are most ashamed. . . . I could imagine how somebody with something precious and vulnerable to hide would roll through life, rude and round like an old green wine barrel.

Furthermore, behind all these considerations, let me remind you of our perhaps premature attempt to find out what the definitions of evil might have been according to Socratic teaching on the one hand, to the preaching and living example of Jesus of Nazareth on the other. According to Socrates, wrong would be whatever I cannot bear to have done, and the wrongdoer would be somebody unfit for intercourse, especially for the thinking intercourse of him with himself. You find the same position in Nietzsche's much quoted aphorism: "My memory tells me: I did this. My pride replies: I could not have done it. Pride is unrelenting. Finally my memory gives in" (*Beyond Good and Evil*, no. 68). For our purposes, let us disregard the modern form in which the old position reappears and where suppression, still unknown in the ancient household of the soul, appears as the supreme remedy. For us, it is decisive that, as we mentioned before, the faculty of remembering is what prevents wrongdoing. We saw that the criterion here is highly subjective in two ways: what I can bear to have done without losing my integrity as a person might change from individual to individual, from country to country, from century to century. But it is also subjective in that the issue finally turns on the question of with whom I wish to be together, and not about "objective" standards and rules. I quoted to you the curious and curiously agreeing statements from Cicero and Meister Eckhart, the former declaring that he would prefer to go astray with Plato rather than share the truth with some charlatans, and the latter stating that he'd much rather be in hell with God than in paradise without him. On a popular level, you find the same attitude in the Roman proverb *"Quod licet Jovi non licet bovi"*—what is permitted to Jove is not permitted to an ox. In other words, what somebody does, depends upon who he is. What is permitted to some is not permitted to others, from which it follows that many things may be permitted to an ox that are not permitted to Jove.

Evil according to Jesus is defined as a "stumbling stone," *skandalon*, which human powers cannot remove, so that the real wrongdoer appears as the man who should never have been born—"it were better for him that a millstone were hanged about his neck and he cast into the sea." The criterion is no longer the self and what the self can or cannot bear to live with, but the performance and the consequences of the deed at large. The *skandalon* is what is not in our power to repair—by forgiving or by punishment—and what therefore remains an obstacle for all further performances and doings. And the agent is not somebody who, in the Platonic understanding, can be reformed through punishment or, if he is beyond improvement, will offer through his sufferings a deterrent example for others; the agent is an offender to the world order as such. He is, to take another of Jesus' metaphors, like the weed, "the tares in the field," with which one can't do anything except destroy them, burn them in the fire. Jesus never said what this evil is that can't be forgiven by men or God, and the interpretation of the *skandalon*, the stumbling stone, as being the sin against the Holy Ghost, does not tell us much more about it, except that this is the evil to which I wholeheartedly assent, which I commit willingly. I find this interpretation difficult to reconcile with the sayings in the Gospels, where the question of free will is not yet raised. But what is stressed here beyond doubt is the harm done to the community, the danger arising to all.

It seems obvious to me that this is the position of the man of action as distinguished from the position of the man whose main concern and preoccupation is thinking. Jesus' radicalism in the question of evil—a radicalism all the more impressive as it is so intimately bound up with the greatest possible large-mindedness toward all sorts of wrongdoers, including adulterers, prostitutes, thieves, and publicans—has never been accepted, as far as I know, by any philosopher who ever touched upon the problem. You need only to think of Spinoza, to whom what we call evil is but an aspect under which the unquestionable goodness of everything that is appears to human eyes, or of Hegel, to whom evil as the negative is the powerful force that drives on the dialectic of becoming, and in whose philosophy the evildoers, far from being the tares among the wheat, will even appear as the fertilizers of the field. To justify evil in the two-fold sense of wickedness and misfortune has always belonged among the perplexities of metaphysics. Philosophy in the traditional sense, which is confronted with the problem of Being as a whole, has always felt obligated to affirm and find an appropriate place for everything that is. I shall again turn to Nietzsche in order to sum up this side of our problem: He said (*Will to Power*, no. 293), "The notion of an action to be rejected, to be cast away [*verwerfliche Handlung*], creates difficulties. Nothing that happens at all can be such as to be rejected; one should not want to eliminate it, for everything is so intimately connected with everything else that to reject one thing means to reject all. One outcast action, that means an outcast world." The

notion of which Nietzsche speaks here, that I could say an unqual-
ified no to a particular event or to one particular person in the
sense of "It shouldn't have happened, he shouldn't have been
born," is indeed a notion abhorred by all philosophers. And when
he claimed that "the wicked and the misfortunate are in a more
favorable position to discover certain parts of truth" (*Beyond
Good and Evil*, no. 39), he was firmly anchored in this tradition
except that he translated into very concrete terms the rather
abstract ideas of his predecessors; that such statements sounded
heretical in his own ears, which were still the ears of a Protestant
minister's son, is another matter. It is true, however, that he goes
beyond this tradition when, in the same aphorism, he mentions
"the wicked people who are happy—a species of men whom the
moralists pass over in silence." This observation may not be particularly deep and it seems Nietzsche never came back to it, but it
actually hits the very center of the whole problem, at least of the
problem posed in traditional terms.

For when I said during the last lecture that according to traditional philosophy it is the will, and neither reason nor mere desire,
that prompts man into action, I stated a half-truth. To be sure, the
will, as we saw, is understood as the arbiter between desires or the
arbiter between reason and desires, and as such, it must be free
from being determined by either reason or desire. And, as has
been pointed out since Augustine and Duns Scotus, since Kant
and Nietzsche, the will is either free or does not exist; it must be
the "total cause of itself" (Duns Scotus), for if you wish to assign
it a cause, you immediately find yourself in an infinite regress of
causes, asking of each what is the cause of this cause? Augustine
pointed this out in *De libero arbitrio* 3.17. It is a mental faculty, discovered by Paul, elaborated by Augustine, and from then on
interpreted and reinterpreted as no other human faculty has been.

But the question of its actual existence has also always been debated to a far greater extent than that of reason, desire, or any other of our faculties. The paradox, briefly stated, is this: only with the discovery of the will as the harborer of human freedom did it ever occur to men that they might not be free, even if they were coerced neither by natural forces nor by fate nor by their fellowmen. Of course, it has always been known that man may be a slave to his desires and that moderation and self-control are the signs of a free man. Men who did not know how to control themselves were judged to have slavish souls, as was the man defeated in warfare who permitted himself to be taken prisoner and sold into servitude instead of committing suicide. One would yield and change from one status into another if one were a coward or a fool. The problem arose, as we saw, when it was discovered that the I-will and the I-can are not the same, regardless of external circumstances. Furthermore, the I-will-but-I-cannot is not the same as when a paralyzed man says, "I want to move my limbs but cannot," in which case the body resists the mind. On the contrary, the perplexities of the will become obvious only when the mind tells itself what to do. This is depicted as the brokenness of the will which at the same time wills and wills not. The question then is, can I be said to be free, uncoerced by others or by necessity, if I do what I will not, or, conversely, am I free if I succeed in doing what I will? Now this question of whether or not men are free when they start to act cannot be demonstrably resolved, for the act itself always falls into a sequence of occurrences in whose context it appears to be caused by other occurrences—that is, it falls into a context of causality. On the other side it has been said, over and over again, that no precept of either a moral or a religious nature could possibly make sense without the assumption of human freedom, which is true and obvious enough; but it is a mere hypothesis. And the most we can say about it is what Nietzsche stated: There exist two hypotheses, the hypothesis of science that there is no will, and the commonsense hypothesis that the will is free. And the latter is "a dominant sentiment of which we cannot liberate ourselves even if the scientific hypothesis were demonstrated" (*Will to Power*, no. 667). In other words, the moment we start to act, we assume that we are free, no matter what the truth of the matter may be. This, it seems, would be fine and sufficient proof, as it were, if we were only acting beings. But the trouble is that we are not, and that the moment we stop acting and start considering what we have done with others, or even how this specific act fits into the whole texture of our life, the matter becomes again highly doubtful. In retrospect, everything seems explicable by causes, by precedents or circumstances, so that we must admit the legitimacy of both hypotheses, each valid for its own field of experience.

The device which philosophy traditionally used to apply to get out of this predicament is actually quite simple, though it may appear complicated in some particular instances. The difficulty lies in there being something that is not determined by anything and yet is still not arbitrary; that the arbiter should not arbitrate arbitrarily. And what stands behind the will as the arbiter between desires or between reason and desires is that *omnes homines beatus esse volunt*, that all men tend to be happy, gravitate as it were, toward happiness. I use the word "gravitate" here on purpose in order to indicate that more is meant here than desires, strivings, appetites and the like, all of which can be fulfilled only piecemeal and still leave man as a whole, seen in the whole of his life, "unhappy." Hence, in this interpretation, the will, though not determined by any specific cause, rises out of this ground of gravitation which supposedly is common to all men. To put it bluntly: it is not only as if man, at every moment of his life, wanted to be able to say, "I am happy, I am happy, I am happy"; but rather, as if man at the end of his life wanted to be able to say, "I have been happy." According to the moralists this should be possible only for nonwicked people, which, alas, is no more than an assumption. If we go back to our old Socratic criterion where happiness would mean to be at peace with oneself, one could say that wicked people have lost the capacity even to raise the question and to answer it insofar as they, being at odds with themselves, have lost the capacity of becoming two-in-one in the dialogue of thought. This argument appears in a different form in Augustine who maintained: "The man who, knowing the right, fails to do it, loses the power to know what is right; and the man who, having the power to do right, is unwilling, loses the power to do what he wills" (*De libero arbitrio* 3.19.53). In other words, the man acting against the gravitational pull towards happiness loses the power of being either happy or unhappy. This is difficult to maintain if happiness is actually the gravitational center of one's whole being, and no matter how plausible or implausible we may find the argument, the truth of the matter is that it loses much, if not all, of its credibility through the simple fact that the very same people who advanced it in one form or another—from Plato to Christian ethicists up to the revolutionary statesmen of the end of the eighteenth century—believed it necessary to threaten the "wicked" with great "unhappiness" in a future life; the latter indeed took practically for granted that "species of men" whom the moralists, theoretically speaking, used to pass over in silence.

We therefore shall leave this bothersome question of happiness out of account. The happiness of the wicked in their success has always been one of the more uncomfortable facts of life which it would do no good to explain away. We need only to summon up the complementary notion of people who do good or are decent *because* they want to be happy. It is with this reason as with all reasons in this matter (quoting Nietzsche again): "If someone told us he needed reasons to remain decent we could hardly trust him any longer; certainly, we would avoid his company"—after all, can't he change his mind? And with this, we've come back to that faculty of pure spontaneity that prompts us into doing *and* arbitrates between reasons without being subject to them. Until now, we have spoken indiscriminately about these two functions of the will, its instigating and its arbitrating powers. All our descriptions drawn from Paul and Augustine about the two-fold brokenness of the will, the I-will-and-cannot in Paul, the I-will-and-will-not in Augustine, actually apply only to the will insofar as it prompts into action, and not to its arbitrating function. For this latter function is in fact the same as judgment; the will is called upon to judge between different and opposite propositions, and whether this faculty of judgment, one of the most mysterious faculties of the human mind, should be said to be the will or reason or perhaps a third mental capacity, is at least an open question.

As far as the first function of the will, its instigating power, is concerned, we find in Nietzsche two curiously unconnected and, as we will see, contradictory descriptions. Let me start with the description that follows the traditional, that is, Augustinian understanding. "To will is not the same as to desire, to strive for, to want: from all these, it is distinguished through the element of Command. . . . That something is commanded, that is inherent in willing" (*Will To Power*, no. 668). And in another context:

Someone who wills gives orders to something in him that obeys. . . . The strangest aspect of this multiple phenomenon we call Will is that we have but one word for it, and especially only one word for the fact that we are in every given case at the same time those who issue the orders and those who obey them; insofar as we obey, we experience the feelings of coercion, urging, pressing, resisting which usually begin to manifest themselves immediately after the act of willing; insofar however . . . as we are in command, . . . we experience a sensation of pleasure, and this all the more strongly as we are used to overcome the dichotomy through the notions of the I, the Ego, and this in such a way that we take the obedience in ourselves for granted and therefore identify to will and to perform, to will and to act. (*Beyond Good and Evil*, no. 19)

This interpretation is traditional insofar as it insists on the brokenness of the will whose inner paralysis, according to Christian or Pauline teachings, can only be healed through divine grace. It deviates decisively from this interpretation only in that it believes it detects within the inner household of the will a kind of tricky device, by virtue of which we are enabled to identify ourselves only with the commanding part, and to overlook as it were the unpleasant, paralyzing sentiments of being coerced and hence of being called upon to resist. Nietzsche himself calls this a self-delusion, albeit a wholesome one. By identifying ourselves with the one who issues the commands, we experience the feeling of superiority which comes from wielding power. This description, one is inclined to think, would be accurate if willing could ever exhaust itself in the mere act of willing, without having to go on toward performing. The brokenness of the will, as we saw, becomes manifest when it comes to performance, and the sentiments which a blissful self-delusion overcomes as long as I am not called upon to deliver the goods, so to speak, ceases when it is discovered that *velle* and *posse*, the I-will and the I-can are not the same. Or, to put it into Nietzschean terms: "The will wants to be master of himself" and learns that if the mind commands itself and not merely the body (where it is obeyed instantly, as Augustine told us), this means that I make a slave of myself—that I drag, as it were, the master-slave relationship, whose essence is the denial of freedom, into the intercourse and the relationship which I establish between me and myself. Hence, the famous harborer of freedom turns out to be the destroyer of all freedom.[20]

And yet there is an important new factor thrown into this discussion not mentioned before, the element of pleasure, which Nietzsche understood as inherent in the feeling of having power over others. Nietzsche's philosophy therefore rests on his equation of the will with will-to-power; he does not deny the brokenness of the will into two which he calls the "oscillations between yes and no" (*Will to Power*, no. 693), the simultaneous presence of pleasure and displeasure in every act of willing, but he counts these negative feelings of being coerced and of resisting among the necessary obstacles without which the will would not know its own power. Obviously, this is an accurate description of the pleasure principle; the mere absence of pain cannot cause pleasure, and a will that does not overcome resistance could not awaken pleasant feelings. Nietzsche, wittingly following the ancient hedonist philosophies which had been somewhat reformulated by modern sensualism, especially by Bentham's "calculus of pain and pleasure," relied in his description of pleasure on the experience of being released from pain, and neither on absence of pain nor on sheer presence of pleasure. The intensity of this sensation of being released from pain is beyond doubt; in intensity it is matched only by the sensation of pain itself which is always more intense than any pleasure unrelated to pain could possibly be. No doubt, the pleasure of drinking the most exquisite wine cannot be compared in intensity to the pleasure felt by a desperately thirsty man who gets a drink of water. However, this self-interpretation is faulty even according to Nietzsche's own descriptions. The source of pleasure was put by him in the feeling "that will and action are somehow united" (*dass Wille und Aktion irgendwie eins seien—Beyond Good and Evil*, no. 19), that is, in the I-will-and-I-can, independently of negative feelings—pain and release from pain—as the joy in drinking a glass of wine is independent of and unrelated to the feelings of thirst and the pleasure of quenching it.

Hence, we find in Nietzsche another analysis of the will which takes up the pleasure motif but explains it differently. In the equation of will with will-to-power, power is by no means that which the will desires or wills, it is not its aim and not its content! Will and power, or feeling of power, are the same (*Will to Power*, no. 692). The goal of the will is to will, as the goal of life is to live. Powerfulness is inherent in willing no matter what the object or the goal might be. Hence, the will whose goal is humility is no less powerful than the will whose goal is to rule over others. This powerfulness, the sheer potency of the willing act itself, Nietzsche explains as a phenomenon of abundance, as an indication of a strength that goes beyond the force necessary to meet the demands of everyday life. "By the word 'freedom of will' we signify this feeling of a surplus of strength." There is still a faint analogy to the pleasure principle: just as you can enjoy a good glass of wine only when you are not thirsty, in which case just any liquid would do, so the faculty of the will would arise in you only after you have got everything which is really indispensable for your sheer survival. This overflow of strength is then identified by Nietzsche with the creative impulse; it is the root of all productivity. If this is true (and I think all data of experience speak in favor of this interpretation) we could explain why the will is seen as the source of spontaneity that prompts into action—whereas the understanding of the will as disclosing the ultimate impotence of man through its dialectical nature could only lead to a complete paralysis of all forces unless one relies on divine help as is done in all strictly Christian ethics. And it is of course also this abundance of strength, this extravagant generosity or "lavish will" that prompts men in wanting and loving to do good (*Will to Power*, no. 749). What is most obvious in those few men we know of who devoted their whole lives to "doing good," like Jesus of Nazareth or St. Francis of Assisi, is certainly not meekness but rather an overflowing strength, maybe not of character but of their very nature.

It is important to understand that this outline of the "lavishness of the will" rising out of a surplus of strength does not indicate any specific goals. Nietzsche underlined this in the following (*Gay Science* 360): we must "distinguish between the cause of acting and the cause of acting in such or such a way, in this particular direction, with this or that aim in mind. The first cause is a quantity of surplus strength that only waits to be used up no matter in what form or with what content. The second cause, [the goal or content] is insignificant compared with this force, often a small incident, that releases this quantity—like the match put to dynamite." No doubt, this contains a serious underestimation of these so-called secondary causes which, after all, include the morally decisive question of whether the will to do turns in the direction of doing right or doing wrong. The underestimation is comprehensible within the framework of Nietzsche's philosophy—if the astounding accumulation of questions and problems and the constant experimentation with them that never leaves an unequivocal result can be called a philosophy.

But we are not interested in Nietzsche's philosophy here, but exclusively in certain discoveries regarding the faculty of the will. And we are grateful that he at least made the distinction between two factors which, in the traditional as well as in the modern discussions of the will, are left in confusion, namely, its commanding function and its function as arbiter, the will as called upon and then sitting in judgment over conflicting claims, whereby the assumption is that it knows how to tell right from wrong. Within the tradition, you find the whole question of free will usually discussed under the title of *liberum arbitrium,* free arbitration, so that in the discussion of moral issues the emphasis has shifted entirely from the cause of action as such to the question of what goals to seek and which decisions to make. In other words, the commanding function of the will (which raised such difficulties in Paul's and Augustine's minds) disappeared into the background, and its judging function (that it could clearly and freely distinguish between right and wrong) came to the foreground. The reason is not difficult to guess. With Christianity becoming an institution, the "Thou shalt" or the "Thou shalt not," that which commands, appeared more and more exclusively as a voice from outside, be it the voice of God speaking directly to man or the voice of the ecclesiastical authority in charge of making the voice of God heard among the believers. And the question was more and more only whether or not man possessed an organ within himself that could distinguish between conflicting voices. This organ, according to the meaning of the Latin word *liberum arbitrium,* was characterized by the same disinterestedness which we demand for the judging function in legal proceedings, where judge or jury are disqualified when they have a stake in the matter under jurisdiction. The arbiter was originally the man who approached *(ad-bitere)* an occurrence as an unconcerned spectator, an eyewitness, and because of this unconcern was held to be capable of impartial judgment. Hence, the freedom of the will as *liberum arbitrium* means its impartiality—it does not mean this inexplicable source of spontaneity that prompts into action.[21]

But these are matters of history, and we shall now turn our attention to the question of judgment, the true arbiter between right and wrong, beautiful and ugly, true and untrue. We are interested here only in the question of how we tell right from wrong, but curiously enough, Kant himself, though he was by no means particularly sensitive to the arts, approached this problem with the question, how do I tell beautiful from ugly? He originally thought of his *Critique of Judgment* as a Critique of Taste. Kant assumed that no such problem existed for Truth and Right, since he believed that just as human reason in its theoretical capacity knows truth by itself, without any help from another mental faculty, the same reason in its practical capacity knows "the moral law within me." He defined judgment as the faculty which always comes into play when we are confronted with particulars; judgment decides about the relation between a particular instance and the general, be the general a rule or a standard or an ideal or some other kind of measurement. In all instances of reason and knowledge, judgment subsumes the particular under its appropriate general rule. Even this apparently simple operation has its difficulties, for since there are no rules for the subsumption, this must be decided freely. Hence "deficiency in judgment is just what is ordinarily called stupidity, and for such a failing there is no remedy. An obtuse and narrow-minded person . . . may indeed be trained through study even to the extent of becoming learned. But as such people are commonly lacking in judgment, it is not unusual to meet learned men who . . . betray that original want, which can never be made good" (*Critique of Pure Reason* B172–173). The matter gets a bit worse when it comes to those judgments where no fixed rules and standards are applicable, as in questions of taste, and where, therefore, the "general" must be seen as contained in the particular. No one can define Beauty; and when I say that this particular tulip is beautiful, I don't mean, all tulips are beautiful, therefore this one is too, nor do I apply a concept of beauty valid for all objects. What Beauty, something general, is, I know because I see it and state it when confronted with it in particulars. How do I know and why do I claim a certain validity for such judgments? These are in a very simplified form the central guiding questions in the *Critique of Judgment*.

But more generally, we can say that lack of judgment shows itself in all fields: we call it stupidity in intellectual (cognitive) matters, lack of taste in aesthetic issues, and moral obtuseness or insanity when it comes to conduct. And the opposite of all these specific failings, the very ground from which judgment springs wherever it is exercised, according to Kant, is common sense. Kant himself analyzed primarily aesthetic judgments, because it seemed to him that only in this field do we judge without having general rules which are either demonstrably true or self-evident to go by. If therefore I shall now use his results for the field of morality, I assume that the field of human intercourse and conduct and the phenomena we confront in it are somehow of the same nature. In justification, I'll remind you of our first session when I explained the not very pleasant background of factual experience which gave rise to these considerations.

I mentioned the total collapse of moral and religious standards among people who to all appearances had always firmly believed in them, and I also mentioned the undeniable fact that the few who managed not to be sucked into the whirlwind were by no means the "moralists," people who had always upheld rules of right conduct, but on the contrary very often those who had been convinced, even before the debacle, of the objective non-validity of these standards per se. Hence, theoretically, we find ourselves today in the same situation in which the eighteenth century found itself with respect to mere judgments of taste. Kant was outraged that the question of beauty should be decided arbitrarily, without possibility of dispute and mutual agreement, in the spirit of *de gustibus non disputandum est*. More often than not, even in circumstances which are very far from any catastrophic indication, we find ourselves today in exactly the same position when it comes to discussions of moral issues. So, let us return to Kant.

Common sense for Kant did not mean a sense common to all of us, but strictly that sense which fits us into a community with others, makes us members of it and enables us to communicate things given by our five private senses. This it does with the help of another faculty, the faculty of imagination (to Kant the most mysterious faculty). Imagination or representation—there is a difference between the two which we can neglect here—designates my ability to have an image in my mind of something that is not present. Representation makes present what is absent—for instance the George Washington Bridge. But while I can conjure up before the eye of my mind the faraway bridge, I actually have two imaginations or representations in my mind: first, this particular bridge which I have seen often and, second, a schematic image of bridge as such, by which I can recognize and identify any particular bridge, including this one, as being a bridge. This second schematic bridge never appears before my bodily eyes; the moment I put it down on paper it becomes a particular bridge, it is no longer a mere schema. Now, the same representative capacity without which no knowledge would be possible at all, stretches out to other people, and the schemata that appear in knowledge become examples in judgment. Common sense, by virtue of its imaginative capacity, can have present in itself all those who actually are absent. It can think, as Kant says, in the place of everybody else, so that when somebody makes the judgment, this is beautiful, he does not mean merely to say this pleases me (as if, for instance, chicken soup may please me but may not be pleasant to others), but he claims assent from others because in judging he has already taken them into account and hence hopes that his judgments will carry a certain general, though perhaps not universal, validity. The validity will reach as far as the community of which my common sense makes me a member—Kant, who thought of himself as a citizen of the world, hoped it would reach to the community of all mankind. Kant calls this an "enlarged mentality," meaning that without such an agreement man is not fit for civilized intercourse. The point of the matter is that my judgment of a particular instance does not merely depend upon my perception but upon my representing to myself something which I do not perceive. Let me illustrate this: suppose I look at a specific slum dwelling and I perceive in this particular building the general notion which it does not exhibit directly, the notion of poverty and misery. I arrive at this notion by representing to myself how I would feel if I had to live there, that is, I try to think in the place of the slum-dweller. The judgment I shall come up with will by no means necessarily be the same as that of the inhabitants whom time and hopelessness may have dulled to the outrage of their condition, but it will become an outstanding example for my further judging of these matters. Furthermore, while I take into account others when judging, this does not mean that I conform in my judgment to their's. I still speak with my own voice and I do not count noses in order to arrive at what I think is right. But my judgment is no longer subjective either, in the sense that I arrive at my conclusions by taking only myself into account.

However, while I take into account others in rendering my judgment, these others do not include everybody; Kant says explicitly that the validity of such judgments can extend only "over the whole sphere of judging subjects," of people who also judge. To put it differently, it is not for those who refuse to judge to dispute the validity of my judgment. The common sense with which I judge is a general sense, and to the question, "How can anyone judge according to a common sense as he contemplates the object according to his private sense?" Kant would reply that the community among men produces a common sense. The validity of common sense grows out of the intercourse with people—just as we say that thought grows out of the intercourse with myself. ("To think is to talk with oneself, hence also to listen to oneself internally" *Anthrop.* no. 36.) However, with these restrictions we can say that the more people's positions I can make present in my thought and hence take into account in my judgment, the more *representative* it will be. The validity of such judgments would be neither objective and universal nor subjective, depending on personal whim, but intersubjective or representative. This kind of representative thought, which is possible only through imagination, demands certain sacrifices. Kant says, "We must so to speak renounce ourselves for the sake of others"—and it is more than a mere curiosity that this denial of selfishness should not occur in the context of his moral philosophy but in this context of merely aesthetic judgments. The reason is common sense. If common sense, the sense through which we are members of a community, is the mother of judgment, then not even a painting or a poem, let alone a moral issue, can be judged without invoking and weighing silently the judgments of others, to which I refer just as I refer to the schema of the bridge to recognize other bridges. "In taste," Kant says, "egoism is overcome"—we are considerate in the original sense of the word, we consider the existence of others and we must try to win their agreement, to "woo their consent," as Kant put it. In Kantian morality, nothing of this sort is necessary: we act as intelligible beings and the laws we follow would have validity for all intelligible beings—including the inhabitants of other planets, the angels, and God himself. We are not considerate for we need not consider the positions of others and we don't consider the consequences of our act which are immaterial for the law or for the goodness of the will from which the act springs. Only when it comes to these judgments of taste does Kant find a situation in which the Socratic "It is better to be at odds with the whole world than, being one, to be at odds with myself" loses some of its validity. Here I can't be at odds with the whole world, though I may still find myself at odds with a good part of it. If we consider morality in more than its negative aspect—the refraining from doing wrong, which may mean the refraining from doing anything—then we shall have to consider human conduct in terms which Kant thought appropriate only for aesthetic conduct, so to speak. And the reason why he discovered moral significance in this seemingly so different sphere of human life was that only here did he consider men in the plural, as living in a community. It is therefore in this context that we meet the impartial arbiter of the will as *liberum arbitrium*. "Disinterested appreciation," as you know, is Kant's definition of what we feel in the face of beauty. Hence, egoism cannot be overcome by moral preaching which, on the contrary, always sends me back to myself; but, in Kant's words, "Egoism can be opposed only by plurality, which is a frame of mind in which the self, instead of being enwrapped in itself as if it were the whole world, regards itself as a citizen of the world" (*Anthrop.*, no. 2).

When we now think back to the objective standards and rules of behavior according to which we conduct ourselves in everyday life, without much thinking and without much judging in Kant's sense, that is, where we actually subsume particular cases under general rules without ever questioning the rules, the question arises whether there is really nothing to hold onto when we are called upon to decide that this is right and this is wrong, as we decide that this is beautiful and this is ugly. And the answer to this question is yes and no. Yes—if we mean by it generally accepted standards as we have them in every community with regard to manners and convention, that is, with regard to the *mores* of morality. Matters of right and wrong, however, are not decided like table manners, as though nothing were at stake but acceptable conduct. And there is indeed something to which common sense, when it rises to the level of judging, can and does hold us to, and this is the example. Kant said, "Examples are the go-cart of judgment" (*Critique of Pure Reason* B174), and he also called the "representative thought" present in judgment where particulars cannot be subsumed under something general, by the name of "exemplary thought." We cannot hold on to anything general, but to some particular that has become an example. In a way, this example resembles the schematic building I carry in my mind to recognize as buildings all structures that are housing something or somebody. But the example, in contradistinction to the schema, is supposed to give us a difference in quality. Let me illustrate this difference with an instance outside the moral sphere, and let us ask, what is a table? In answer to this question, you either call upon the form or the (Kantian) schema of a table present in your imagination, to which every table must conform in order to be a table at all. Let's call this the *schematic table* (which incidentally is pretty much the same as the "ideal" table, the Idea of table in Plato). Or you can gather together all sorts of tables, strip them of their secondary qualities, such as color, number of legs, material, etc., until you arrive at the minimum qualities common to all of them. Let us call this the *abstract table*. Or you can finally choose the best among all tables you know of or can imagine, and say this is an *example* of how tables should be constructed and how they should look. Let us call this the *exemplary table*. What you have done is to single out, *eximere*, some particular instance which now *becomes* valid for other particular instances. There are many concepts in the historical and political sciences which are arrived at in this way. Most political virtues and vices are thought of in terms of exemplary individuals: Achilles for courage, Solon for insight (wisdom), etc. Or take the instance of Caesarism or Bonapartism: you have taken Napolean or Caesar as an example, that is, as some particular person exhibiting qualities that are valid for other instances. To be sure, no one who does not know who Caesar or Napolean were can understand what you are talking about if you speak of Caesarism or Bonapartism. Hence the validity of the concept is restricted, but within its restrictions, it is valid nevertheless.

Examples, which are indeed the "go-cart" of all judging activities, are also and especially the guideposts of all moral thought. The extent to which the old and once very paradoxical statement "It is better to suffer wrong than to do wrong," has won the agreement of civilized men is due primarily to the fact that Socrates gave an example and hence became an example for a certain way of conduct and a certain way of deciding between right and wrong. This position is summed up again in Nietzsche—the last philosopher, one is tempted to think, who took moral issues seriously and who therefore analyzed and thought through all former moral positions. He said as follows: "It is a denaturation of morality to separate the act from the agent, to direct hatred or contempt against the 'sin' [the deed instead of the doer], to believe that an action could be good or evil in itself. . . . [In every action] all depends upon who does it, the same 'crime' may be in one case the highest privilege, and in another the stigma [of evil]. Actually, it is the self-relatedness of him who judges that interprets an action or rather its actor with respect to . . . resemblance or 'non-affinity' between the agent and the judge" (*Will to Power*, no. 292). We judge and tell right from wrong by having present in our mind some incident and some person, absent in time or space, that have become examples. There are many such examples. They can lie far back in the past or they can be among the living. They need not be historically real; as Jefferson once remarked: "the fictitious murder of Duncan by Macbeth" excites in us "as great a horror of villainy, as the real one of Henri IV" and a "lively and lasting sense of filial duty is more effectually impressed on a son or daughter by reading *King Lear,* than by all the dry volumes of ethics and divinity that ever were written." (This is what every ethics teacher should say but no other teacher.)

Well, obviously I have neither the time nor probably the ability to cross all the t's and dot all the i's, that is, to answer even in the briefest form all the questions I myself have raised during these four lectures. I can only hope that at least some indication of how we can think and move in these difficult and urgent matters has become apparent. In conclusion, permit me just two further comments. From our discussion today about Kant, I hope it became clearer why I raised, by way of Cicero and Meister Eckhart, the question of whom we wish to be together with. I tried to show that our decisions about right and wrong will depend upon our choice of company, of those with whom we wish to spend our lives. And again, this company is chosen by thinking in examples, in examples of persons dead or alive, real or fictitious, and in examples of incidents, past or present. In the unlikely case that someone should come and tell us that he would prefer Bluebeard for company, and hence take him as his example, the only thing we could do is to make sure that he never comes near us. But the likelihood that someone would come and tell us that he does not mind and that any company will be good enough for him is, I fear, by far greater. Morally and even politically speaking, this indifference, though common enough, is the greatest danger. And connected to this, only a bit less dangerous, is another very common modern phenomenon, the widespread tendency to refuse to judge at all. Out of the unwillingness or inability to choose one's examples and one's company, and out of the unwillingness or inability to relate to others through judgment, arise the real *skandala*, the real stumbling blocks which human powers can't remove because they were not caused by human and humanly understandable motives. Therein lies the horror and, at the same time, the banality of evil.

1965–66

COLLECTIVE RESPONSIBILITY

There is such a thing as responsibility for things one has not done; one can be held liable for them. But there is no such thing as being or feeling guilty for things that happened without oneself actively participating in them. This is an important point, worth making loudly and clearly at a moment when so many good white liberals confess to guilt feelings with respect to the Negro question. I do not know how many precedents there are in history for such misplaced feelings, but I do know that in postwar Germany, where similar problems arose with respect to what had been done by the Hitler regime to Jews, the cry "We are all guilty" that at first hearing sounded so very noble and tempting has actually only served to exculpate to a considerable degree those who actually were guilty. Where all are guilty, nobody is. Guilt, unlike responsibility, always singles out; it is strictly personal. It refers to an act, not to intentions or potentialities. It is only in a metaphorical sense that we can say we *feel* guilty for the sins of our fathers or our people or mankind, in short, for deeds we have not done, although the course of events may well make us pay for them. And since sentiments of guilt, *mens rea* or bad conscience, the awareness of wrong doing, play such an important role in our legal and moral judgment, it may be wise to refrain from such metaphorical statements which, when taken literally, can only lead into a phony sentimentality in which all real issues are obscured.

We call compassion what I feel when somebody else suffers; and this feeling is authentic only so long as I realize that it is, after all, not I but somebody else who suffers. But it is true, I think, that "solidarity is a necessary condition" for such emotions; which, in our case of collective guilt feelings would mean that the cry "We are all guilty" is actually a declaration of solidarity with the wrongdoers.

I do not know when the term "collective responsibility" first made its appearance, but I am reasonably sure that not only the term but also the problems it implies owe their relevance and general interest to political predicaments as distinguished from legal or moral ones. Legal and moral standards have one very important thing in common—they always relate to the person and what the person has done; if the person happens to be involved in a common undertaking as in the case of organized crime, what is to be judged is still this very person, the degree of his participation, his specific role, and so on, and not the group. The fact of his membership plays a role only insofar as it makes his having committed a crime more probable; and this is in principle not different from bad reputation or having a criminal record. Whether the defendant was a member of the Mafia or a member of the SS or some other criminal or political organization, assuring us that he was a mere cog who acted only upon superior orders and did what everybody else would have done just as well, the moment he appears in a court of justice he appears as a person and is judged according to what he did. It is the grandeur of court proceedings that even a cog can become a person again. And the same seems true to an even higher degree for moral judgment, for which the excuse: My only alternative would have led to suicide, is not as binding as it is for legal proceedings. It is not a case of responsibility but of guilt.

No *collective* responsibility is involved in the case of the thousand experienced swimmers, lolling at a public beach and letting a man drown in the sea without coming to his help, because they were no collectivity to begin with; no collective *responsibility* is involved in the case of conspiracy to rob a bank, because here the fault is not vicarious; what is involved are various degrees of guilt. And if, as in the case of the postbellum Southern social system, only the "alienated residents" or the "outcasts" are innocent, we have again a clear-cut case of guilt; for all the others have indeed done something which is by no means "vicarious." [These three "cases" are taken from the paper to which Arendt was responding.—Ed.]

Two conditions have to be present for collective responsibility: I must be held responsible for something I have not done, and the reason for my responsibility must be my membership in a group (a collective) which no voluntary act of mine can dissolve, that is, a membership which is utterly unlike a business partnership which I can dissolve at will. The question of "contributory group fault" must be left in abeyance because every participation is already nonvicarious. This kind of responsibility in my opinion is always political, whether it appears in the older form, when a whole community takes it upon itself to be responsible for whatever one of its members has done, or whether a community is being held responsible for what has been done in its name. The latter case is of course of greater interest for us because it applies, for better and worse, to all political communities and not only to representative government. Every government assumes responsibility for the deeds and misdeeds of its predecessors and every nation for the deeds and misdeeds of the past. This is even true for revolutionary governments which may deny liability for contractual agreements their predecessors have entered into. When Napoleon Bonaparte became the ruler of France, he said: I assume responsibility for everything France has done from the time of Charlemagne to the terror of Robespierre. In other words, he said, all this was done in my name to the extent that I am a member of this nation and the representative of this body politic. In this sense, we are always held responsible for the sins of our fathers as we reap the rewards of their merits; but we are of course not guilty of their misdeeds, either morally or legally, nor can we ascribe their deeds to our own merits.

We can escape this political and strictly collective responsibility only by leaving the community, and since no man can live without belonging to some community, this would simply mean to exchange one community for another and hence one kind of responsibility for another. It is true that the twentieth century has created a category of men who were truly outcasts, belonging to no internationally recognizable community whatever, the refugees and stateless people, who indeed can not be held politically responsible for anything. Politically, regardless of their group or individual character, they are the absolutely innocent ones; and it is precisely this absolute innocence that condemns them to a position outside, as it were, of mankind as a whole. If there were such a thing as collective, namely vicarious guilt, this would be the case of collective, namely, vicarious innocence. Actually, they are the only totally nonresponsible people; and while we usually think of responsibility, especially collective responsibility, as a burden and even as a kind of punishment, I think it can be shown that the price paid for collective nonresponsibility is considerably higher.

What I am driving at here is a sharper dividing line between political (collective) responsibility, on one side, and moral and/or legal (personal) guilt, on the other, and what I have chiefly in mind are those frequent cases in which moral and political considerations and moral and political standards of conduct come into conflict. The main difficulty in discussing these matters seems to lie in the very disturbing ambiguity of the words we use in discussions of these issues, to wit, morality or ethics. Both words mean originally no more than customs or manners and then, in an elevated sense, the customs and manners that are most appropriate for the citizen. From the *Nicomachean Ethics* to Cicero, ethics or morals were part of politics, that part that dealt not with the institutions but with the citizen, and all the virtues in Greece or in Rome are definitely political virtues. The question is never whether an individual *is* good but whether his conduct is good for the world he lives in. In the center of interest is the world and not the self. When we talk about moral questions, including the question of conscience, we mean something altogether different, something, as a matter of fact, for which we don't have a ready-made word. On the other hand, since we use these ancient words in our discussions, this very old and very different connotation is always present. There is one exception where moral considerations in our sense can be detected in a classical text, and that is the Socratic proposition "It is better to suffer wrong than to do wrong," which I shall have to discuss in a moment. Before doing so, I would like to mention another difficulty which comes from the opposite side, as it were, namely from the side of religion. That moral matters concern such a thing as the well-being of a soul rather than that of the world is of course part and parcel of the Hebrew-Christian heritage. If, for instance—to give the most common example from Greek antiquity—in Aeschylus Orestes kills his mother upon the strict command of Apollo and is then, nevertheless, haunted by the Erinyes, it is the order of the world that has twice been disturbed and must be restored. Orestes did the right thing when he avenged the death of his father and killed his mother; and still he was guilty because he had violated another "taboo," as we would say today. The tragedy is that only an evil deed can pay back the original crime, and the solution, as we all know, is brought about by Athena or rather by the foundation of a tribunal which from now on will take it upon itself to maintain the right order and lift the curse of an unending chain of evildoing which was necessary to maintain the order of the world. It is the Greek version of the Christian insight that every resisting of the evil done in the world necessarily entails some implication in evil, and the solution of the predicament for the individual.

With the rise of Christianity, the emphasis shifted entirely from care for the world and the duties connected with it, to care for the soul and its salvation. In the early centuries, the polarization of the two was absolute; the epistles in the New Testament are full of recommendations to shun public, political involvement and to mind one's own, strictly private business, caring for one's soul—until Tertullian summed up this attitude *nec ulla magis res aliena quam publica*—"no matter is more alien to us than what matters publicly." What we even today understand by moral standards and prescriptions has this Christian background. In present-day thinking about these matters, the standards of strictness are obviously the highest for moral matters, the lowest for matters of customs and manners, whereas legal standards are somewhere in between. My point here is that morality owes this high position in our hierarchy of "values" to its religious origin; whether the divine law prescribing the rules of human conduct was understood to be directly revealed as in the Ten Commandments or indirectly as in natural law notions is of no importance in this context. The rules were *absolute* because of their divine origin, and their sanctions consisted in "future rewards and punishments." It is more than doubtful that these originally religiously rooted rules of conduct can survive the loss of faith in their origin and, especially, the loss of transcendent sanctions. (John Adams, in a strangely prophetic way, predicted that this loss would "make murder as indifferent as shooting plover, and the extermination of the Rohilla nation as innocent as the swallowing of mites on a morsel of cheese.") As far as I can see, there are but two of the Ten Commandments to which we still feel morally bound, the "Thou shalt not kill" and the "Thou shalt not bear false witness"; and these two have recently been quite successfully challenged by Hitler and Stalin, respectively.

In the center of moral considerations of human conduct stands the self; in the center of political considerations of conduct stands the world. If we strip moral imperatives of their religious connotations and origins, we are left with the Socratic proposition "It is better to suffer wrong than to do wrong," and its strange substantiation, "For it is better for me to be at odds with the whole world than, being one, to be at odds with myself." However we may interpret this invocation of the axiom of noncontradiction in moral matters, as though the one and the same imperative, "Thou shalt not contradict yourself," is axiomatic for logic and ethics (which incidentally is still Kant's chief argument for the categorical imperative), one thing seems clear: the presupposition is that I live together not only with others but also with my self, and that this togetherness, as it were, has precedence over all others. The political answer to the Socratic proposition would be "What is important in the world is that there be no wrong; suffering wrong and doing wrong are equally bad." Never mind who suffers it; your duty is to prevent it. Or, to invoke for brevity's sake another famous saying, this time of Machiavelli who precisely for this reason wanted to teach princes "how not to be good": writing about Florentine patriots who had dared to defy the pope, he praised them because they had shown "how much higher they placed their city than their souls." Where religious language speaks of the soul, secular language speaks of the self.

There are many ways in which political and moral standards of conduct can come into conflict with each other, and in political theory they are usually dealt with in connection with the reason-of-state doctrine and its so-called double standard of morality. We are here concerned with only one special case, with the case of collective and vicarious responsibility in which the member of a community is held responsible for things he did not participate in but which were done in his name. Such nonparticipation can have many causes: the form of government of the country may be such that its inhabitants, or large strata of them, are not admitted to the public realm at all so that nonparticipation is not a matter of choice. Or, on the contrary, in free countries a certain group of citizens may not want to participate, to have anything to do with politics, but not for moral reasons but simply because they have chosen to take advantage of one of our liberties, the one usually not mentioned when we count our freedoms because it is so much taken for granted, and that is freedom from politics. This freedom was unknown in antiquity, and it has been quite effectively abolished in a number of twentieth-century dictatorships, especially of course in the totalitarian variety. In contrast to absolutism and other forms of tyranny, where nonparticipation was a matter of course and not of choice, we deal here with a situation where participation, and that as we know can mean complicity in criminal activities, is a matter of course, and nonparticipation a matter of decision. And we have finally the case in free countries where nonparticipation is actually a form of resistance—as in the case of those who refuse to be drafted into the war in Vietnam. This resistance is often argued on moral grounds; but so long as there is freedom of association and with it the hope that resistance in the form of refusal to participate will bring about a change of policy, it is essentially political. What is in the center of consideration is not the self—I don't go because I don't want to dirty my hands, which, of course, may also be a valid argument—but the fate of the nation and its conduct toward other nations in the world.

Nonparticipation in the political affairs of the world has always been open to the reproach of irresponsibility, of shirking one's duties toward the world we share with one another and the community we belong to. And this reproach is by no means successfully countered if nonparticipation is argued on moral grounds. We know from recent experiences that active and sometimes heroic resistance to evil governments comes much rather from men and women who participated in them than from outsiders who were innocent of any guilt. This is true, as a rule with exceptions, for the German resistance against Hitler and is even truer for the few cases of rebellion against communist regimes. Hungary and Czechoslovakia are cases in point. Otto Kirchheimer, discussing these matters from a legal viewpoint (in his *Political Justice*), rightly stressed that for the question of legal or moral innocence, namely absence of any complicity in crimes committed by a regime, "active resistance" would be an "illusory yardstick, withdrawal from significant participation in public life, . . . willingness to disappear into oblivion" and obscurity "is a standard which may be rightfully imposed by those sitting in judgement" (pp 331 f) By the same token, though, he somehow justifies those defendants who said that their sense for responsibility did not permit them to choose this way; that they served in order to prevent worse, etc.—arguments, which, to be sure, in the case of the Hitler regime sounded rather absurd and indeed usually were not much more than hypocritical rationalizations of an ardent desire to pursue one's career, but that is another matter. What is true is that the nonparticipants were not resisters and that they did not believe that their attitude had any political consequences.

What the moral argument, which I quoted in the form of the Socratic proposition, actually says is the following: If I would do what is now demanded of me as the price of participation, either as mere conformism or even as the only chance of eventually successful resistance, I could no longer live with myself; my life would cease to be worthwhile for me. Hence, I much rather suffer wrong now, and even pay the price of a death penalty in case I am forced to participate, than do wrong and then have to live together with such a wrongdoer. If it is a question of killing, the argument would not be that the world would be better off without the murder being done, but the unwillingness to live with an assassin. This argument, it seems to me, is unanswerable from even the strictest political point of view, but it is clearly an argument which can be valid only in extreme, that is, in marginal situations. It is often such situations which are most apt to bring clarification into otherwise rather obscure and equivocal matters. The marginal situation in which moral propositions become absolutely valid in the realm of politics is impotence. Powerlessness which always presupposes isolation is a valid excuse for doing nothing. The trouble with this argument is of course that it is entirely subjective; its authenticity can be demonstrated only by the willingness to suffer. There are no general rules, as in legal proceedings, which could be applied and which would be valid for all. But this, I am afraid, will be the bane of all moral judgments which are not supported by or derived from religious commands. Socrates, as we know, was never able to prove his proposition; and Kant's categorical imperative, the only competitor as a strictly nonreligious and nonpolitical moral prescription, cannot be proved either. The even deeper trouble with the argument is that it is applicable only to people who are used to living explicitly with themselves, which is only another way of saying that its validity will be plausible only to men who have a conscience; and, the prejudices of jurisprudence that so often in perplexity appeal to conscience as something every sane man must have notwithstanding, the evidence is that quite a number of men have it, but by no means all, and that those who have it can be found in all walks of life and, more specifically, with all degrees of education and noneducation. No objective sign of social or educational standing can assure its presence or absence.

The only activity that seems to correspond to these *secular* moral propositions and to validate them is the activity of thinking, which in its most general, entirely nonspecialized sense can be defined with Plato as the silent dialogue between me and myself. If applied to matters of conduct, the faculty of imagination would be involved in such thought to a high degree, that is, the ability to represent, to make present to myself what is still absent— any contemplated deed. To what extent this faculty of thought, which is exercised in solitude, extends into the strictly political sphere, where I am always together with others, is another question. But whatever our answer to this question, which we hope will be answered by political philosophy, might turn out to be, no moral, individual and personal, standards of conduct will ever be able to excuse us from collective responsibility. This vicarious responsibility for things we have not done, this taking upon ourselves the consequences for things we are entirely innocent of, is the price we pay for the fact that we live our lives not by ourselves but among our fellow men, and that the faculty of action, which, after all, is the political faculty par excellence, can be actualized only in one of the many and manifold forms of human community.

1968

THINKING AND MORAL
CONSIDERATIONS

For W. H. Auden

To talk about thinking seems to me so presumptuous that I feel I owe you a justification. Some years ago, reporting the trial of Eichmann in Jerusalem, I spoke of "the banality of evil" and meant with this no theory or doctrine but something quite factual, the phenomenon of evil deeds, committed on a gigantic scale, which could not be traced to any particularity of wickedness, pathology, or ideological conviction in the doer, whose only personal distinction was a perhaps extraordinary shallowness. However monstrous the deeds were, the doer was neither monstrous nor demonic, and the only specific characteristic one could detect in his past as well as in his behavior during the trial and the preceding police examination was something entirely negative: it was not stupidity but a curious, quite authentic inability to think. He functioned in the role of prominent war criminal as well as he had under the Nazi regime; he had not the slightest difficulty in accepting an entirely different set of rules. He knew that what he had once considered his duty was now called a crime, and he accepted this new code of judgment as though it were nothing but another language rule. To his rather limited supply of stock phrases he had added a few new ones, and he was utterly helpless only when he was confronted with a situation to which none of them would apply, as in the most grotesque instance when he had to make a speech under the gallows and was forced to rely on clichés used in funeral oratory which were inapplicable in his case because he was not the survivor.[1] Considering what his last words should be in case of a death sentence, which he had expected all along, this simple fact had not occurred to him, just as inconsistencies and flagrant contradictions in examination and cross-examinations during the trial had not bothered him. Clichés, stock phrases, adherence to conventional, standardized codes of expression and conduct have the socially recognized function of protecting us against reality, that is, against the claim on our thinking attention which all events and facts arouse by virtue of their existence. If we were responsive to this claim all the time, we would soon be exhausted; the difference in Eichmann was only that he clearly knew of no such claim at all.

This total absence of thinking attracted my interest. Is evildoing, not just the sins of omission but the sins of commission, possible in the absence of not merely "base motives" (as the law calls it) but of any motives at all, any particular prompting of interest or volition? Is wickedness, however we may define it, this being "determined to prove a villain," *not* a necessary condition for evildoing? Is our ability to judge, to tell right from wrong, beautiful from ugly, dependent upon our faculty of thought? Do the inability to think and a disastrous failure of what we commonly call conscience coincide? The question that imposed itself was, could the activity of thinking as such, the habit of examining and reflecting upon whatever happens to come to pass, regardless of specific content and quite independent of results, could this activity be of such a nature that it "conditions" men against evildoing? (The very word *con-science*, at any rate, points in this direction insofar as it means "to know with and by myself," a kind of knowledge that is actualized in every thinking process.) Finally, is not the urgency of these questions enforced by the well-known and rather alarming fact that only good people are ever bothered by a bad conscience whereas it is a very rare phenomenon among real criminals? A good conscience does not exist except as the absence of a bad one.

Such were the questions. To put it differently and use Kantian language, after having been struck by a phenomenon—the *quaestio facti*—which willy-nilly "put me into the possession of a concept" (the banality of evil), I could not help raising the *quaestio juris* and asked myself, "with what right did I possess and use it."[2]

I

To raise such questions as "What is thinking?" "What is evil?" has its difficulties. They belong to philosophy or metaphysics, terms that designate a field of inquiry which, as we all know, has fallen into disrepute. If this were merely a matter of positivist and neopositivist assaults, we need perhaps not be concerned.[3] Our difficulty with raising such questions is caused less by those to whom they are "meaningless" anyhow than by those who are under attack. Just as the crisis in religion reached its climax when theologians, as distinguished from the old crowd of nonbelievers, began to talk about the "God is dead" propositions, the crisis in philosophy and metaphysics came into the open when philosophers themselves began to declare the end of philosophy and metaphysics. Now, this could have its advantage; I trust it will once it has been understood what these "ends" actually mean, not that God has "died"—an obvious absurdity in every respect—but that the way God has been thought of for thousands of years is no longer convincing; and not that the old questions which are coeval with the appearance of men on earth have become "meaningless," but that the way they were framed and answered has lost plausibility.

What has come to an end is the basic distinction between the sensual and the supersensual, together with the notion, at least as old as Parmenides, that whatever is not given to the senses—God or Being or the First Principles and Causes (*archai*) or the Ideas— is more real, more truthful, more meaningful than what appears, that it is not just *beyond* sense perception but *above* the world of the senses. What is "dead" is not only the localization of such "eternal truths" but the distinction itself. Meanwhile, in increasingly strident voices the few defenders of metaphysics have warned us of the danger of nihilism inherent in this development; and although they themselves seldom invoke it, they have an important argument in their favor: it is indeed true that once the supersensual realm is discarded, its opposite, the world of appearances as understood for so many centuries, is also annihilated. The sensual, as still understood by the positivists, cannot survive the death of the supersensual. No one knew this better than Nietzsche who, with his poetic and metaphorical description of the assassination of God in *Zarathustra,* has caused so much confusion in these matters. In a significant passage in *The Twilight of Idols,* he clarifies what the word "God" meant in *Zarathustra.* It was merely a symbol for the suprasensual realm as understood by metaphysics; he now uses instead of "God" the term "true world" and says, "We have abolished the true world. What has remained? The apparent one perhaps? Oh no! With the true world we have also abolished the apparent one."[4]

These modern "deaths" of God, of metaphysics, of philosophy, and, by implication, of positivism may be events of great importance, but they are after all thought events, and though they concern most intimately our ways of thinking, they do not concern our ability to think, the sheer fact that man is a thinking being. By this, I mean that man has an inclination and, unless pressed by more urgent needs of living, even a need (Kant's "need of reason") to think beyond the limitations of knowledge, to do more with his intellectual abilities, his brain power, than to use them as an instrument for knowing and doing. Our desire to know, whether arising out of practical necessities, theoretical perplexities, or sheer curiosity can be fulfilled by reaching its intended goal; and while our thirst for knowledge may be unquenchable because of the immensity of the unknown, so that every region of knowledge opens up further horizons of knowables, the activity itself leaves behind a growing treasure of knowledge that is retained and kept in store by every civilization as part and parcel of its world. The activity of knowing is no less a world-building activity than the building of houses. The inclination or the need to think, on the contrary, even if aroused by none of the time-honored metaphysical, unanswerable "ultimate questions," leaves nothing so tangible behind, nor can it be stilled by allegedly definite insights of "wise men." The need to think can be satisfied only through thinking, and the thoughts which I had yesterday will satisfy this need today only to the extent that I can think them anew.

We owe to Kant the distinction between thinking and knowing, between reason, the urge to think and to understand, and the intellect, which desires and is capable of certain, verifiable knowledge. Kant himself believed that the need to think beyond the limitations of knowledge was aroused only by the old metaphysical questions of God, freedom, and immortality, and that he had "found it necessary to deny knowledge to make room for faith"; by doing so he had thrown the foundations of a future "systematic metaphysics" as a "bequest to posterity."[5] But this shows only that Kant, still bound by the tradition of metaphysics, never became fully aware of what he had done, and his "bequest to posterity" turned out to be the destruction of all possible foundations of metaphysical systems. For the ability and the need to think are by no means restricted to any specific subject matter, such as the questions which reason raises and knows it will never be able to answer. Kant has not "denied knowledge" but separated knowing from thinking, and he has made room not for faith but for thought. He has indeed, as he once suggested, "eliminated the obstacles by which reason hinders itself."[6]

In our context and for our purposes, this distinction between knowing and thinking is crucial. If the ability to tell right from wrong should have anything to do with the ability to think, then we must be able to "demand" its exercise in every sane person no matter how erudite or ignorant, how intelligent or stupid he may prove to be. Kant, in this respect almost alone among the philosophers, was much bothered by the common opinion that philosophy is only for the few, precisely because of this opinion's moral implications. In this vein he once remarked, "Stupidity is caused by a wicked heart,"[7] a statement which in this form is not true. Inability to think is not stupidity; it can be found in highly intelligent people, and wickedness is hardly its cause, if only because thoughtlessness as well as stupidity are much more frequent phenomena than wickedness. The trouble is precisely that no wicked heart, a relatively rare phenomenon, is necessary to cause great evil. Hence, in Kantian terms, one would need philosophy, the exercise of reason as the faculty of thought, to prevent evil.

And this is demanding a great deal, even if we assume and welcome the decline of those disciplines, philosophy and metaphysics, which for so many centuries have monopolized this faculty. For thinking's chief characteristic is that it interrupts all doing, all ordinary activities no matter what they happen to be. Whatever the fallacies of the two-world theories might have been, they arose out of genuine experiences. For it is true that the moment we start thinking on no matter what issue we stop everything else, and this everything else, again whatever it may happen to be, interrupts the thinking process; it is as though we moved into a different world. Doing and living in the most general sense of *inter homines esse*, "being among my fellowmen"—the Latin equivalent for being alive—positively prevents thinking. As Valéry once put it: *"Tantôt je suis, tantôt je pense,"* now I am, now I think.

Closely connected with this situation is the fact that thinking always deals with objects that are absent, removed from direct sense perception. An object of thought is always a re-presentation, that is, something or somebody that is actually absent and present only to the mind which, by virtue of imagination, can make it present in the form of an image.[8] In other words, when I am thinking, I move outside the world of appearances, even if my thought deals with ordinary sense-given objects and not with such invisibles as concepts or ideas, the old domain of metaphysical thought. In order to think about somebody, he must be removed from our senses; so long as we are together with him we don't think of him—though we may gather impressions that later become food for thought; to think about somebody who is present implies removing ourselves surreptitiously from his company and acting as though he were no longer there.

These remarks may indicate why thinking, the quest for meaning—rather than the scientist's thirst for knowledge for its own sake—can be felt to be "unnatural," as though men, when they begin to think, engage in some activity contrary to the human condition. Thinking as such, not only the thinking about extraordinary events or phenomena or the old metaphysical questions, but every reflection that does not serve knowledge and is not guided by practical purposes—in which cases thinking is the handmaiden of knowledge, a mere instrument for ulterior purposes—is, as Heidegger once remarked, "out of order."[9] There is, to be sure, the curious fact that there have always been men who chose the *bios theōrētikos* as their way of life, which is no argument against the activity being "out of order." The whole history of philosophy, which tells us so much about the objects of thought and so little about the process of thinking itself, is shot through with intramural warfare between man's common sense, this highest, sixth sense that fits our five senses into a common world and enables us to orient ourselves in it, and man's faculty of thinking by virtue of which he willfully removes himself from it.

And not only is this faculty for the ordinary course of affairs "good for nothing" while its results remain uncertain and unverifiable, but it also is somehow self-destructive. Kant, in the privacy of his posthumously published notes, wrote: "I do not approve of the rule that if the use of pure reason has proved something, this result should later no longer be doubted as though it were a solid axiom"; and "I do not share the opinion . . . that one should not doubt once one has convinced oneself of something. In pure philosophy this is impossible. *Our mind has a natural aversion against it*"[10] (my italics). From which it seems to follow that the business of thinking is like the veil of Penelope: it undoes every morning what it had finished the night before.

Let me sum up my three main propositions in order to restate our problem, the inner connection between the ability or inability to think and the problem of evil.

First, if such a connection exists at all, then the faculty of thinking, as distinguished from the thirst for knowledge, must be ascribed to everybody; it cannot be a privilege of the few.

Second, if Kant is right and the faculty of thought has a "natural aversion" against accepting its own results as "solid axioms," then we cannot expect any moral propositions or commandments, no final code of conduct from the thinking activity, least of all a new and now allegedly final definition of what is good and what is evil.

Third, if it is true that thinking deals with invisibles, it follows that it is out of order because we normally move in a world of appearances in which the most radical experience of *dis*appearance is death. The gift for dealing with things that do not appear has often been believed to exact a price—the price of blinding the thinker or the poet to the visible world. Think of Homer, whom the gods gave the divine gift by striking him with blindness; think of Plato's *Phaedo* where those who do philosophy appear to those who don't, the many, like people who pursue death. Think of Zeno, the founder of Stoicism, who asked the Delphic oracle what he should do to attain the best life and was answered, "Take on the color of the dead."[11]

Hence the question is unavoidable: How can anything relevant for the world we live in arise out of so resultless an enterprise? An answer, if at all, can come only from the thinking activity, the performance itself, which means that we have to trace experiences rather than doctrines. And where do we turn for these experiences? The "everybody" of whom we demand thinking writes no books; he has more urgent business to attend to. And the few, whom Kant once called the "professional thinkers," were never particularly eager to write about the experience itself, perhaps because they knew that thinking is resultless by nature. For their books with their doctrines were inevitably composed with an eye to the many, who wish to see results and don't care to draw distinctions between knowing and thinking, between truth and meaning. We do not know how many of the "professional" thinkers whose doctrines constitute the tradition of philosophy and metaphysics had doubts about the validity and even the possible meaningfulness of their results. We know only Plato's magnificent denial (in the *Seventh Letter*) of what others proclaimed as his doctrines:

> On the subjects that concern me nothing is known since there exists nothing in writing on them nor will there ever exist anything in the future. People who write about such things know nothing; they don't even know themselves. For there is no way of putting it in words like other things which one can learn. Hence, no one who possesses the very faculty of thinking (*nous*) and therefore knows the weakness of words, will ever risk putting down thoughts in discourse, let alone fixing them into so unflexible a form as written letters.[12]

II

The trouble is that few thinkers ever told us what made them think and even fewer have cared to describe and examine their thinking experience. In this difficulty, unwilling to trust our own experiences because of the obvious danger of arbitrariness, I propose to look for a model, for an example that, unlike the "professional" thinkers, could be representative for our "everybody," i.e., to look for a man who counted himself neither among the many nor among the few—a distinction at least as old as Pythagoras; who did not aspire to being a ruler of cities or claim to know how to improve and take care of the citizens' souls; who did not believe that men could be wise and did not envy the gods their divine wisdom in case they should possess it; and who therefore had never even tried his hand at formulating a doctrine that could be taught and learned. In brief, I propose to use a man as our model who did think without becoming a philosopher, a citizen among citizens, doing nothing, claiming nothing that, in his view, every citizen should do and had a right to claim. You will have guessed that I intend to speak about Socrates, and I hope that no one will seriously dispute that my choice is historically justifiable.

But I must warn you: there is a great deal of controversy about the historical Socrates, about how and to what extent he can be distinguished from Plato, what weight to assign to Xenophon's Socrates, etc., and though this is one of the more fascinating topics of learned contention, I shall ignore it here altogether. Still, to use or, rather, to transform a historical figure into a model and assign to it a definite representative function stands in need of some justification. Etienne Gilson, in his great book *Dante and Philosophy,* shows how in the *Divine Comedy* "a character conserves as much of its historical reality as the representative function Dante assigns to it required."[13] Such freedom in handling historical, factual data, it seems, can be granted only to poets, and if nonpoets try their hand at it, the scholars will call it license and worse. And still, with or without justification, this is precisely what the broadly accepted custom of construing "ideal types" amounts to; for the great advantage of the ideal type is precisely that he is not a personified abstraction with some allegorical meaning ascribed to it, but that he was chosen out of the crowd of living beings, in the past or the present, because he possessed a representative significance in reality which only needed some purification in order to reveal its full meaning. Gilson explains how this purification works in his discussion of the part assigned by Dante to Thomas Aquinas in the *Divine Comedy*. In the 10th canto of "Paradiso," Aquinas glorifies Siger of Brabant who had been condemned for heresy and whom "the Thomas Aquinas of history would never have undertaken to eulogize in the way in which Dante makes him eulogize him," because he would have refused "to carry the distinction between philosophy and theology to the point of holding . . . the radical separatism that Dante had in mind." For Dante, Aquinas would thus have "forfeited the right to symbolize in the *Divine Comedy* the Dominican wisdom of faith," a right to which, on all other accounts, he could lay claim. It was, as Gilson brilliantly shows, that "part of his make-up, which [even Aquinas] had to leave at the gate of the *Paradiso* before he could enter."[14] There are a number of traits in the Xenophonian Socrates, whose historical credibility need not be doubted, which Socrates might have had to leave at the gate of paradise if Dante had used him.

The first thing that strikes us in Plato's Socratic dialogues is that they are all aporetic. The argument either leads nowhere or it goes around in circles. To know what justice is you must know what knowledge is, and to know knowing you must have a previous, unexamined notion of knowledge. (Thus in *Theaetetus* and *Charmides*.) Hence, "A man cannot try to discover either what he knows or what he does not know." If he knows, there is no need of inquiry; if he does not know. . . he does not even know what he is to look for" (*Meno* 80). Or, in the *Euthyphro:* In order to be pious I must know what piety is. Pious are the things that please the gods; but are they pious because they please the gods or do they please the gods because they are pious? None of the *logoi*, the arguments, ever stays put; they move about, because Socrates, asking questions to which he does *not* know the answers, sets them in motion. And once the statements have come full circle, it is usually Socrates who cheerfully proposes to start all over again and inquire what justice or piety or knowledge or happiness are.

For the topics of these early dialogues deal with very simple, everyday concepts, such as arise whenever people open their mouths and begin to talk. The introduction usually runs as follows: To be sure, there are happy people, just deeds, courageous men, beautiful things to see and admire, everybody knows about them; the trouble starts with our usage of nouns, presumably derived from those adjectives which we apply to particular cases as they *appear* to us (we *see* a happy man, *perceive* the courageous deed or the just decision), that is, with such words as "happiness," "courage," "justice," etc., which we now call concepts and which Solon called the "non-appearing measure" (*aphanēs metron*) "most difficult for the mind to comprehend, but nevertheless holding the limits of all things"[15]—and Plato somewhat later called ideas perceivable only by the eyes of the mind. These words, used to group together seen and manifest qualities and occurrences but nevertheless relating to something unseen, are part and parcel of our everyday speech, and still we can give no account of them; when we try to define them, they get slippery; when we talk about their meaning, nothing stays put anymore, everything begins to move. So instead of repeating what we learned from Aristotle, that Socrates was the man who discovered the "concept," we should ask ourselves what Socrates did when he discovered it. For surely, these words were part of the Greek language before he tried to force the Athenians and himself to give an account of what they and he meant when they uttered them, being convinced that no speech would be possible without them.

This conviction has become questionable. Our knowledge of the so-called primitive languages has taught us that this grouping together of many particulars into a name common to all of them is by no means a matter of course, for these languages, whose vocabulary is often much richer than ours, lack such abstract nouns even if they relate to clearly visible objects. To simplify matters, let us take such a noun which to us no longer sounds abstract at all. We can use the word "house" for a great number of objects—for the mud-hut of a tribe, for the palace of a king, the country home of a city dweller, the cottage in the village or the apartment house in town—but we can hardly use it for the tents of some nomads. The house in and by itself, *auto kath'auto*, that which makes us use the word for all these particular and very different buildings, is never seen, neither by the eyes of the body nor by the eyes of the mind; every imagined house, be it ever so abstract, having the bare minimum to make it recognizable, is already a particular house. This house as such, of which we must have a notion in order to recognize particular buildings as houses, has been explained in different ways and called by different names in the history of philosophy; with this we are not concerned here, although we might have perhaps less trouble defining it than such words as "happiness" or "justice." The point here is that it implies something considerably less tangible than the structure perceived by our eyes. It implies "housing somebody" and being "dwelt in" as no tent could house or serve as a dwelling place which is put up today and taken down tomorrow. The word "house," Solon's "unseen measure," "holds the limits of all things" pertaining to dwelling; it is a word that could not exist unless one presupposes thinking about being housed, dwelling, having a home. As a word, "house" is shorthand for all these things, the kind of shorthand without which thinking and its characteristic swiftness— "swift as a thought" as Homer used to say—would not be possible at all. *The word "house" is something like a frozen thought which thinking must unfreeze*, defrost as it were, whenever it wants to find out its original meaning. In medieval philosophy, this kind of thinking was called meditation, and the word should be heard as different from, even opposed to, contemplation. In any event, this kind of pondering reflection does not produce definitions and in this sense is entirely without results; it might however be that those who, for whatever reason, have pondered the meaning of the word "house" will make their apartments look a bit better— though not necessarily so and certainly without being conscious of anything so verifiable as cause and effect. Meditation is not the same as deliberation, which indeed is supposed to end in tangible results; and meditation does not aim at deliberation although it sometimes, by no means very often, turns into it.

Socrates, however, who is commonly said to have believed in the teachability of virtue, seems indeed to have held that talking and thinking about piety, justice, courage, and the rest were liable to make men more pious, more just, more courageous, even though they were not given either definitions or "values" to direct their further conduct. What Socrates actually believed in in such matters can best be illustrated by the similes he applied to himself. He called himself a gadfly and a midwife, and, according to Plato, was called by somebody else an "electric ray," a fish that paralyzes and numbs by contact, a likeness whose appropriateness he recognized under the condition that it be understood that "the electric ray paralyzes others only through being paralyzed itself. It isn't that, knowing the answers myself I perplex other people. The truth is rather that I infect them also with the perplexity I feel myself."[16] Which, of course, sums up neatly the only way thinking can be taught—except that Socrates, as he repeatedly said, did not teach anything for the simple reason that he had nothing to teach; he was "sterile" like the midwives in Greece who were beyond the age of childbearing. (Since he had nothing to teach, no truth to hand out, he was accused of never revealing his own view [*gnōmē*]—as we learn from Xenophon, who defended him against this charge.)[17] It seems that he, unlike the professional philosophers, felt the urge to check with his fellowmen if his perplexities were shared by them—and this urge is quite different from the inclination to find solutions for riddles and then to demonstrate them to others.

Let us look briefly at the three similes. *First,* Socrates is a gadfly: he knows how to arouse the citizens who, without him, will "sleep on undisturbed for the rest of their lives," unless somebody else comes along to wake them up again. And what does he arouse them to? To thinking, to examining matters, an activity without which life, according to him, was not only not worth much but was not fully alive.[18]

Second, Socrates is a midwife: here the implication is threefold—the "sterility" I mentioned before, the expert knowledge of delivering others of their thoughts, that is, of the implications of their opinions, and the Greek midwife's function of deciding whether the child was fit to live or, to use Socratic language, was a mere "wind egg," of which the bearer must be cleansed. In this context, only the last two of these implications matter. For looking at the Socratic dialogues, there is nobody among Socrates' interlocutors who ever brought forth a thought that was no wind egg. He rather did what Plato, certainly thinking of Socrates, said of the Sophists: he purged people of their "opinions," that is, of those unexamined prejudgments which prevent thinking by suggesting that we know where we not only don't know but cannot know, helping them, as Plato remarks, to get rid of what was bad in them, their opinions, without however making them good, giving them truth.[19]

Third, Socrates, knowing that we don't know and still unwilling to let it go at that, remains steadfast with his own perplexities and, like the electric ray, paralyzes with them whomever he comes into contact with. The electric ray, at first glance, seems to be the opposite of the gadfly; it paralyzes where the gadfly arouses. Yet, what cannot but look like paralysis from the outside and the ordinary course of human affairs is felt as the highest state of being alive. There exist, despite the scarcity of documentary evidence for the thinking experience, a number of utterances of the thinkers throughout the centuries to this effect. Socrates himself, very much aware that thinking deals with invisibles and is itself invisible, lacking all the outside manifestation of other activities, seems to have used the metaphor of the wind for it: "The winds themselves are invisible, yet what they do is manifest to us and we somehow feel their approach."[20] (The same metaphor, incidentally, is used by Heidegger, who also speaks of the "storm of thought.")

In the context in which Xenophon, always anxious to defend the master against vulgar accusations with vulgar arguments, mentions this metaphor, it does not make much sense. Still, even he indicates that the manifestations of the invisible wind of thought are those concepts, virtues and "values," with which Socrates dealt in his examinations. The trouble—and the reason why the same man can be understood and understand himself as gadfly as well as electric ray—is that this same wind, whenever it is aroused, has the peculiarity of doing away with its own previous manifestations. It is in its nature to undo, unfreeze as it were, what language, the medium of thinking, has frozen into thought—words (concepts, sentences, definitions, doctrines), whose "weakness" and inflexibility Plato denounces so splendidly in the *Seventh Letter.* The consequence of this peculiarity is that thinking inevitably has a destructive, undermining effect on all established criteria, values, measurements for good and evil, in short on those customs and rules of conduct we treat of in morals and ethics. These frozen thoughts, Socrates seems to say, come so handy you can use them in your sleep; but if the wind of thinking, which I shall now arouse in you, has roused you from your sleep and made you fully awake and alive, then you will see that you have nothing in your hand but perplexities, and the most we can do with them is share them with each other.

Hence, the paralysis of thought is twofold: it is inherent in the *stop* and think, the interruption of all other activities, and it may have a paralyzing effect when you come out of it, no longer sure of what had seemed to you beyond doubt while you were unthinkingly engaged in whatever you were doing. If your action consisted in applying general rules of conduct to particular cases as they arise in ordinary life, then you will find yourself paralyzed because no such rules can withstand the wind of thought. To use once more the example of the frozen thought inherent in the word "house," once you have thought about its implied meaning—dwelling, having a home, being housed—you are no longer likely to accept for your own home whatever the fashion of the time may prescribe; but this by no means guarantees that you will be able to come up with an acceptable solution for your own housing problems. You may be paralyzed.

This leads to the last and, perhaps, even greatest danger of this dangerous and resultless enterprise. In the circle around Socrates, there were men like Alcibiades and Critias—God knows, by no means the worst among his so-called pupils—and they turned out to be a very real threat to the polis, and this not by being paralyzed by the electric ray but, on the contrary, by having been aroused by the gadfly. What they had been aroused to was license and cynicism. They had not been content with being taught how to think without being taught a doctrine, and they changed the nonresults of the Socratic thinking examination into negative results: if we cannot define what piety is, let us be impious—which is pretty much the opposite of what Socrates had hoped to achieve by talking about piety.

The quest for meaning, which relentlessly dissolves and examines anew all accepted doctrines and rules, can at every moment turn against itself, as it were, produce a reversal of the old values, and declare these as "new values." This, to an extent, is what Nietzsche did when he reversed Platonism, forgetting that a reversed Plato is still Plato, or what Marx did when he turned Hegel upside down, producing a strictly Hegelian system of history in the process. Such negative results of thinking will then be used as sleepily, with the same unthinking routine, as the old values; the moment they are applied to the realm of human affairs, it is as though they had never gone through the thinking process. What we commonly call nihilism—and are tempted to date historically, decry politically, and ascribe to thinkers who allegedly dared to think "dangerous thoughts"—is actually a danger inherent in the thinking activity itself. There are no dangerous thoughts; thinking itself is dangerous, but nihilism is not its product. Nihilism is but the other side of conventionalism; its creed consists of negations of the current, so-called positive values to which it remains bound. All critical examinations must go through a stage of at least hypothetically negating accepted opinions and "values" by finding out their implications and tacit assumptions, and in this sense nihilism may be seen as an ever-present danger of thinking. But this danger does not arise out of the Socratic conviction that an unexamined life is not worth living but, on the contrary, out of the desire to find results which would make further thinking unnecessary. Thinking is equally dangerous to all creeds and, by itself, does not bring forth any new creed.

However, nonthinking, which seems so recommendable a state for political and moral affairs, also has its dangers. By shielding people against the dangers of examination, it teaches them to hold fast to whatever the prescribed rules of conduct may be at a given time in a given society. What people then get used to is not so much the content of the rules, a close examination of which would always lead them into perplexity, as the possession of rules under which to subsume particulars. In other words, they get used to never making up their minds. If somebody then should show up who, for whatever reasons and purposes, wishes to abolish the old "values" or virtues, he will find it easy enough provided he offers a new code, and he will need no force and no persuasion—no proof that the new values are better than the old ones—to establish it. The faster men held to the old code, the more eager will they be to assimilate themselves to the new one; the ease with which such reversals can take place under certain circumstances suggests indeed that everybody is asleep when they occur. This century has offered us some experience in such matters: How easy it was for the totalitarian rulers to reverse the basic commandments of Western morality—"Thou shalt not kill" in the case of Hitler's Germany, "Thou shalt not bear false testimony against thy neighbor" in the case of Stalin's Russia.

To come back to Socrates. The Athenians told him that thinking was subversive, that the wind of thought was a hurricane which sweeps away all the established signs by which men orient themselves in the world; it brings disorder into the cities and it confuses the citizens, especially the young ones. And though Socrates denied that thinking corrupts, he did not pretend that it improves, and though he declared that "no greater good has ever befallen" the polis than what he was doing, he did not pretend that he started his career as a philosopher in order to become such a great benefactor. If "an unexamined life is not worth living,"[21] then thinking accompanies living when it concerns itself with such concepts as justice, happiness, temperance, pleasure, with words for invisible things which language has offered us to express the meaning of whatever happens in life and occurs to us while we are alive.

Socrates calls this quest for meaning *erōs*, a kind of love which is primarily a need—it desires what it has not—and which is the only matter he pretends to be an expert in.[22] Men are in love with wisdom and do philosophy (*philosophein*) because they are not wise, just as they are in love with beauty and "do beauty," so to speak (*philokalein,* as Pericles called it),[23] because they are not beautiful. Love, by desiring what is not there, establishes a relationship with it. To bring this relationship into the open, make it appear, men speak about it in the same way the lover wants to speak about his beloved.[24] Since the quest is a kind of love and desire, the objects of thought can only be lovable things—beauty, wisdom, justice, etc. Ugliness and evil are excluded by definition from the thinking concern, although they may occasionally turn up as deficiencies, as lack of beauty, injustice, and evil (*kakia*) as lack of good. This means that they have no roots of their own, no essence of which thought could get hold. Evil, we are told, cannot be done voluntarily because of its "ontological status," as we would say today; it consists in an absence, in something that is not. If thinking dissolves normal, positive concepts into their original meaning, then the same process dissolves these negative "concepts" into their original meaninglessness, into nothing. This incidentally is by no means only Socrates' opinion; that evil is a mere privation, negation, or exception from the rule is the nearly unanimous opinion of all thinkers.[25] (The most conspicuous and most dangerous fallacy in the proposition, as old as Plato, "Nobody does evil voluntarily," is the implied conclusion, "Everybody wants to do good." The sad truth of the matter is that most evil is done by people who never made up their mind to be either bad or good.)

Where does this leave us with respect to our problem—inability or refusal to think and the capacity of doing evil? We are left with the conclusion that only people filled with this *erōs*, this desiring love of wisdom, beauty, and justice, are capable of thought—that is, we are left with Plato's "noble nature" as a prerequisite for thinking. And this was precisely what we were not looking for when we raised the question whether the thinking activity, the very performance itself—as distinguished from and regardless of whatever qualities a man's nature, his soul, may possess—conditions him in such a way that he is incapable of evil.

III

Among the very few positive statements that Socrates, this lover of perplexities, ever made there are two propositions, closely connected with each other, which deal with our question. Both occur in the *Gorgias*, the dialogue about rhetoric, the art of addressing and convincing the many. The *Gorgias* does not belong to the early Socratic dialogues; it was written shortly before Plato became the head of the Academy. Moreover, it seems that its very subject matter deals with a form of discourse which would lose all sense if it were aporetic. And yet, this dialogue is still aporetic; only the last Platonic dialogues from which Socrates either disappears or is no longer the center of the discussion have entirely lost this quality. The *Gorgias*, like the *Republic*, concludes with one of the Platonic myths of a hereafter with rewards and punishments which apparently, that is ironically, resolve all difficulties. Their seriousness is purely political; it consists in their being addressed to the multitude. These myths, certainly non-Socratic, are of importance because they contain, albeit in a nonphilosophical form, Plato's admission that men can and do commit evil voluntarily, and even more importantly, the implied admission that he, no more than Socrates, knew what to do philosophically with this disturbing fact. We may not know whether Socrates believed that ignorance causes evil and that virtue can be taught; but we do know that Plato thought it wiser to rely on threats.

The two positive Socratic propositions read as follows: The *first:* "It is better to be wronged than to do wrong"—to which Callicles, the interlocutor in the dialogue, replies what all Greece would have replied: "To suffer wrong is not the part of a man at all, but that of a slave for whom it is better to be dead than alive, as it is for anyone who is unable to come either to his own assistance when he is wronged or to that of anyone he cares about" (474). The *second:* "It would be better for me that my lyre or a chorus I directed should be out of tune and loud with discord, and that multitudes of men should disagree with me rather than that I, *being one,* should be out of harmony with myself and contradict *me.*" Which causes Callicles to tell Socrates that he is "going mad with eloquence," and that it would be better for him and everybody else if he would leave philosophy alone (482).

And there, as we shall see, he has a point. It was indeed philosophy, or rather the experience of thinking, that led Socrates to make these statements—although, of course, he did not start his enterprise in order to arrive at them. For it would be a serious mistake, I believe, to understand them as the results of some cogitation about morality; they are insights, to be sure, but insights of experience, and as far as the thinking process itself is concerned they are at best incidental by-products.

We have difficulties realizing how paradoxical the first statement must have sounded when it was made; after thousands of years of use and misuse, it reads like cheap moralizing. And the best demonstration of how difficult it is for modern minds to understand the thrust of the second is the fact that its key words, *"being one"* it would be worse for me to be at odds with myself than in disagreement with multitudes of men, are frequently left out in translation. As to the first, it is a subjective statement, meaning, it is better *for me* to suffer wrong than to do wrong, and it is countered by the opposite, equally subjective statement which, of course, sounds much more plausible. If, however, we were to look at the propositions from the viewpoint of the world, as distinguished from that of the two gentlemen, we would have to say what counts is that a wrong has been committed; it is irrelevant who is better off, the wrongdoer or the wrong-sufferer. As citizens we must prevent wrongdoing since the world we all share, wrongdoer, wrong-sufferer, and spectator, is at stake; the City has been wronged. (Thus our law codes distinguish between crimes, where indictment is mandatory, and transgressions, where only private individuals are being wronged who may or may not want to sue. In the case of a crime, the subjective states of mind of those involved are irrelevant—the one who suffered may be willing to forgive, the one who did may be entirely unlikely to do it again—because the community as a whole has been violated.)

In other words, Socrates does not talk here as a citizen who is supposed to be more concerned with the world than with his own self. It is rather as though he said to Callicles: If you were like me, in love with wisdom and in need of examining, and if the world should be as you depict it—divided into the strong and the weak where "the strong do what they can and the weak suffer what they must" (Thucydides)—so that no alternative exists but to either do or suffer wrong, then you would agree with me that it is better to suffer than to do. The presupposition is if you were thinking, if you were to agree that "an unexamined life is not worth living."

To my knowledge there exists only one other passage in Greek literature that, in almost the same words, says what Socrates said. "More unfortunate (*kakodaimonesteros*) than the wronged one is the wrong doer," reads one of the few fragments of Democritus (B45), the great adversary of Parmenides who probably for this reason was never mentioned by Plato. The coincidence seems noteworthy because Democritus, in distinction from Socrates, was not particularly interested in human affairs but seems to have been quite interested in the experience of thinking. "The mind (*logos*)," he said, makes abstinence easy because "it is used to getting joys out of itself (*auton ex heautou*)" (B146). It looks as though what we are tempted to understand as a purely moral proposition actually arises out of the thinking experience as such.

And this brings us to the second statement, which is the prerequisite of the first one. It, too, is highly paradoxical. Socrates talks of being one and *therefore* not being able to risk getting out of harmony with himself. But nothing that is identical with itself, truly and absolutely *one* like A is A, can be either in or out of harmony with itself; you always need at least two tones to produce a harmonious sound. To be sure, when I appear and am seen by others, I am one; otherwise I would be unrecognizable. And so long as I am together with others, barely conscious of myself, I am as I appear to others. We call *consciousness* (literally, "to know with myself") the curious fact that in a sense I also am for myself, though I hardly appear to me, which indicates that the Socratic "being-one" is not so unproblematic as it seems; I am not only for others but for myself, and in this latter case, I clearly am not just one. A difference is inserted into my Oneness.

We know of this difference in other respects. Everything that exists among a plurality of things is not simply what it is, in its identity, but it is also different from other things; this being different belongs to its very nature. When we try to get hold of it in thought, wanting to define it, we must take this otherness (*alteritas*) or difference into account. When we say what a thing is, we always also say what it is not; every determination, as Spinoza has it, is a negation. Related to itself alone it is the same (*auto* [i.e., *hekaston*] *heautō tauton:* "each for itself the same"),[26] and all we can say about it in its sheer identity is "A rose is a rose is a rose." But this is not at all the case if I in my identity ("being one") relate to myself. This curious thing that I am needs no plurality in order to establish difference; it carries the difference within itself when it says: "I am I." So long as I am conscious, that is, conscious of myself, I am identical with myself only for others to whom I appear as one and the same. For myself, articulating this being-conscious-of-myself, I am inevitably *two-in-one*—which incidentally is the reason why the fashionable search for identity is futile and our modern identity crisis could be resolved only by losing consciousness. Human consciousness suggests that difference and otherness, which are such outstanding characteristics of the world of appearances as it is given to man as his habitat among a plurality of things, are the very conditions for the existence of man's ego as well. For this ego, the I-am-I, experiences difference in identity precisely when it is not related to the things that appear but only to itself. Without this original split, which Plato later used in his definition of thinking as the soundless dialogue (*eme emautō*) between me and myself, the two-in-one, which Socrates presupposes in his statement about harmony with myself, would not be possible.[27] Consciousness is not the same as thinking; but without it, thinking would be impossible. What thinking actualizes in its process is the difference given in consciousness.

For Socrates, this two-in-one meant simply that if you want to think you must see to it that the two who carry on the thinking dialogue be in good shape, that the partners be friends. It is better for you to suffer than to do wrong because you can remain the friend of the sufferer; who would want to be the friend of and have to live together with a murderer? Not even a murderer. What kind of dialogue could you lead with him? Precisely the dialogue which Shakespeare let Richard III lead with himself after a great number of crimes had been committed:

> What do I fear? Myself? There's none else by.
> Richard loves Richard: that is, I am I.
> Is there a murderer here? No. Yes, I am:
> Then fly. What from myself? Great reason why—
> Lest I revenge. What, myself upon myself?
> O no! Alas, I rather hate myself
> For hateful deeds committed by myself.
> I am a villain. Yet I lie, I am not.
> Fool, of thyself speak well. Fool, do not flatter.

A similar encounter of the self with itself, undramatic, mild, and almost harmless in comparison, can be found in one of the contested Socratic dialogues, the *Hippias Major* (which, even though not written by Plato, may still give authentic evidence of Socrates). At its end, Socrates tells Hippias, who has proved to be an especially empty-headed partner, "how blissfully fortunate" he is compared with himself who, when he goes home, is awaited by a very obnoxious fellow "who always cross-examines [him], a close relative, living in the same house." Hearing Socrates give utterance to Hippias' opinions, he will ask him "whether he is not ashamed of himself talking about a beautiful way of life when questioning makes it evident that he does not even know the meaning of the word 'beauty' " (304). In other words, when Hippias goes home he remains one; although he certainly does not lose consciousness, he also will do nothing to actualize the difference within himself. With Socrates or, for that matter, Richard III, it is a different story. They have not only intercourse with others, they have intercourse with themselves. The point here is that what the one calls "the other fellow" and the other "conscience" is never present except when they are alone. When midnight is over and Richard has joined again the company of his friends, then

> Conscience is but a word that cowards use,
> Devised at first to keep the strong in awe.

And even Socrates, so attracted by the marketplace, must go home where he will be alone, in solitude, to meet the other fellow.

I chose the passage in *Richard III*, because Shakespeare, though he uses the word "conscience," does not use it here in the accustomed way. It took language a long time until it separated the word "consciousness" from "conscience," and in some languages, for instance in French, such a separation never happened. Conscience, as we use it in moral or legal matters, supposedly is always present within us, just like consciousness. And this conscience is also supposed to tell us what to do and what to repent of; it was the voice of God before it became the *lumen naturale* or Kant's practical reason. Unlike this conscience, the fellow Socrates is talking about has been left at home; he fears him, as the murderers in *Richard III* fear their conscience—as something that is absent. Conscience appears as an afterthought, that thought which is aroused either by a crime, as in the case of Richard himself, or by unexamined opinions, as in the case of Socrates, or as the anticipated fear of such afterthoughts, as in the case of the hired murderers in *Richard III*. This conscience, unlike the voice of God within us or the *lumen naturale,* gives no positive prescriptions—even the Socratic *daimonion,* his divine voice, only tells him what *not* to do; in the words of Shakespeare, "it fills a man full of obstacles." What makes a man fear this conscience is the anticipation of the presence of a witness who awaits him only *if* and when he goes home. Shakespeare's murderer says: "Every man that means to live well endeavors . . . to live without it," and success in this endeavor comes easy because all he has to do is never to start the soundless solitary dialogue we call thinking, never to go home and examine things. This is not a matter of wickedness or goodness, as it is not a matter of intelligence or stupidity. He who does not know the intercourse between me and myself (in which we examine what we say and what we do) will not mind contradicting himself, and this means he will never be either able or willing to give account of what he says or does; nor will he mind committing any crime, since he can be sure that it will be forgotten the next moment.

Thinking in its noncognitive, nonspecialized sense as a natural need of human life, the actualization of the difference given in consciousness, is not a prerogative of the few but an ever-present faculty of everybody; by the same token, inability to think is not the "prerogative" of those many who lack brain power but the ever-present possibility for everybody—scientists, scholars, and other specialists in mental enterprises not excluded—to shun that intercourse with oneself whose possibility and importance

Socrates first discovered. We were here not concerned with wickedness, with which religion and literature have tried to come to terms, but with evil; not with sin and the great villains who became the negative heroes in literature and usually acted out of envy and resentment, but with the nonwicked everybody who has no special motives and for this reason is capable of *infinite* evil; unlike the villain, he never meets his midnight disaster.

For the thinking ego and its experience, conscience, which "fills a man full of obstacles," is a side effect. And it remains a marginal affair for society at large except in emergencies. For thinking as such does society little good, much less than the thirst for knowledge in which it is used as an instrument for other purposes. It does not create values, it will not find out, once and for all, what "the good" is, and it does not confirm but rather dissolves accepted rules of conduct. Its political and moral significance comes out only in those rare moments in history when "Things fall apart; the centre cannot hold; / Mere anarchy is loosed upon the world," when "The best lack all conviction, while the worst / Are full of passionate intensity."

At these moments, thinking ceases to be a marginal affair in political matters. When everybody is swept away unthinkingly by what everybody else does and believes in, those who think are drawn out of hiding because their refusal to join is conspicuous and thereby becomes a kind of action. The purging element in thinking, Socrates' midwifery, that brings out the implications of unexamined opinions and thereby destroys them—values, doctrines, theories, and even convictions—is political by implication. For this destruction has a liberating effect on another human faculty, the faculty of judgment, which one may call, with some justification, the most political of man's mental abilities. It is the faculty to judge *particulars* without subsuming them under those general rules which can be taught and learned until they grow into habits that can be replaced by other habits and rules.

The faculty of judging particulars (as Kant discovered it), the ability to say, "this is wrong," "this is beautiful," etc., is not the same as the faculty of thinking. Thinking deals with invisibles, with representations of things that are absent; judging always concerns particulars and things close at hand. But the two are interrelated in a way similar to the way consciousness and conscience are interconnected. If thinking, the two-in-one of the soundless dialogue, actualizes the difference within our identity as given in consciousness and thereby results in conscience as its by-product, then judging, the by-product of the liberating effect of thinking, realizes thinking, makes it manifest in the world of appearances, where I am never alone and always much too busy to be able to think. The manifestation of the wind of thought is no knowledge; it is the ability to tell right from wrong, beautiful from ugly. And this indeed may prevent catastrophes, at least for myself, in the rare moments when the chips are down.

1971

❖❖❖ II ❖❖❖
JUDGMENT

REFLECTIONS ON LITTLE ROCK

Introduction

The point of departure of my reflections was a picture in the newspapers showing a Negro girl on her way home from a newly integrated school: she was persecuted by a mob of white children, protected by a white friend of her father, and her face bore eloquent witness to the obvious fact that she was not precisely happy. The picture showed the situation in a nutshell because those who appeared in it were directly affected by the Federal court order, the children themselves. My first question was, what would I do if I were a Negro mother? The answer: under no circumstances would I expose my child to conditions which made it appear as though it wanted to push its way into a group where it was not wanted. Psychologically, the situation of being unwanted (a typically social predicament) is more difficult to bear than outright persecution (a political predicament) because personal pride is involved. By pride, I do not mean anything like being "proud of being a Negro," or a Jew, or a white Anglo-Saxon Protestant, etc., but that untaught and natural feeling of identity with whatever we happen to be by the accident of birth. Pride, which does not compare and knows neither inferiority nor superiority complexes, is indispensable for personal integrity, and it is lost not so much by persecution as by pushing, or rather being pushed into pushing, one's way out of one group and into another. If I were a Negro mother in the South, I would feel that the Supreme Court ruling, unwillingly but unavoidably, has put my child into a more humiliating position than it had been in before.

Moreover, if I were a Negro I would feel that the very attempt to start desegregation in education and in schools had not only, and very unfairly, shifted the burden of responsibility from the shoulders of adults to those of children. I would in addition be convinced that there is an implication in the whole enterprise of trying to avoid the real issue. The real issue is equality before the law of the country, and equality is violated by segregation laws, that is, by laws enforcing segregation, not by social customs and the manners of educating children. If it were only a matter of equally good education for my children, an effort to grant them equality of opportunity, why was I not asked to fight for an improvement of schools for Negro children and for the immediate establishment of special classes for those children whose scholastic record now makes them acceptable to white schools? Instead of being called upon to fight a clear-cut battle for my indisputable rights—my right to vote and be protected in it, to marry whom I please and be protected in my marriage (though, of course, not in attempts to become anybody's brother-in-law*), or my right to equal opportunity—I would feel I had become involved in an affair of social climbing; and if I chose this way of bettering myself, I certainly would prefer to do it by myself, unaided by any government agencies. To be sure, even pushing and using my elbows might not entirely depend upon my own inclinations. I might be forced into it in order to make a decent

*"Brother-in-law" refers to one of Arendt's critics' misunderstanding of her position on antimiscegenation laws, which to her were unconstitutional and should be struck down by the Supreme Court.—Ed.

living or raise the standard of life for my family. Life can be very unpleasant, but whatever it may force me to do—and it certainly does not force me to buy my way into restricted neighborhoods—I can retain my personal integrity precisely to the extent that I act under compulsion and out of some vital necessity, and not merely for social reasons.

My second question was: what would I do if I were a white mother in the South? Again I would try to prevent my child's being dragged into a political battle in the schoolyard. In addition, I would feel that my consent was necessary for any such drastic changes no matter what my opinion of them happened to be. I would agree that the government has a stake in the education of my child insofar as this child is supposed to grow up into a citizen, but I would deny that the government had any right to tell me in whose company my child received its instruction. The rights of parents to decide such matters for their children until they are grown-ups are challenged only by dictatorships.

If, however, I were strongly convinced that the situation in the South could be materially helped by integrated education, I would try—perhaps with the help of the Quakers or some other body of like-minded citizens—to organize a new school for white and colored children and to run it like a pilot project, as a means to persuade other white parents to change their attitudes. To be sure, there, too, I would use the children in what is essentially a political battle, but at least I would have made sure that the children in school are all there with the consent and the help of their parents; there would be no conflict between home and school, though there might arise a conflict between home and school, on one side, and the street on the other. Let us now assume that in the course of such an enterprise, Southern citizens who object to integrated education also organized themselves and even succeeded in persuading the state authorities to prevent the opening and functioning of the school. This would be the precise moment when, in my opinion, the federal government should be called upon to intervene. For here we would have again a clear case of segregation enforced by governmental authority.

This now brings us to my third question. I asked myself: what exactly distinguishes the so-called Southern way of life from the American way of life with respect to the color question? And the answer, of course, is simply that while discrimination and segregation are the rule in the whole country, they are enforced by legislation only in the Southern states. Hence, whoever wishes to change the situation in the South can hardly avoid abolishing the marriage laws and intervening to effect free exercise of the franchise. This is by no means an academic question. It is partly a matter of constitutional principle which by definition is beyond majority decisions and practicality; and it also involves, of course, the rights of citizens, as, for instance, the rights of those twenty-five or so Negro men from Texas who, while in the Army, had married European women and therefore could not go home because in the eyes of Texas legislation they were guilty of a crime.

The reluctance of American liberals to touch the issue of the marriage laws, their readiness to invoke practicality and shift the ground of the argument by insisting that the Negroes themselves have no interest in this matter, their embarrassment when they are reminded of what the whole world knows to be the most outrageous piece of legislation in the whole Western Hemisphere, all this recalls to mind the earlier reluctance of the founders of the Republic to follow Jefferson's advice and abolish the crime of slavery. Jefferson, too, yielded for practical reasons, but he, at least, still had enough political sense to say after the fight was lost: "I tremble when I think that God is just." He trembled not for the

Negroes, not even for the whites, but for the destiny of the Republic because he knew that one of its vital principles had been violated right at the beginning. Not discrimination and social segregation, in whatever forms, but racial legislation constitutes the perpetuation of the original crime in this country's history.

One last word about education and politics. The idea that one can change the world by educating the children in the spirit of the future has been one of the hallmarks of political utopias since antiquity. The trouble with this idea has always been the same: it can succeed only if the children are really separated from their parents and brought up in state institutions, or are indoctrinated in school so that they will turn against their own parents. This is what happens in tyrannies. If, on the other hand, public authorities are unwilling to draw the consequences of their own vague hopes and premises, the whole educational experiment remains at best without result, while, at worst, it irritates and antagonizes both parents and children who feel that they are deprived of some essential rights. The series of events in the South that followed the Supreme Court ruling, after which this administration committed itself to fight its battle for civil rights on the grounds of education and public schools, impresses one with a sense of futility and needless embitterment as though all parties concerned knew very well that nothing was being achieved under the pretext that something was being done.

I

It is unfortunate and even unjust (though hardly unjustified) that the events at Little Rock should have had such an enormous echo in public opinion throughout the world and have become a major stumbling block to American foreign policy. For unlike other domestic problems which have beset this country since the end of World War II (a security hysteria, a runaway prosperity, and the concomitant transformation of an economy of abundance into a market where sheer superfluity and nonsense almost wash out the essential and the productive), and unlike such long-range difficulties as the problem of mass culture and mass education—both of which are typical of modern society in general and not only of America—the country's attitude to its Negro population is rooted in American tradition and nothing else. The color question was created by the one great crime in America's history and is soluble only within the political and historical framework of the Republic. The fact that this question has also become a major issue in world affairs is sheer coincidence as far as American history and politics are concerned; for the color problem in world politics grew out of the colonialism and imperialism of European nations—that is, the one great crime in which America was never involved. The tragedy is that the unsolved color problem within the United States may cost her the advantages she otherwise would rightly enjoy as a world power.

For historical and other reasons, we are in the habit of identifying the Negro question with the South, but the unsolved problems connected with Negroes living in our midst concern of course the whole country, not the South alone. Like other race questions, it has a special attraction for the mob and is particularly well fitted to serve as the point around which a mob ideology and a mob organization can crystallize. This aspect may one day even prove more explosive in the big Northern urban centers than in the more tradition-bound South, especially if the number of Negroes in Southern cities continues to decline while the Negro population of non-Southern cities increases at the same rate as in recent years. The United States is not a nation-state in the European sense and never was. The principle of its political structure is, and always has been, independent of a homogeneous population and of a common past. This is somewhat less true of the South, whose population is more homogeneous and more rooted in the past than that of any other part of the country. When William Faulkner recently declared that in a conflict between the South and Washington he would ultimately have to act as a citizen of Mississippi, he sounded more like a member of a European nation-state than a citizen of this Republic. But this difference between North and South, though still marked, is bound to disappear with the growing industrialization of Southern states and plays no role in some of them even today. In all parts of the country, in the East and North with its host of nationalities no less than in the more homogeneous South, the Negroes stand out because of their "visibility." They are not the only "visible minority," but they are the most visible one. In this respect, they somewhat resemble new immigrants, who invariably constitute the most "audible" of all minorities and therefore are always the most likely to arouse xenophobic sentiments. But while audibility is a temporary phenomenon, rarely persisting beyond one generation, the Negroes' visibility is unalterable and permanent. This is not a trivial matter. In the public realm, where nothing counts that cannot make itself seen and heard, visibility and audibility are of prime importance. To argue that they are merely exterior appearances is to beg the question. For it is precisely appearances that "appear" in public, and inner qualities, gifts of heart or mind, are political only to the extent that their owner wishes to expose them in public, to place them in the limelight of the marketplace.

The American Republic is based on the equality of all citizens, and while equality before the law has become an inalienable principle of all modern constitutional government, equality as such is of greater importance in the political life of a republic than in any other form of government. The point at stake, therefore, is not the well-being of the Negro population alone, but, at least in the long run, the survival of the Republic. Tocqueville saw over a century ago that equality of opportunity and condition, as well as equality of rights, constituted the basic "law" of American democracy, and he predicted that the dilemmas and perplexities inherent in the principle of equality might one day become the most dangerous challenge to the American way of life. In its all-comprehensive, typically American form, equality possesses an enormous power to equalize what by nature and origin is different—and it is only due to this power that the country has been able to retain its fundamental identity against the waves of immigrants who have always flooded its shores. But the principle of equality, even in its American form, is not omnipotent; it cannot equalize natural, physical characteristics. This limit is reached only when inequalities of economic and educational condition have been ironed out, but at that juncture a danger point, well known to students of history, invariably emerges: the more equal people have become in every respect, and the more equality permeates the whole texture of society, the more will differences be resented, the more conspicuous will those become who are visibly and by nature unlike the others.

It is therefore quite possible that the achievement of social, economic, and educational equality for the Negro may sharpen the color problem in this country instead of assuaging it. This, of course, does not have to happen, but it would be only natural if it did, and it would be very surprising if it did not. We have not yet reached the danger point, but we shall reach it in the foreseeable future, and a number of developments have already taken place which clearly point toward it. Awareness of future trouble does not commit one to advocating a reversal of the trend which happily for more than fifteen years now has been greatly in favor of the Negroes. But it does commit one to advocating that government intervention be guided by caution and moderation rather than by impatience and ill-advised measures. Since the Supreme Court decision to enforce desegregation in public schools, the general situation in the South has deteriorated. And while recent events indicate that it will not be possible to avoid Federal enforcement of Negro civil rights in the South altogether, conditions demand that such intervention be restricted to the few instances in which the law of the land and the principle of the Republic are at stake. The question therefore is where this is the case in general, and whether it is the case in public education in particular.

The administration's Civil Rights program covers two altogether different points. It reaffirms the franchise of the Negro population, a matter of course in the North, but not at all in the South. And it also takes up the issue of segregation, which is a matter of fact in the whole country and a matter of discriminatory legislation only in Southern states. The present massive resistance throughout the South is an outcome of enforced desegregation, and not of legal enforcement of the Negroes' right to vote. The results of a public opinion poll in Virginia showing that 92 percent of the citizens were totally opposed to school integration, that 65 percent were willing to forgo public education under these conditions, and that 79 percent denied any obligation to accept the Supreme Court decision as binding, illustrate how serious the situation is. What is frightening here is not the 92 percent opposed to integration, for the dividing line in the South was never between those who favored and those who opposed segregation—practically speaking, no such opponents existed—

but the proportion of people who prefer mob rule to law-abiding citizenship. The so-called liberals and moderates of the South are simply those who are law-abiding, and they have dwindled to a minority of 21 percent.

No public opinion poll was necessary to reveal this information. The events in Little Rock were quite sufficiently enlightening; and those who wish to blame the disturbances solely on the extraordinary misbehavior of Governor Faubus can set themselves right by listening to the eloquent silence of Arkansas' two liberal senators. The sorry fact was that the town's law-abiding citizens left the streets to the mob, that neither white nor black citizens felt it their duty to see the Negro children safely to school. That is, even prior to the arrival of Federal troops, law-abiding Southerners had decided that enforcement of the law against mob rule and protection of children against adult mobsters were none of their business. In other words, the arrival of troops did little more than change passive into massive resistance.

It has been said, I think again by Mr. Faulkner, that enforced integration is no better than enforced segregation, and this is perfectly true. The only reason that the Supreme Court was able to address itself to the matter of desegregation in the first place was that segregation has been a legal, and not just a social, issue in the South for many generations. For the crucial point to remember is that it is not the social custom of segregation that is unconstitutional, but its *legal enforcement*. To abolish this legislation is of great and obvious importance and in the case of that part of the Civil Rights bill regarding the right to vote, no Southern state in fact dared to offer strong opposition. Indeed, with respect to unconstitutional legislation, the Civil Rights bill did not go far enough, for it left untouched the most outrageous law of Southern states—the law which makes mixed marriage a criminal offense. The right to marry whoever one wishes is an elementary human right compared to which "the right to attend an integrated school, the right to sit where one pleases on a bus, the right to go into any hotel or recreation area or place of amusement, regardless of one's skin or color or race" are minor indeed. Even political rights, like the right to vote, and nearly all other rights enumerated in the Constitution, are secondary to the inalienable human rights to "life, liberty and the pursuit of happiness" proclaimed in the Declaration of Independence; and to this category the right to home and marriage unquestionably belongs. It would have been much more important if this violation had been brought to the attention of the Supreme Court; yet had the Court ruled the antimiscegenation laws unconstitutional, it would hardly have felt compelled to encourage, let alone enforce, mixed marriages.

However, the most startling part of the whole business was the Federal decision to start integration in, of all places, the public schools. It certainly did not require too much imagination to see that this was to burden children, black and white, with the working out of a problem which adults for generations have confessed themselves unable to solve. I think no one will find it easy to forget the photograph reproduced in newspapers and magazines throughout the country, showing a Negro girl, accompanied by a white friend of her father, walking away from school, persecuted and followed into bodily proximity by a jeering and grimacing mob of youngsters. The girl, obviously, was asked to be a hero—that is, something neither her absent father nor the equally absent representatives of the NAACP felt called upon to be. It will be hard for the white youngsters, or at least those among them who outgrow their present brutality, to live down this photograph which exposes so mercilessly their juvenile delinquency. The picture looked to me like a fantastic caricature of progressive education which, by abolishing the authority of adults, implicitly denies their responsibility for the world into which they have borne their children and refuses the duty of guiding them into it. Have we now come to the point where it is the children who are being asked to change or improve the world? And do we intend to have our political battles fought out in the school yards?

Segregation is discrimination enforced by law, and desegregation can do no more than abolish the laws enforcing discrimination; it cannot abolish discrimination and force equality upon society, but it can, and indeed must, enforce equality within the body politic. For equality not only has its origin in the body politic; its validity is clearly restricted to the political realm. Only there are we all equals. Under modern conditions, this equality has its most important embodiment in the right to vote, according to which the judgment and opinion of the most exalted citizen are on a par with the judgment and opinion of the hardly literate. Eligibility, the right to be voted into office, is also an inalienable right of every citizen; but here equality is already restricted, and though the necessity for personal distinction in an election arises out of the numerical equality, in which everybody is literally reduced to being one, it is distinction and qualities which count in the winning of votes and not sheer equality.

Yet unlike other differences (for example, professional specialization, occupational qualification, or social and intellectual distinction) the political qualities needed for winning office are so closely connected with being an equal among equals, that one may say that, far from being specialties, they are precisely those distinctions to which all voters equally aspire—not necessarily as human beings, but as citizens and political beings. Thus the qualities of officials in a democracy always depend upon the qualities of the electorate. Eligibility, therefore, is a necessary corollary of the right to vote; it means that everyone is given the opportunity to distinguish himself in those things in which all are equals to begin with. Strictly speaking, the franchise and eligibility for office are the only political rights, and they constitute in a modern democracy the very quintessence of citizenship. In contrast to all other rights, civil or human, they cannot be granted to resident aliens.

What equality is to the body politic—its innermost principle—discrimination is to society. Society is that curious, somewhat hybrid realm between the political and the private in which, since the beginning of the modern age, most men have spent the greater part of their lives. For each time we leave the protective four walls of our private homes and cross over the threshold into the public world, we enter first, not the political realm of equality, but the social sphere. We are driven into this sphere by the need to earn a living or attracted by the desire to follow our vocation or enticed by the pleasure of company, and once we have entered it, we become subject to the old adage of "like attracts like" which controls the whole realm of society in the innumerable variety of its groups and associations. What matters here is not personal distinction but the differences by which people belong to certain groups whose very identifiability demands that they discriminate against other groups in the same domain. In American society, people group together, and therefore discriminate against each other, along lines of profession, income, and ethnic origin, while in Europe the lines run along class origin, education, and manners. From the viewpoint of the human person, none of these discriminatory practices makes sense; but then it is doubtful whether the human person as such ever appears in the social realm. At any rate, without discrimination of some sort, society would simply cease to exist and very important possibilities of free association and group formation would disappear.

Mass society—which blurs lines of discrimination and levels group distinctions—is a danger to society as such, rather than to the integrity of the person, for personal identity has its source beyond the social realm. Conformism, however, is not a characteristic of mass society alone, but of every society insofar as only those are admitted to a given social group who conform to the general traits of difference which keep the group together. The danger of conformism in this country—a danger almost as old as the Republic—is that, because of the extraordinary heterogeneity of its population, social conformism tends to become an absolute and a substitute for national homogeneity. In any event, discrimination is as indispensable a social right as equality is a political right. The question is not how to abolish discrimination, but how to keep it confined within the social sphere, where it is legitimate, and prevent its trespassing on the political and the personal sphere, where it is destructive.

In order to illustrate this distinction between the political and the social, I shall give two examples of discrimination, one in my opinion entirely justified and outside the scope of government intervention, the other scandalously unjustified and positively harmful to the political realm.

It is common knowledge that vacation resorts in this country are frequently "restricted" according to ethnic origin. There are many people who object to this practice; nevertheless it is only an extension of the right to free association. If as a Jew I wish to spend my vacations only in the company of Jews, I cannot see how anyone can reasonably prevent my doing so; just as I see no reason why other resorts should not cater to a clientele that wishes not to see Jews while on a holiday. There cannot be a "right to go into any hotel or recreation area or place of amusement," because many of these are in the realm of the purely social where the right to free association, and therefore to discrimination, has greater validity than the principle of equality. (This does not apply to theaters and museums, where people obviously do not congregate for the purpose of associating with each other.) The fact that the "right" to enter social places is silently granted in most countries and has become highly controversial only in American democracy is due not to the greater tolerance of other countries but in part to the homogeneity of their population and in part to their class system, which operates socially even when its economic foundations have disappeared. Homogeneity and class working together assure a "likeness" of clientele in any given place that even restriction and discrimination cannot achieve in America.

It is, however, another matter altogether when we come to "the right to sit where one pleases in a bus" or a railroad car or station, as well as the right to enter hotels and restaurants in business districts—in short, when we are dealing with services which, whether privately or publicly owned, are in fact public services that everyone needs in order to pursue his business and lead his life. Though not strictly in the political realm, such services are clearly in the public domain where all men are equal; and discrimination in Southern railroads and buses is as scandalous as discrimination in hotels and restaurants throughout the country. Obviously the situation is far worse in the South because segregation in public services is enforced by law and plainly visible to all. It is unfortunate indeed that the first steps toward clearing up the segregation situation in the South after so many decades of complete neglect did not begin with its most inhuman and its most conspicuous aspects.

The third realm, finally, in which we move and live together with other people—the realm of privacy—is ruled neither by equality nor by discrimination, but by exclusiveness. Here we choose those with whom we wish to spend our lives, personal friends and those we love; and our choice is guided not by likeness or qualities shared by a group of people—it is not guided, indeed, by any objective standards or rules—but strikes, inexplicably and unerringly, at one person in his uniqueness, his unlikeness to all other people we know. The rules of uniqueness and exclusiveness are, and always will be, in conflict with the standards of society precisely because social discrimination violates the principle, and lacks validity for the conduct, of private life. Thus every mixed marriage constitutes a challenge to society and means that the partners to such a marriage have so far preferred personal happiness to social adjustment that they are willing to bear the burden of discrimination. This is and must remain their private business. The scandal begins only when their challenge to society and prevailing customs, to which every citizen has a right, is interpreted as a criminal offense so that by stepping outside the social realm they find themselves in conflict with the law as well. Social standards are not legal standards and if legislature follows social prejudice, society has become tyrannical.

For reasons too complicated to discuss here, the power of society in our time is greater than it ever was before, and not many people are left who know the rules of and live a private life. But this provides the body politic with no excuse for forgetting the rights of privacy, for failing to understand that the rights of privacy are grossly violated whenever legislation begins to enforce social discrimination. While the government has no right to interfere with the prejudices and discriminatory practices of society, it has not only the right but the duty to make sure that these practices are not legally enforced.

Just as the government has to ensure that social discrimination never curtails political equality, it must also safeguard the rights of every person to do as he pleases within the four walls of his own home. The moment social discrimination is legally enforced, it becomes persecution, and of this crime many Southern states have been guilty. The moment social discrimination is legally abolished, the freedom of society is violated, and the danger is that thoughtless handling of the Civil Rights issue by the Federal government will result in such a violation. The government can legitimately take no steps against social discrimination because government can act only in the name of equality—a principle which does not obtain in the social sphere. The only public force that can fight social prejudice is the churches, and they can do so in the name of the uniqueness of the person, for it is on the principle of the uniqueness of souls that religion (and especially the Christian faith) is based. The churches are indeed the only communal and public place where appearances do not count, and if discrimination creeps into the houses of worship, this is an infallible sign of their religious failing. They then have become social and are no longer religious institutions.

Another issue involved in the present conflict between Washington and the South is the matter of states' rights. For some time it has been customary among liberals to maintain that no such issue exists at all but is only a ready-made subterfuge of Southern reactionaries who have nothing in their hands except "abstruse arguments and constitutional history." In my opinion, this is a dangerous error. In contradistinction to the classical principle of the European nation-state that power, like sovereignty, is indivisible, the power structure of this country rests on the principle of division of power and on the conviction that the body politic as a whole is strengthened by the division of power. To be sure, this principle is embodied in the system of checks and balances between the three branches of government; but it is no less rooted in the government's Federal structure which demands that there also be a balance and a mutual check between Federal power and the powers of the forty-eight states. If it is true (and I am convinced it is) that unlike force, power generates more power when it is divided, then it follows that every attempt of the Federal government to deprive the states of some of their legislative sovereignty can be justified only on grounds of legal argument and constitutional history. Such arguments are not abstruse; they are based on a principle which indeed was uppermost in the minds of the founders of the Republic.

All this has nothing to do with being a liberal or a conservative, although it may be that where the nature of power is at stake, liberal judgment with its long and honorable history of deep distrust of power in any form can be less trusted than on other questions. Liberals fail to understand that the nature of power is such that the power potential of the Union as a whole will suffer if the regional foundations on which this power rests are undermined. The point is that force can, indeed must, be centralized in order to be effective, but power cannot and must not. If the various sources from which it springs are dried up, the whole structure becomes impotent. And states' rights in this country are among the most authentic sources of power, not only for the promotion of regional interests and diversity, but for the Republic as a whole.

The trouble with the decision to force the issue of desegregation in the field of public education rather than in some other field in the campaign for Negro rights has been that this decision unwittingly touched upon an area in which every one of the different rights and principles we have discussed is involved. It is perfectly true, as Southerners have repeatedly pointed out, that the Constitution is silent on education and that legally as well as traditionally, public education lies in the domain of state legislation. The counterargument that all public schools today are Federally supported is weak, for Federal subvention is intended in these instances to match and supplement local contributions and does not transform the schools into Federal institutions, like the Federal district courts. It would be very unwise indeed if the Federal government—which now must come to the assistance of more and more enterprises that once were the sole responsibility of the states—were to use its financial support as a means of whipping the states into agreement with positions they would otherwise be slow or altogether unwilling to adopt.

The same overlapping of rights and interests becomes apparent when we examine the issue of education in the light of the three realms of human life—the political, the social, and the private. Children are first of all part of family and home, and this means that they are, or should be, brought up in that atmosphere of idiosyncratic exclusiveness which alone makes a home a home, strong and secure enough to shield its young against the demands of the social and the responsibilities of the political realm. The right of parents to bring up their children as they see fit is a right of privacy, belonging to home and family. Ever since the introduction of compulsory education, this right has been challenged and restricted, but not abolished, by the right of the body politic to prepare children to fulfill their future duties as citizens. The stake of the government in the matter is undeniable—as is the right of the parents. The possibility of private education provides no way out of the dilemma, because it would make the safeguarding of certain private rights dependent upon economic status and consequently underprivilege those who are forced to send their children to public schools.

Parents' rights over their children are legally restricted by compulsory education and nothing else. The state has the unchallengeable right to prescribe minimum requirements for future citizenship and beyond that to further and support the teaching of subjects and professions which are felt to be desirable and necessary to the nation as a whole. All this involves, however, only the content of the child's education, not the context of association and social life which invariably develops out of his attendance at school; otherwise one would have to challenge the right of private schools to exist. For the child himself, school is the first place away from home where he establishes contact with the public world that surrounds him and his family. This public world is not political but social, and the school is to the child what a job is to an adult. The only difference is that the element of free choice which, in a free society, exists at least in principle in the choosing of jobs and the associations connected with them, is not yet at the disposal of the child but rests with his parents.

To force parents to send their children to an integrated school against their will means to deprive them of rights which clearly belong to them in all free societies—the private right over their children and the social right to free association. As for the children, forced integration means a very serious conflict between home and school, between their private and their social life, and while such conflicts are common in adult life, children cannot be expected to handle them and therefore should not be exposed to them. It has often been remarked that man is never so much of a conformer—that is, a purely social being—as in childhood. The reason is that every child instinctively seeks authorities to guide him into the world in which he is still a stranger, in which he cannot orient himself by his own judgment. To the extent that parents and teachers fail him as authorities, the child will conform more strongly to his own group, and under certain conditions the peer group will become his supreme authority. The result can only be a rise of mob and gang rule, as the news photograph we mentioned above so eloquently demonstrates. The conflict between a segregated home and a desegregated school, between family prejudice and school demands, abolishes at one stroke both the teachers' and the parents' authority, replacing it with the rule of public opinion among children who have neither the ability nor the right to establish a public opinion of their own.

Because the many different factors involved in public education can quickly be set to work at cross purposes, government intervention, even at its best, will always be rather controversial. Hence it seems highly questionable whether it was wise to begin enforcement of civil rights in a domain where no basic human and no basic political right is at stake, and where other rights—social and private—whose protection is no less vital, can so easily be hurt.

1959

THE DEPUTY

Guilt by Silence?

Rolf Hochhuth's play *The Deputy* has been called "the most controversial literary work of this generation," and in view of the controversy it has aroused in Europe and is about to arouse in this country, this superlative seems justified. The play deals with the alleged failure of Pope Pius XII to make an unequivocal public statement on the massacre of European Jews during World War II, and concerns by implication Vatican policy toward the Third Reich.

The facts themselves are not in dispute. No one has denied that the Pope was in possession of all pertinent information regarding the Nazi deportation and "resettlement" of Jews. No one has denied that the Pope did not even raise his voice in protest when, during the German occupation of Rome, the Jews, including Catholic Jews (that is, Jews converted to Catholicism), were rounded up, right under the windows of the Vatican, to be included in the Final Solution. Thus, Hochhuth's play might as well be called the most factual literary work of this generation as "the most controversial." The play is almost a report, closely documented on all sides, using actual events and real people, reinforced by 65 pages of "historical sidelights" written by Hochhuth and anticipating nearly all arguments that have been raised against it. The author himself seems at least as interested in literal, factual truth as he is in literary quality, for he says almost apologetically in his "sidelights" that for artistic reasons he had "to advance a better opinion of Pius XII than may be historically justified, and a better one than I privately hold." With this sentence, however, he touches upon one of the really controversial—that is, debatable—points at issue: is it true, as Hochhuth clearly thinks, that the Vatican would not have been silent "had there been a better Pope"?

There have been a few instances in which the Church tried to dodge the grave issues at stake either by imputing a thesis to the play which it does not contain—nowhere does Hochhuth claim that "Pope Pius was responsible for Auschwitz" or that he was the "arch-culprit" of this period—or by referring to the help given to Jews by the local hierarchy in some countries. The fact that local hierarchies did so, especially in France and Italy, was never in dispute. To what extent the Pope initiated or even supported these activities is not known, since the Vatican does not open its archives for contemporary history. But it may be assumed that most of the good, as well as the bad, done must be ascribed to local and often, I suspect, to strictly individual initiative. "During the deportation of Catholic Jews from Holland," Hochhuth reports, "a dozen members of various orders were actually handed over from Dutch religious houses." But who would dare blame Rome for that? And since another question Hochhuth raises—"How could the Gestapo have discovered that this one nun [Edith Stein, a German convert and famous philosophical writer] had Jewish blood?"—has never been answered, who would blame Rome for that? But by the same token, the Church as an institution can hardly book on her account the few great demonstrations of true Christian charity—the distribution of forged documents to thousands of Jews in southern France in order to facilitate their emigration; the attempt of Provost Bernhard Lichtenberg of St. Hedwig's Cathedral in Berlin to accompany the Jews to the East; the martyrdom of Father Maximilian Kolbe, a Polish priest in Auschwitz, to quote only some of the best known examples.

What the Church as an institution and the Pope as her sovereign ruler can book on their account is the systematic work of information done by the nuncios all over Nazi-occupied Europe to enlighten at least the heads of government in Catholic countries—France, Hungary, Slovakia, Romania—about the true, murderous meaning of the word "resettlement." This was important because the moral and spiritual authority of the Pope vouched for the truth of what otherwise could be only too easily dismissed as enemy propaganda, especially in countries that welcomed this opportunity of "solving the Jewish question," though not at the price of mass murder. However, the Vatican's exclusive use of diplomatic channels meant also that the Pope did not think fit to tell the people—for instance, the Hungarian Gendarmerie, all good Catholics, who were busy rounding up Jews for the Eichmann Kommando in Budapest—and, by implication, seemed to discourage the bishops (if such discouragement was necessary) from telling their flocks. What has appeared—first to the victims and the survivors, then to Hochhuth, and finally through him to many others—as such outrageous inadequacy was the frightening equanimity which the Vatican and its nuncios apparently thought it wise to affect, the rigid adherence to a normality that no longer existed in view of the collapse of the whole moral and spiritual structure of Europe. At the end of the 4th act of *The Deputy*, Hochhuth uses a quotation from a public statement of Pope Pius, changing only one word: where Pius had said "Poles," Hochhuth has Pius say "Jews," as follows: "As the flowers in the countryside wait beneath winter's mantle of snow for the

warm breezes of spring, so the Jews must wait praying and trust-
ing that the hour of heavenly comfort will come." It is a prime
example not merely of what Hochhuth has called "Pacelli's flow-
ery loquacity," but of something more common, a disastrous loss
of all feeling for reality.

Still, what the Vatican did during the war years, when the Pope
was the only man in Europe free from any taint of propaganda,
was considerably more than nothing, and it would have been
enough if it were not for the uncomfortable fact that the man on
St. Peter's chair is no ordinary ruler but "the Vicar of Christ."
Regarded as a secular ruler, the Pope did what most, though not
all, secular rulers did under the circumstances. Regarded as an
institution among institutions, the Church's inclination to accommodate "itself to any regime which affirms its willingness to
respect Church property and prerogatives" (which Nazi Germany,
but not Soviet Russia, at least pretended to do) has understandably
almost become, as Gordon Zahn, a distinguished Catholic sociolo-
gist, has said, "an unchallengeable truism in Catholic political
philosophy." But the Pope's negligible secular power—as ruler
of fewer than a thousand inhabitants of Vatican City—depends
"upon the spiritual sovereignty of the Holy See" which is indeed
sui generis and wields an enormous, though imponderable "world
spiritual authority." The matter is succinctly summed up in Stalin's
remark, "How many divisions has the Pope?" and in Churchill's
answer, "A number of legions not always visible on parade." The
accusation leveled by Hochhuth against Rome is that the Pope
failed to mobilize these legions—roughly 400 million all over
the earth.

The answer from the side of the Church up to now has fallen
into three parts. First, there are the words of Cardinal Montini
before he became Pope Paul VI: "An attitude of protest and con-

demnation . . . would have been not only futile but harmful: that is the long and the short of the matter." (This seems a very debatable point, since more than 40 percent of the Reich's population was Catholic at the outbreak of the war and almost all Nazi-occupied countries as well as most of Germany's allies had Catholic majorities.) Second, much less profiled but actually the argument that validates the first claim, these legions could not be mobilized by Rome. (This argument has more force. The view that the "Catholic Church [compared with the Protestant Church] bears the greater guilt, for it was an organized, supranational power in a position to do something," as Albert Schweitzer has argued in his preface to the Grove Press edition of the play, may have overestimated the Pope's power and underestimated the extent to which he depends upon the national hierarchies and the extent to which the local episcopate depends upon its flocks. And it can hardly be denied than an *ex cathedra* pronouncement of the Pope in the midst of the war might have caused a schism.)

The third argument on the side of the Church rests on the necessity for the Church to remain neutral in case of war, even though this neutrality—the fact that in modern wars the bishops always bless the armies on either side—implies that the old Catholic distinction between just and unjust war has become practically inapplicable. (Obviously, this was the price the Church had to pay for the separation of Church and State and the resulting generally smooth and peaceful coexistence of an international spiritual sovereignty, binding the local hierarchy in ecclesiastical matters only, with the national secular authority of the state.)

Even if the Pope had seen in Hitler's wars "the classic example of the unjust war," as Zahn has characterized it, which he evidently did not, since according to one of his secretaries, Father Robert Leiber, he "had always looked upon Russian Bolshevism as more dangerous than German National Socialism" (quoted from the very informative article by Guenter Lewy, "Pius XII, the Jews, and the German Catholic Church," in *Commentary*)— he almost certainly would not have intervened.[1] The point of the matter is rather that despite his conviction "that the fate of Europe depended upon a German victory on the Eastern front" (Lewy), and though very prominent figures in the German and Italian hierarchy tried to persuade him "to declare [the war against Russia] a holy war or crusade," the Pope maintained publicly what another historian, Robert A. Graham, S.J., has called a "significant silence." And this silence is all the more significant as the Pope had broken his neutrality twice—first at the occasion of Russia's attack on Finland, and shortly thereafter when Germany violated the neutrality of Holland, Belgium, and Luxembourg.

However one may try to reconcile these apparent contradictions, there can hardly be any doubt that one reason why the Vatican did not protest against the massacres in the East, where, after all, not only Jews and Gypsies but Poles and Polish priests were involved, was the mistaken notion that these killing operations were part and parcel of the war. The very fact that the Nuremberg trials also counted these atrocities, which had not the slightest connection with military operations, among "war crimes" shows how plausible this argument must have sounded during the war. Despite a whole literature on the criminal nature of totalitarianism, it is as though the world has needed nearly two decades to realize what actually had happened in those few years and how disastrously almost all men in high public position had failed to understand even when they were in possession of all factual data.

Yet even if we take all this into account, it is not possible to let the matter rest there. Hochhuth's play concerns Rome's attitude during the massacres, certainly the most dramatic moment of the whole development; only marginally does it concern the relations between German Catholicism and the Third Reich in the preceding years and the role played by the Vatican under Pacelli's predecessor, Pope Pius XI. To a certain extent, the culpability of "official Christianity in Germany" has been settled, especially its Catholic page. Prominent Catholic scholars—Gordon Zahn, already mentioned, at Loyola University in this country, the eminent historian Friedrich Heer in Austria, the group of writers and publicists around the Frankfurter Hefte in Germany, and for the early period of the Hitler regime the late Waldemar Gurian, professor at Notre Dame University—have done a remarkably thorough job, fully aware, of course, that German Protestantism would fare hardly better, and possibly even worse if studied in the same admirable spirit of truthfulness.

Heer notes that it is a matter of public record that Catholics who tried to resist Hitler "could count on the sympathy of their church leaders neither in prison, nor on the scaffold." And Zahn tells the incredible story of two men who, having refused to serve in the war because of their Christian faith, were denied the sacraments by the prison chaplains until just before they were to be executed. (They were accused of "disobedience" to their spiritual leaders—suspect, one may assume, of seeking martyrdom and of the sin of perfectionism.)

All this proves no more and no less than that Catholics behaved in no way differently from the rest of the population. And this had been obvious from the very beginning of the new regime. The German episcopate had condemned racism, neo-Paganism, and the rest of the Nazi ideology in 1930 (one of the diocesan authorities went so far as to forbid "Catholics to become registered members of the Hitler party under pain of being excluded from the sacraments") and then it withdrew all prohibitions and warnings promptly in March 1933—that is, at the very moment when all public organizations (with the exception, of course, of the Communist party and its affiliations) were "co-ordinated." To be sure, this came after the election of March 5th when, as Waldemar Gurian noted in 1936 in his *Hitler and the Christians,* it had become "clear, especially in Bavaria, that even Catholics had succumbed to the National Socialist whirlwind." All that remained of the former solemn condemnations was a not too prominent warning against "an *exclusive* preoccupation with race and blood" (italics added), in one of the pastoral letters signed by all bishops and issued from Fulda. And when shortly thereafter the help of the churches was enlisted in determining all persons of Jewish descent, "the Church co-operated as a matter of course," and continued to do so right to the bitter end, Guenter Lewy reported in *Commentary.* Hence, the German shepherds followed their flocks, they did not lead them. And if it is true that "the conduct of the French, Belgian and Dutch bishops" in the war years "stands in marked contrast to the conduct" of their German brethren, one is tempted to conclude that this was, at least partly, due to the different conduct of the French, Belgian, and Dutch people.

However, what may be true with respect to the national hierarchies is certainly not true for Rome. The Holy See had its own policy with regard to the Third Reich, and up to the outbreak of the war this policy was even a shade friendlier than that of the German episcopate. Thus, Waldemar Gurian observed that prior to the Nazi seizure of power, when in 1930 the German bishops had condemned the National Socialist party, the Vatican newspaper, *Osservatore Romano,* "pointed out that the condemnation of its religious and cultural program did not necessarily imply refusal to co-operate politically," while, on the other hand, neither the Dutch bishops' protestation against the deportation of Jews nor Galen's condemnation of euthanasia were ever backed by Rome. The Vatican, it will be remembered, signed a Concordat with the Hitler regime in the summer of 1933, and Pius XI, who even before had praised Hitler "as the first statesman to join him in open disavowal of Bolshevism," thus became, in the words of the German bishops, "the first foreign sovereign to extend to [Hitler] the handclasp of trust." The Concordat was never terminated, either by Pius XI or by his successor.

Moreover, the excommunication of the Action Française, a French group of the extreme right whose teachings of a *catholicisme cérébral* had been condemned in 1926 as heresy, was withdrawn by Pius XII in July 1939—that is, at a time when the group was no longer merely reactionary but outright fascist. No prudence, finally, and no considerations for the difficult position of local, national hierarchies prevailed when, in July 1949, the Holy Office excommunicated all persons "who were members of the Communist Party, or furthered its aims," including those who read Communist books and magazines or wrote for them, and renewed this decree in April 1959. (That socialism is irreconcilable with the teachings of the Church had been stated before, in 1931, by Pius XI's encyclical *Quadragesimo anno*. Encyclicals, incidentally, are not identical with *ex-cathedra* pronouncements in which alone the Pope claims to be "infallible." But there can hardly be any doubt about their binding authority for the majority of the believers.) And even long after the war, when we read in the official Catholic Encyclopedia in Germany (Herder) that communism "is the greatest and most cruel persecutor of Christian churches since the Roman Empire," Nazism is not even mentioned. The Nazi regime had started violating the provisions of the Concordat before the ink on it was dry, but all the time it was in force there had been only one strong protest against the Third Reich—Pius XI's encyclical *Mit brennender Sorge* (With Burning Care) of 1937. It condemned "heathenism" and warned against elevating racist and national values to absolute priority, but the words "Jew" or "anti-Semitism" do not occur, and it is chiefly concerned with the anti-Catholic and especially the anticlerical slander campaign of the Nazi party. Neither racism in general nor anti-Semitism in particular has ever been absolutely condemned by the Church. There exists the strangely moving story of the German-Jewish nun, Edith Stein, already mentioned, who, in 1938, still unmolested in her German convent, wrote a letter to Pius XI, asking him to issue an encyclical about the Jews. That she did not succeed is not surprising, but is it also so natural that she never received an answer?

Hence, the political record of Vatican policies between 1933 and 1945 is reasonably clear. Only its motives are open to dispute. Obviously the record was shaped by the fear of communism and of Soviet Russia, although without Hitler's help Russia would hardly have been able or even willing to occupy half of Europe. This error in judgment is understandable and was widespread, and the same can be said about the Church's inability to judge correctly the total evil of Hitler's Germany. The worst one can say—and it has been said frequently—is that Catholic "medieval anti-Semitism" must be blamed for the Pope's silence about the massacres of the Jews. Hochhuth touches upon the matter in passing, but wisely left it out of his play because he "wanted to keep only to provable facts."

Even if it could be proved that the Vatican approved of a certain amount of anti-Semitism among the faithful—and this anti-Semitism, where it existed, was quite up to date although not racist: it saw in the modern assimilated Jews an "element of decomposition" of Western culture—it would be quite beside the point. For Catholic anti-Semitism had two limitations which it could not transgress without contradicting Catholic dogma and the efficacy of the sacraments—it could not agree to the gassing of the Jews any more than it could agree to the gassing of the mentally ill, and it could not extend its anti-Jewish sentiments to those who were baptized. Could these matters also be left to the decision of the national hierarchies? Were they not matters of the highest ecclesiastical order, subject to the authority of the head of the Church?

For, in the beginning, they were understood as such. When the Nazi government's intention to issue race laws which would forbid mixed marriages became known, the Church warned the German authorities that she could not comply and tried to persuade them that such laws would run counter to the provisions of the Concordat. However, this was difficult to prove. The Concordat stipulated "the right of the Catholic Church to settle her own affairs independently *within the limits of universally binding laws*" (italics added), and this meant of course that a civil ceremony had to precede the receiving of the marriage sacrament in Church. The Nuremberg laws put the German clergy into the impossible position of having to withhold the sacraments from persons of the Catholic faith who according to ecclesiastical law were entitled to them. Wasn't this a matter of Vatican jurisdiction? In any event, when the German hierarchy decided to conform to these laws, which implicitly denied that a baptized Jew was a Christian and belonged to the Church like everybody else, with equal rights and duties, something very serious had happened.

From then on, the segregation of Catholics of Jewish descent within the German Church became a matter of course. And in 1941, when the deportations of Jews from Germany began, the bishops of Cologne and Paderborn could actually recommend "that non-Aryan or half-Aryan priests and nuns volunteer to accompany the deportees" to the East (Guenter Lewy in *Commentary*)—that is, those members of the Church who were subject to deportation anyhow. I can't help thinking that if there was any group of people during the years of the Final Solution who were more forsaken by all mankind than the Jews traveling to their death, it must have been these Catholic "non-Aryans" who had left Judaism and who now were singled out, as a group apart, by the highest dignitaries of the Church. We don't know what they thought on their way to the gas chambers—are there no survivors among them?—but it is difficult to gainsay Hochhuth's remark that they were "abandoned by everyone, abandoned even by the Deputy of Christ. So it was in Europe from 1941 to 1944."

Indeed "so it was," and against Hochhuth's "historical truth . . . in its full ghastliness" all protests that passivity was the best policy because it was the lesser evil, or that disclosure of the truth comes "at the wrong psychological moment," are of no avail. To be sure, no one can say what actually would have happened had the Pope protested in public. But, quite apart from all immediate practical considerations, did no one in Rome realize what so many inside and outside the Church at that time realized, namely, that—in the words of Reinhold Schneider, the late German Catholic writer—a protest against Hitler "would have elevated the Church to a position it has not held since the Middle Ages"?

It has been Rolf Hochhuth's good fortune that a considerable part of Catholic learned and public opinion has sided with him. Professor Gordon Zahn has praised the play's "impressive historical accuracy." And Friedrich Heer in Austria has said all there needs to be said about truth which, alas, always comes at the "wrong psychological moment" and, in the period under discussion, would have come at the wrong physical moment as well: "Only the truth will make us free. The whole truth which is always awful."

1964

AUSCHWITZ ON TRIAL

I

Of about 2,000 SS men posted at Auschwitz between 1940 and 1945 (and many must still be alive), "a handful of intolerable cases" had been selected and charged with murder, the only offense not covered by the statute of limitation, in December 1963, when the Frankfurt trial began. Investigation into the Auschwitz complex had lasted many years—documents ("not very informative," according to the court) had been collected and 1,300 witnesses questioned—and other Auschwitz trials were to follow. (Only one subsequent trial has so far taken place. This second trial began in December 1965; one of the defendants, Gerhard Neubert, had been among those originally accused in the first trial. In contrast to the first trial, the second has been so poorly covered by the press that it took some "research" to determine whether it had occurred at all.) Yet in the words of the prosecutors in Frankfurt: *"The majority of the German people do not want to conduct any more trials against the Nazi criminals."*

Exposure for twenty months to the monstrous deeds and the grotesquely unrepentant, aggressive behavior of the defendants, who more than once almost succeeded in turning the trial into a farce, had no impact on this climate of public opinion, although the proceedings were well covered by German newspapers and radio stations. (Bernd Naumann's highly perceptive reportage, which originally appeared in the *Frankfurter Allgemeine Zeitung*, was the most substantial.) This came to light during the heated debates in the first months of 1965—in the midst of the Auschwitz proceedings—over the proposed extension of the statute of limitation for Nazi criminals, when even Bonn's minister of justice, Mr. Bucher, pleaded that the "murderers among us" be left in peace. And yet, these "intolerable cases" in the "proceedings against Mulka and others," as the Auschwitz trial was officially called, were no desk murderers. Nor—with a few exceptions—were they even "regime criminals" who executed orders. Rather, they were the parasites and profiteers of a criminal system that had made mass murder, the extermination of millions, a legal duty. Among the many awful truths with which this book confronts us is the perplexing fact that German public opinion in this matter was able to survive the revelations of the Auschwitz trial.

For what the majority think and wish constitutes public opinion even though the public channels of communication—the press, radio, and television—may run counter to it. It is the familiar difference between *le pays réel* and the country's public organs; and once this difference has widened into a gap, it constitutes a sign of clear and present danger to the body politic. It was just this kind of public opinion, which can be all-pervasive and still only rarely come into the open, that the trial in Frankfurt revealed in its true strength and significance. It was manifest in the behavior of the defendants—in their laughing, smiling, smirking impertinence toward prosecution and witnesses, their lack of respect for the court, their "disdainful and threatening" glances toward the public in the rare instances when gasps of horror were heard. Only once does one hear a lonely voice shouting back, "Why don't you kill him and get it over with?" It was manifest in the behavior of the lawyers who kept reminding the judges that they must pay no attention to "what one will think of us in the outside world," implying over and over again that not a German desire for justice but world opinion influenced by the victims' desire for "retribution" and "vengeance" was the true cause of their clients' present trouble. Foreign correspondents, but no German reporter so far as I know, were shocked that "those of the accused who still live at home are by no means treated as outcasts by their communities."[1] Naumann reports an incident in which two defendants passed the uniformed guard outside the building, greeted him cordially with "Happy Holidays," and were greeted in return with "Happy Easter." Was this the *vox populi?*

It is, of course, because of this climate of public opinion that the defendants had been able to lead normal lives under their own names for many years before they were indicted. These years, according to the worst among them—Boger, the camp's specialist for "rigorous interrogations" with the help of the "Boger swing," his "talking machine" or "typewriter"—had "proved that Germans stick together, because [where he lived] everyone knew who [he] was." Most of them lived peacefully unless they had the misfortune to be recognized by a survivor and denounced either to the International Auschwitz Committee in Vienna or to the Central Office for Prosecution of National Socialist Crimes in West Germany, which late in 1958 had begun to collect material for the prosecution of Nazi criminals in local courts. But even this risk was not too great, for the local courts—with the exception of Frankfurt, where the state's attorney's office was under Dr. Fritz Bauer, a German Jew—had not been eager to prosecute, and German witnesses were notoriously unwilling to cooperate.

Who then were the witnesses at Frankfurt? The court had called them, Jews and non-Jews, from many lands—from Russia, Poland, Austria, East Germany, Israel, America. Few of those residing in West Germany were Jews; most were either former

SS men who risked self-incrimination (the court heard many such cases and one such witness was arrested) or former political prisoners who, according to the "majority of the German people," represented at Frankfurt by a gentleman from IG Farben, were "mostly asocial elements" anyhow. As it turned out, this was an opinion now shared by some of the former inmates themselves: "The SS men were infected" by the inmates; not the guards but the prisoners "were beasts in human form"; the brutality of the guards was understandable because their victims, especially "the Galician Jews, were highly undisciplined"; and the SS became "bad" because of the influence of the capos, the trustee prisoners. But even those German witnesses who did not indulge in this kind of talk were unwilling to repeat in court what they had said in the pretrial examinations: They denied their testimony, didn't remember it, and talked of having been bullied (certainly untrue): maybe they were drunk, maybe they had lied, and so on in monotonous repetition. The discrepancies are glaring, irritating, embarrassing, and behind them one can sense public opinion, which the witnesses had not faced when they testified *in camera*. Almost every one of them would rather admit that he is a liar than risk having his neighbors read in the newspapers that he does not belong among the Germans who "stick together."

What a predicament for the judges in a case that must "rely exclusively on witness testimony," notoriously unreliable even under the best of circumstances. But the weak link in the evidence of this trial was not so much the lack of objective "incontrovertible" proof—the "small, mosaic-like pieces" of fingerprints, footprints, postmortem reports on the cause of death, and the like—nor was it the inevitable memory lapses of witnesses testifying on dates and details of events that happened more than twenty years ago, or the almost irresistible temptation to project "things others described vividly in that setting as his own experiences." It was rather the fantastic discrepancy between pretrial testimony and testimony in court in the case of most of the German witnesses; the justified suspicion that the testimony of the Polish witnesses had been doctored by some governmental agency for the prosecution of Nazi crimes in Warsaw; the less justified suspicion that the testimony of some Jewish witnesses may have been manipulated by the International Auschwitz Committee in Vienna; the unavoidable admission to the witness stand of former capos, stool pigeons, and Ukrainians who "were working hand in glove with the camp Gestapo"; and, finally, the sad fact that the most reliable category, the survivors, consisted of two very different groups—those who had survived by sheer luck, which in effect meant holding an inside job in office, hospital, or kitchen, and those who, in the words of one of them, had understood immediately that "only a few could be saved and I was going to be among them."

The court, under the guidance of the able and calm presiding judge Hans Hofmeyer, tried hard to exclude all political issues— "Political guilt, moral and ethical guilt, were not the subject of its concern"—and to conduct the truly extraordinary proceedings as "an ordinary criminal trial, regardless of its background." But the political background of both past and present—the legally criminal state order of the Third Reich, to which the Federal Republic is the successor, and the present opinions of the majority of the German people about this past—made itself felt factually and juridically in every single session.

Even more striking than the discrepancies between the witnesses' pretrial and trial testimony—and inexplicable except on the grounds of public opinion outside the courtroom—was the fact that exactly the same should happen with the testimony of the defendants. To be sure, these men had now probably been told by their lawyers that the safest course was to deny everything regardless of the most elementary credibility: "I have yet to meet anyone who did anything in Auschwitz," said Judge Hofmeyer. "The commandant was not there, the officer in charge only happened to be present, the representative of the Political Section only carried lists, and still another one only came with the keys." This explains "the wall of silence" and the persistent, though not consistent, lying of the defendants, many of whom simply were not intelligent enough to be consistent. (In Germany, defendants do not testify under oath.) It explains why Kaduk—a former butcher and a sly, primitive brute who, after identification by a former inmate, had been sentenced to death by a Soviet military tribunal and then pardoned in 1956—will not boast in court, as he had done in the pretrial examination, of having been "a sharp cookie . . . not the type to break down" or voice his regret at having only beaten but not killed Polish President Cyrankiewicz. (Immediately after the war, such boasts could still be heard in court. Naumann mentions the Sachsenhausen trial of 1947 before an Allied tribunal in which a defendant could say proudly that other guards might have been "exceptionally brutal, but they couldn't hold a candle to me.") And it was also probably upon advice from their lawyers that the defendants, who before the pretrial examining judge had charged each other freely and "could only laugh" about their colleagues' claims to innocence, could "not seem to remember this portion of their deposition" in court. All this is no more than would be expected of murderers who had in mind least of all what Judge Hofmeyer called "expiation."

We learn little about these pretrial examinations here, but the information we get seems to indicate that the discrepancies mentioned were a matter not only of deposition but of general attitude and behavior as well. The outstanding example of this more

fundamental aspect—and perhaps the most interesting psychological phenomenon that came to light during the trial—is the
case of Pery Broad, one of the youngest defendants, who wrote
an excellent, entirely trustworthy description of the Auschwitz
camp shortly after the end of the war for the British occupation
authorities. The Broad Report—dry, objective, matter-of-fact—
reads as though its author were an Englishman who knows how
to conceal his fury behind a facade of supreme sobriety. Yet there
is no doubt that Broad—who had taken part in the Boger-swing
game, was described by witnesses as "clever, intelligent, and cun-
ning," had been known among the inmates as "death in kid
gloves," and seemed "amused by all that went on in Auschwitz"—
was its sole author and wrote it voluntarily. And there is even less
doubt that he now greatly regrets having done so. During his
pretrial examination before a police officer, he had been "commu-
nicative," admitted to having shot at least one inmate ("I am not
sure that the person I shot wasn't a woman"), and said he felt
"relieved" by his arrest. The judge calls him a many-faceted
(*schillernde*) personality, but that says little and could just as well
apply, though on an altogether different level, to the brute Kaduk,
whom the patients in the West Berlin hospital where he worked as
a male nurse used to call Papa Kaduk. These seemingly inexplicable differences in behavior, most striking in the case of Pery
Broad—first in Auschwitz, then before the British authorities,
then before the examining officer, and now back again among the
old "comrades" in court—must be compared with the behavior of
Nazi criminals before non-German courts. In the context of the
Frankfurt proceedings there was hardly any occasion to mention
non-German trials, except when statements of dead people whose
depositions had incriminated the defendants were read into the
record. This happened with the statement of an Auschwitz medical officer, Dr. Fritz Klein, who had been examined by British

interrogators at the very moment of defeat, in May 1945, and who before his execution had signed a confession of guilt: "I recognize that I am responsible for the slaying of thousands, particularly in Auschwitz, as are all the others, from the top down."

The point of the matter is that the defendants at Frankfurt, like almost all other Nazi criminals, not only acted out of self-protection but showed a remarkable tendency to fall in line with whoever happened to constitute their surroundings—to "coordinate" themselves, as it were, at a moment's notice. It is as though they had become sensitized not to authority and not to fear but to the general climate of opinion to which they happened to be exposed. (This atmosphere did not make itself felt in the lonely confrontation with examining officers, who, in the case of those in Frankfurt and in Ludwigsburg—where the Central Office for the Prosecution of Nazi Crimes is located and where some of the defendants had undergone their first interrogation—were clearly and openly in favor of conducting these trials.) What made Broad, who had concluded his report to the British authorities twenty years earlier with a kind of cheer for England and America, the outstanding example of this sensitization was not so much his dubious character as the simple fact that he was the most intelligent and articulate of this company.

Only one of the defendants, the physician Dr. Lucas, does not show open contempt for the court, does not laugh, insult witnesses, demand that the prosecuting attorneys apologize, and try to have fun with the others. One doesn't quite understand why he is there at all, for he seems the very opposite of an "intolerable case." He spent only a few months in Auschwitz and is praised by numerous witnesses for his kindness and desperate eagerness to help; he is also the only one who agrees to accompany the court on the trip to Auschwitz, and who sounds entirely convincing when he mentions in his closing statement that he "will never recover" from his experiences in concentration and extermination camps, that he sought, as many witnesses testified, "to save the lives of as many Jewish prisoners as possible," and that "today as then, [he is] torn by the question: And what about the others?" His codefendants show by their behavior what only Baretzki, whose chief claim to notoriety in the camp was his ability to kill inmates with one blow of his hand, is stupid enough to say openly: *"If today I were to talk, who knows, if everything should change tomorrow I could be shot."*

For the point of the matter is that none of the defendants, except Dr. Lucas, takes the proceedings before the district court very seriously. The verdict here is not deemed to be the last word of either history or justice. And in view of German jurisdiction and the climate of public opinion, it is difficult to maintain that they are altogether wrong. The last word at Frankfurt was a verdict that sentenced seventeen of the defendants to many years of hard labor—six of them for life—and acquitted three. But only two of the sentences (both acquittals) have become operative. In Germany, the defendant must either accept the sentence or ask the higher court to review it; naturally, the defense filed appeals in all cases that did not end with acquittal. The same right to appeal is open to the prosecution, and the prosecution also appealed ten cases, including the acquittal of Dr. Schatz. Once the appeal is filed, the convicted is free until notified of the verdict of the Court of Appeals, unless the judge signs a new warrant of confinement, which was done in all cases for the next six months. Since then, however, a whole year has elapsed, and no review proceedings have as yet taken place; nor has a date for any been set. I do not know if new warrants were signed or if the defendants, with the exception of those who were in prison for other offenses, have gone home. The case, at any rate, is not closed.

Boger smiled when he heard that the prosecution had demanded a life sentence. What did he have in mind? His appeal, or a possible amnesty for all Nazi criminals, or his age (but he is only sixty years old and apparently in good health), or, perhaps, that "everything could change tomorrow"?

II

It would be quite unfair to blame the "majority of the German people" for their lack of enthusiasm for legal proceedings against Nazi criminals without mentioning the facts of life during the Adenauer era. It is a secret to nobody that the West German administration on all levels is shot through with former Nazis. The name of Hans Globke, noted first for his infamous commentary on the Nuremberg laws and then as close adviser to Adenauer himself, has become a symbol for a state of affairs that has done more harm to the reputation and authority of the Federal Republic than anything else. The facts of this situation—not the official statements or the public organs of communication—have created the climate of opinion in the *pays réel,* and it is not surprising under the circumstances that public opinion says: *The small fish are caught, while the big fish continue their careers.*

For it is indeed true that in terms of the Nazi hierarchy the Frankfurt defendants were all small fry: the highest SS officer rank—held by Mulka, adjutant to Camp Commandant Höss, by Höcker, adjutant to Höss's successor, Richard Baer, and by former camp leader Hofmann—was captain (Haupsturmführer). The same is true for their status in German society. Half of them came from the working class, had gone through eight years of elementary school, and worked as manual laborers; and of the ten others, only five belonged to the middle class—the physician, the two dentists, and the two businessmen (Mulka and Capesius)—

while the other five were rather lower middle class. Four of them, moreover, seem to have had previous convictions: Mulka in 1920 for "failing to account for funds"; Boger in 1940, while he was a member of the criminal police, for abortion; Bischoff (who died during the trial) and Dr. Schatz, expelled from the Nazi party in 1934 and 1937, respectively, for unknown (but certainly not political) reasons. These were small fry in every respect, even in terms of criminal record. And as far as the trial is concerned, it must be kept in mind that none of them had volunteered—or even been in a position to volunteer—for duty in Auschwitz. Nor can they be held basically responsible for the main crime committed in the camp, the extermination of millions of people through gas; for the decision to commit the crime of genocide had indeed, as the defense said, "been irrevocably reached by order of Hitler" and was organized with meticulous care by desk murderers in more exalted positions who did not have to dirty their hands.

The defense, curiously inconsistent even apart from the "hollow oratory," based its little-man theory on two arguments: first, that the defendants had been *forced* to do what they did and were in no position to know that it was criminally wrong. But if they had not considered it wrong (and it turned out that most had never given this question a second thought), why had it been necessary to force them? The defense's second argument was that the selections of able-bodied people on the ramp had in effect been a rescue operation because otherwise "all those coming in would have been exterminated." But leaving aside the spurious nature of this argument, had not the selections also taken place upon orders from above? And how could the accused be *credited* with obeying orders when this same obedience constituted their main, and actually, their only possible, excuse?

Still, given the conditions of public life in the Federal Republic, the little-man theory is not without merit. The brute Kaduk sums it up: "The issue is not what we have done, but the men who led us into misfortune. Most of them still are at liberty. Like Globke. That hurts." And on another occasion: "Now we are being made responsible for everything. The last ones get it in the neck, right?" The same theme is sounded by Hofmann, who had been convicted two years before the Auschwitz trial started for two murders in Dachau (two life sentences at hard labor) and who, according to Höss, "wielded real power in the camp," although according to his own testimony, he hadn't done a thing except "set up the children's playground, with sandboxes for the little ones." Hofmann shouts: "But where are the gentlemen who stood on top? They were the guilty ones, the ones who sat at their desks and telephoned." And he mentions names—not Hitler or Himmler or Heydrich or Eichmann, but the higher-ups in Auschwitz, Höss and Aumeier (the officer in charge before him) and Schwarz. The answer to his question is simple: they are all dead, which means to one of his mentality that they have left the "little man" in the lurch, that, like cowards, they have evaded their responsibility for him by allowing themselves to be hanged or by committing suicide.

The matter is not that easily settled, however—especially not at Frankfurt, where the court had called as witnesses former department chiefs of the *Reichssicherheitshauptamt* (the SS Head Office for Reich Security), in charge, among other things, of the organization of the "final solution of the Jewish question," to be executed in Auschwitz. In terms of the military equivalents of their former SS ranks, these gentlemen ranked high above the accused; they were colonels and generals rather than captains or lieutenants or noncoms. Bernd Naumann, who very wisely refrains almost completely from analysis and comment to confront the reader all the more directly with the great drama of court proceedings in the original form of dialogue, considered this little-man issue important enough to add one of his infrequent asides. Faced with these witnesses, he finds, the defendants "have plenty of reason to think how easily, how smoothly, many an 'exalted gentleman' whom they had served either willingly or under some duress has succeeded, without any psychic scruples, in returning from the far-away world of Germanic heroics to today's bourgeois respectability," how "the big man of the past who, as far as the Auschwitz personnel was concerned, had resided in the SS Olympus, leaves the courtroom head held high, with measured steps." And what is a defendant—or, for that matter, anybody else—supposed to think when he reads in the *Süddeutsche Zeitung,* one of the best daily German newspapers, that a former prosecutor at one of the Nazis' "special courts," a man who in 1941 had published a legal commentary that, in the newspaper's opinion, was frankly "totalitarian and anti-Semitic," now "earns his living as a judge of the federal constitutional court at Karlsruhe"?[2]

And if anybody should think that the "big men" were big enough to undergo a change of heart whereas the "little men" were too small for such a heroic internal operation, he need only read this book to know better. To be sure, there were some—for example, Erwin Schulz, a former chief of an *Einsatzkommando* (the mobile killing units of the SS on the Eastern Front), who truthfully and with a shade of regret testified that at the time he "did not have the feeling that it was completely unjustified" to shoot women and children in order "to prevent avengers against the German people from arising," but he himself had successfully asked to be relieved of such duties after he had gone to Berlin and tried to change the order. Much more typical, alas, is the lawyer (and former court officer in the rear of the Eastern Front) Emil

Finnberg, who still quotes Himmler approvingly and announces not without pride: "For me, a Führer order was law." Another example is the former professor and chief of anatomy at the University of Münster (he was stripped of his academic degrees), who without a single word of regret testified as to how he had selected the victims for the defendant Klehr, who then killed them by injections of phenol into the heart. He thought it "humanly understandable" that the murderers needed special rations, and he would doubtless have agreed with his former "assistant," who admitted having injected prisoners and in the same breath justified it: "In plain German, [these prisoners] weren't sick, they were already half dead." (Even this horrible statement turned out to be an understatement—a lie in fact—for many perfectly healthy children were killed in this way.) Finally (but the reader can easily find more examples in the book) there is Wilhelm Boger's lawyer, who in his final address voices "surprise that 'serious men [*sic!*] have written about the Boger swing,' which he does consider as 'the only effective means of physical suasion . . . to which people react.' "

This then is the standpoint of the accused and their attorneys. After their initial attempt at "making Auschwitz into an idyll . . . as far as the staff and their conduct are concerned" has broken down and witness after witness, document after document have demonstrated that they could not have been in the camp without doing something, without seeing something, without knowing what was going on (Höcker, the adjutant to Camp Commandant Baer, hadn't known "anything about the gas chambers" until rather late, when he had heard about them through rumors), they tell the court why they "are sitting here": first, because "the witnesses are testifying out of revenge" ("Why can't the Jews be decent and tell the truth? But obviously they don't want to."); second, because they carried out orders as "soldiers" and "did not ask about right and wrong"; and third, because the little ones are needed as scapegoats for the higher-ups (that's why they are "so bitter today").

All postwar trials of Nazi criminals, from the Trial of Major War Criminals in Nuremberg to the Eichmann trial in Jerusalem and the Auschwitz trial in Frankfurt, have been plagued by legal and moral difficulties in establishing responsibilities and determining the extent of criminal guilt. Public and legal opinion from the beginning has tended to hold that the desk murderers—whose chief instruments were typewriters, telephones, and teletypes—were guiltier than those who actually operated the extermination machinery, threw the gas pellets into the chambers, manned the machine guns for the massacre of civilians, or were busy with the cremation of mountains of corpses. In the trial of Adolf Eichmann, desk murderer par excellence, the court declared that "the degree of responsibility increases as we draw further away from the man who uses the fatal instruments with his own hands." Having followed the proceedings in Jerusalem, one was more than inclined to agree with this opinion. The Frankfurt trial, which in many respects reads like a much-needed supplement to the Jerusalem trial, will cause many to doubt what they had thought was almost self-evident. What stands revealed in these trials is not only the complicated issue of personal responsibility but naked criminal guilt; and the faces of those who did their best, or rather their worst, to obey criminal orders are still very different from those who within a legally criminal system did not so much obey orders as do with their doomed victims as they pleased. The defendants admitted this occasionally in their primitive way— "those on top had it easy . . . issuing orders that prisoners were not to be beaten"—but the defense lawyers to a man conducted the case as though they were dealing here, too, with desk murderers or with "soldiers" who had obeyed their superiors. This was the big lie in their presentation of the cases. The prosecution had indicted for "murder and complicity in murder of *individuals*," together with "mass murder and complicity in mass murder"— that is, for two altogether different offenses.

III

Only at the end of this book, when on the 182nd day of the proceedings Judge Hofmeyer pronounces the sentences and reads the opinion of the court, does one realize how much damage to justice was done—and inevitably done—because the distinctive line between these two different offenses had become blurred. The court, it was said, was concerned not with Auschwitz as an institution but only with "the proceedings against Mulka and others," with the guilt or innocence of the accused men. "The search for truth lay at the heart of the trial," but since the court's considerations were limited by the categories of criminal deeds as they had been known and defined in the German penal code of 1871, it was almost a matter of course that, in the words of Bernd Naumann, "neither the judges nor the jury found the truth—in any event, not the whole truth." For, in the nearly hundred-year-old code, there was no article that covered organized murder as a governmental institution, none that dealt with the extermination of whole peoples as part of demographic policies, with the "regime criminal," or with the everyday conditions under a criminal government (the *Verbrecherstaat*, as Karl Jaspers has termed it)—let alone with the circumstances in an extermination camp where everybody who arrived was doomed to die, either immediately by being gassed or in a few months by being worked to death. The

Broad Report states that "at most 10–15 percent of a given trans-
port were classified as able-bodied and permitted to live," and the
life expectancy of these selected men and women was about three
months. What is most difficult to imagine in retrospect is this
ever-present atmosphere of violent death; not even on the battlefield is death such a certainty and life so completely dependent on
the miraculous. (Nor could the lower ranks among the guards
ever be entirely free from fear; they thought it entirely possible, as
Broad put it, "that to preserve secrecy they might also be marched
off to the gas chambers. Nobody seemed to doubt that Himmler
possessed the requisite callousness and brutality." Broad only for-
got to mention that they must still have reckoned this danger less
formidable than what they might face on the Eastern Front, for
hardly any doubt remains that many of them could have voluntarily transferred from the camp to front-line duty.)

Hence, what the old penal code had utterly failed to take into
account was nothing less than the everyday reality of Nazi Germany in general and of Auschwitz in particular. Insofar as
the prosecution had indicted for mass murder, the assumption of
the court that this could be an "ordinary trial regardless of its
background" simply did not square with the facts. Compared
with ordinary proceedings, everything here could only be topsy-
turvy: for example, a man who had caused the death of thousands
because he was one of the few whose job it was to throw the
gas pellets into the chambers could be criminally less guilty than
another man who had killed "only" hundreds, but upon his own
initiative and according to his perverted fantasies. The background here was administrative massacres on a gigantic scale
committed with the means of mass production—the mass production of corpses. "Mass murder and complicity in mass murder" was a charge that could and should be leveled against every
single SS man who had ever done duty in any of the extermina-

tion camps and against many who had never set foot into one. From this viewpoint, and it was the viewpoint of the indictment, the witness Dr. Heinrich Dürmayer, a lawyer and state councilor from Vienna, was quite right when he implied the need for a reversal of ordinary courtroom procedure—that the defendants under these circumstances should be assumed guilty unless they could prove otherwise: *"I was fully convinced that these people would have to prove their innocence."* And by the same token, people who had "only" participated in the routine operations of extermination couldn't possibly be included among a "handful of intolerable cases." Within the setting of Auschwitz, there was indeed "no one who was not guilty," as the witness said, which for the purposes of the trial clearly meant that "intolerable" guilt was to be measured by rather unusual yardsticks not to be found in any penal code.

All such arguments were countered by the court thus: "National Socialism was also subject to the rule of law." It would seem that the court wanted to remind us that the Nazis had never bothered to rewrite the penal code, just as they had never bothered to abolish the Weimar Constitution. But the carelessness was in appearance only; for the totalitarian ruler realizes early that all laws, including those he gives himself, will impose certain limitations on his otherwise boundless power. In Nazi Germany, then, the Führer's *will* was the *source* of law, and the Führer's order was valid law. What could be more limitless than a man's will, and more arbitrary than an order justified by nothing but the "I will"? In Frankfurt, at any rate, the unhappy result of the court's unrealistic assumptions was that the chief argument of the defense—"a state cannot possibly punish that which it ordered in another phase of its history"—gained considerably in plausibility since the court, too, agreed to the underlying thesis of a "continuity of identity" of the German state from Bismarck's Reich to the Bonn Government.

Moreover, if this continuity of state institutions actually exists—and indeed it does apply to the main body of civil servants whom the Nazis were able to "coordinate" and whom Adenauer, without much ado, simply reemployed—what about the institutions of court and prosecution? As Dr. Laternser—by far the most intelligent among the attorneys for the defense—pointed out, wouldn't it then have been the duty of the prosecution to take action "against flagrant violations of law, like the destruction of Jewish businesses and dwellings in November 1938, the murder of mentally retarded [in 1939 and 1940], and, finally, the murder of Jews? Hadn't the prosecution known at the time that these were crimes? Which judge or state's attorney at the time had protested, let alone resigned?" These questions remained unanswered, indicating just how precarious were the legal foundations of the proceedings. In glaring contrast to the legal assumptions and theories, each and every one of the postwar trials of Nazis has demonstrated the total complicity—and hence, one would hope, the nonexistence of a "continuous identity"—of all state organs, all civil servants, all public figures in high positions in the business world in the crimes of the Nazi regime. Dr. Laternser went on to charge "the Allies with having dissipated the chance of finding a definitive yardstick for future law and thus of having contributed to the confusion of the legal situation." No one who is acquainted with the proceedings at Nuremberg will gainsay this. But why does Laternser not level the same charge against the Federal Republic, which obviously would have a much more immediate interest in correcting the situation? For is it not obvious that all talk about "mastering the past" will remain hollow rhetoric so long as the government has not come to terms

with the very criminality of its predecessor? Instead, it now turned
out at Frankfurt that a decision on the legality of the infamous
Commissar Order—on the basis of which untold thousands of
Russian prisoners of war were killed upon arrival in Auschwitz—
"has not yet been reached by the Federal Court," although the
same court has proclaimed the nonlegality of the extermination of
the Jews "by referring to natural law," which, incidentally and for
reasons outside these considerations, is not a very satisfactory
solution either. (The trouble with the Commissar Order seems
to be that it did not originate clearly enough with Hitler but came
directly from the German High Command; the prisoners "brought
with them a file card that bore the notation 'On orders of the
OKW' [*Oberstes Kommando der Wehrmacht*]." Was that the reason why the court acquitted the defendant Breitwieser, on the
ground that the testimony of the witness Petzold must have been
mistaken, without mentioning the testimony of Eugeniusc Motz,
another witness who had charged Breitwieser with having tried
out Zyklon B in the early gassing experiments on Soviet officers
and commissars?) For the defense, the decision of the highest
German court at any rate represents no more than "*present* legal
thinking," and there is little doubt that these lawyers are in agreement with "the majority of the German people"—and perhaps
with their colleagues in the legal profession as well.

Technically, it was the indictment for "mass murder and complicity in mass murder" that was bound to call forth the trouble-
some "background" of unsolved legal questions, of the absence
of "definitive yardsticks" for meting out justice, thus preventing
the trial from becoming the "essentially very simple case" that
State's Attorney Bauer had hoped it would be. For as far as the
personalities of the defendants and their deeds were concerned,
this was indeed a "very simple case" since nearly all the atrocities

they were accused of by the witnesses had not been covered by superior orders of either the desk murderers or the actual initiator, or initiators, of the "final solution." No one in high position had ever bothered to give instructions for such "details" as the "rabbit chase," the "Boger swing," the "sport," the bunkers, the "standing cells," the "Black Wall," or "cap shooting." No one had issued orders that infants should be thrown into the air as shooting targets, or hurled into the fire alive, or have their heads smashed against walls; there had been no orders that people should be trampled to death, or become the objects of the murderous "sport," including that of killing with one blow of the hand. No one had told them to conduct the selections on the ramp like a "cozy family gathering," from which they would return bragging "about what they had taken from this or the other new arrival. 'Like a hunt party returning from the hunt and telling each other all about it.' " They hadn't been sent to Auschwitz in order to get rich and have "fun." Thus the doubtful legal ruling of all Nazi criminal trials that they were "ordinary criminal trials" and that the accused were not distinct from other criminals for once came true—more true, perhaps, than anybody would have cared to know. Innumerable individual crimes, one more horrible than the next, surrounded and created the atmosphere of the gigantic crime of extermination. And it was these "circumstances"—if this is the name for something that lacks a word in any language— and the "little men" responsible for and guilty of them, not the state crime and not the gentlemen in "exalted" positions, that were fully illuminated in the Auschwitz trial. Here—in contrast to the Jerusalem trial, where Eichmann could have been convicted on the grounds of irrefutable documentary evidence and his own admissions—the testimony of every witness counted, for these men, and not the desk murderers, were the only ones with whom the victims were confronted and whom they knew, the only ones who mattered to them.

Even the otherwise rather spurious argument of the "continuity of identity" of the German state could be invoked in these cases, albeit with some qualifications. For it was not only true that the defendants, as the court said in the case of the trustee prisoner Bednarek, "did not kill the people on order, but *acted contrary to an order* that no prisoner in the camp was to be murdered"—except, of course, by gassing; the fact was that most of these cases could have been prosecuted even by a Nazi or SS court, although this did not often happen. Thus the former head of the Political Section in Auschwitz, a certain Grabner, had been charged by an SS court in 1944 "with having arbitrarily selected 2,000 prisoners for execution"; and two former SS judges, Konrad Morgen and Gerhard Wiebeck, both today practicing lawyers, testified about SS investigations into "corrupt practices and . . . independent killings," which led to charges of murder brought before SS courts. Prosecutor Vogel pointed out that "Himmler had stated that without his special order prisoners were to be neither beaten nor liquidated," which did not prevent him from visiting "the camp a few times to watch the corporal punishment of women."

The lack of definitive yardsticks for judging crimes committed in these extraordinary and horrible conditions becomes painfully conspicuous in the court's verdict against Dr. Franz Lucas. Three years and three months of hard labor—the minimum punishment—for the man who had always been "ostracized by his comrades" and who is now openly attacked by the defendants, who as a rule are very careful to avoid mutual incrimination (only once do they contradict each other, and they retract in court the incriminating remarks made in their pretrial examinations): "If he now claims to have helped people, he may have done so in 1945, when he tried to buy a return ticket." The point is, of course, that this is doubly untrue: Dr. Lucas had helped people from beginning to end; and not only did he not pose as a "savior"— very much in contrast to most of the other defendants—he consistently refused to recognize the witnesses who testified in his favor and to remember the incidents recounted by them. He had discussed sanitary conditions with his colleagues among the inmates, addressing them by their proper titles; he had even stolen in the SS pharmacy "for the prisoners, bought food with his own money," and shared his rations; "he was the only doctor who treated us humanely," who "did not look on us as unacceptable people," who gave advice to the physicians among the inmates on how to "save some fellow prisoners from the gas chambers." To sum up: "We were quite desperate after Dr. Lucas was gone. When Dr. Lucas was with us we were so gay. Really, we learned how to laugh again." And Dr. Lucas says: "I did not know the name of the witness until now." To be sure, none of the acquitted defendants, none of the lawyers for the defense, none of the "exalted gentlemen" who had gone scot-free and had come to testify could hold a candle to Dr. Franz Lucas. But the court, bound by its legal assumptions, could not help but mete out the minimum punishment to this man, although the judges knew quite well that in the words of a witness, he "didn't belong there at all. He was too good." Even the prosecution did not want "to lump him together with the others." It is true, Dr. Lucas had been on the ramp to select the able-bodied, but he had been sent there because he was suspected of "favoring prisoners," and he had been told that he would be "arrested on the spot" if he refused to obey the order. Hence, the charge of "mass murder or complicity in mass murder." When Dr. Lucas had first been confronted with his camp duties, he had sought advice: his bishop had told him that "immoral orders must not be obeyed, but that did not mean that one had to risk one's own life"; a high-ranking jurist justified the horrors because of the war. Neither was very helpful. But let us suppose he had asked the inmates what he ought to do. Wouldn't they have begged him to stay and pay the price of participation in the selections on the ramp—which were an everyday occurrence, a routine horror, as it were—in order to save them from the feeble-minded, Satanic ingenuity of all the others?

IV

Reading the trial proceedings, one must always keep in mind that Auschwitz had been established for *administrative* massacres that were to be executed according to the strictest rules and regulations. These rules and regulations had been laid down by the desk murderers, and they seemed to exclude—probably they were meant to exclude—all individual initiative either for better or for worse. The extermination of millions was planned to function like a machine: the arrivals from all over Europe; the selections on the ramp, and the subsequent selections among those who had been able-bodied on arrival; the division into categories (all old people, children, and mothers with children were to be gassed immediately); the human experiments; the system of "trustee prisoners," the capos, and the prisoner-commandos, who manned the extermination facilities and held privileged positions. Everything seemed foreseen and hence predictable—day after day, month after month, year after year. And yet, what came out of the bureaucratic calculations was the exact opposite of predictability. It was complete arbitrariness. In the words of Dr. Wolken—a former inmate, now a physician in Vienna, and the first and one of the best of the witnesses: *Everything "changed almost from day to day.* It depended on the officer in charge, on the roll-call leader, on the block leader, and on their moods"—most of all, it turns out, on their moods. "Things could happen one day that were completely out of the question two days later. . . . One and the same work detail could be either a death detail . . . or it could be a fairly pleasant affair." Thus, one day the medical officer was in a cheerful mood and had the idea of establishing a block for convalescents; two months later, all the convalescents were rounded up and sent into the gas. What the desk murderers had overlooked, *horribile dictu,* was the human factor. And what makes this so horrible is precisely the fact that these monsters were by no means sadists in a clinical sense, which is amply proved by their behavior under normal circumstances, and they had not been chosen for their monstrous duties on such a basis at all. The reason they came to Auschwitz or similar camps was simply that they were, for one reason or another, not fit for military service.

Upon a first and careless reading of this book, one might be tempted to indulge in sweeping statements about the evil nature of the human race, about original sin, about innate human "aggressiveness," etc., in general—and about the German "national character" in particular. It is easy and dangerous to overlook the not too numerous instances in which the court was told how "occasionally a 'human being' came into the camp" and after one short glance left in a hurry: "No, this is no place for my mother's child." Contrary to the view generally held prior to these trials, it was relatively simple for SS men to escape under one pretext or another—that is, unless one had the bad luck to fall into the hands of someone like Dr. Emil Finnberg, who even today thinks that it was perfectly all right to demand penalties ranging "from prison to death" for the "crime" of physical inability to shoot women and children. It was by far less dangerous to claim "bad nerves" than to stay in the camp, help the inmates, and risk the much greater charge of "favoring the prisoners." Hence those who stayed year in and year out, and did not belong to the select few who became heroes in the process, represented something of an automatic selection of the worst elements in the population. We do not know and are not likely ever to learn anything about percentages in these matters, but if we think of these overt acts of sadism as having been committed by perfectly normal people who in normal life had never come into conflict with the law on such counts, we begin to wonder about the dream world of many an average citizen who may lack not much more than the opportunity.

In any event, one thing is sure, and this one had not dared to believe any more—namely, "that everyone could decide for himself to be either good or evil in Auschwitz." (Isn't it grotesque that German courts of justice today should be unable to render justice to the good as well as the bad?) And this decision depended in no way on being a Jew or a Pole or a German; nor did it even depend upon being a member of the SS. For in the midst of this horror, there was Oberscharführer Flacke, who had established an "island of peace" and didn't want to believe that, as a prisoner said to him, in the end "we'll all be murdered. No witnesses will be allowed to survive." "I hope," he answered, "there'll be enough among us to prevent that."

The clinical normality of the defendants notwithstanding, the chief human factor in Auschwitz was sadism, and sadism is basically sexual. One suspects that the smiling reminiscences of the defendants, who listen delightedly to the recounting of deeds that occasionally make not only the witnesses but the jurors cry and faint; their incredible bows to those who bear testimony against them and recognize them, having once been their helpless victims; their open joy at being recognized (though incriminated) and hence remembered; and their unusually high spirits throughout: that all this reflects the sweet remembrance of great sexual pleasure, as well as indicating blatant insolence. Had not Boger approached a victim with the line of a medieval love song, "Thou art mine" (*Du bist mein / Ich bin dein / des solt du gewiss sein*)—a refinement of which such almost illiterate brutes as Kaduk, Schlage, Baretzki, and Bednarek would hardly have been capable? But here in the courtroom they all behave alike. From what the witnesses describe, there must have been an atmosphere of black magic and monstrous orgies in the ritual of "rigorous interrogation," in the "white gloves" they put on when they went to the bunker, in the cheap bragging about being Satan incarnate, which was the specialty of Boger and the Romanian pharmacist Capesius. The latter—sentenced to death in absentia in Romania and now to nine years at Frankfurt—is the ghoul among them. With the spoils from Auschwitz, he settled in Germany, established his business, and has now charged a "friend" with influencing the witnesses in his favor. His misfortunes in Frankfurt have done his business no harm; his shop in Göppingen, as Sybille Bedford reported in the *Observer*, was "more flourishing than ever."

Only second in importance, as far as the human factor in Auschwitz is concerned, must have been sheer moodiness. What changes more often and swifter than moods, and what is left of the humanity of a man who has completely yielded up to them? Surrounded by a never-ending supply of people who were destined to die in any event, the SS men actually could do as they pleased. These, to be sure, were not the "major war criminals," as the defendants in the Nuremberg trial were called. They were the parasites of the "great" criminals, and when one sees them one begins to wonder whether they were not worse than those whom today they accuse of having caused their misfortunes. Not only had the Nazis, through their lies, elevated the scum of the earth to the elite of the people; but those who lived up to the Nazi ideal of "toughness," and are still proud of it ("sharp cookies" indeed), were in fact like jelly. It was as though their ever-changing moods had eaten up all substance—the firm surface of personal identity, of being either good or bad, tender or brutal, an "idealistic" idiot or a cynical sex pervert. The same man who rightly received one of the most severe sentences—life plus eight years—could on occasion distribute sausages to children; Bednarek, after performing his specialty of trampling prisoners to death, went into his room and prayed, for he was then in the right mood; the same medical officer who handed tens of thousands over to death could also save a woman who had studied at his old alma mater and therefore reminded him of his youth; flowers and chocolates might be sent to a mother who had given birth, although she was to be gassed the next morning. The defendant Hans Stark, a very young man at the time, on one occasion selected two Jews, ordered the capo to kill them, and then proceeded to show him how this was done; and in demonstrating, he killed an additional two Jews. But on another occasion, he mused to an inmate, pointing to a village: "Look how beautifully the village was built. There are so many bricks here. When the war is over *the bricks will bear the names of those who were killed. Perhaps there won't be enough bricks.*"

It certainly is true that there was "almost no SS man who could not claim to have saved someone's life" if he was in the right mood for it; and most of the survivors—about 1 percent of the selected labor force—owed their lives to these "saviors." Death was the supreme ruler in Auschwitz, but side by side with death it was accident—the most outrageous, arbitrary haphazardness, incorporated in the changing moods of death's servants—that determined the destinies of the inmates.

V

Had the judge been wise as Solomon and the court in possession of the "definitive yardstick" that could put the unprecedented crime of our century into categories and paragraphs to help achieve the little that human justice is capable of, it still would be more than doubtful that "the truth, the whole truth," which Bernd Naumann demanded, could have appeared. No generality—and what is truth if it is not general?—can as yet dam up the chaotic flood of senseless atrocities into which one must submerge oneself in order to realize what happens when men say that "everything is possible," and not merely that everything is permitted.

Instead of *the* truth, however, the reader will find *moments of truth,* and these moments are actually the only means of articulating this chaos of viciousness and evil. The moments arise unexpectedly like oases out of the desert. They are anecdotes, and they tell in utter brevity what it was all about.

There is the boy who knows he will die, and so writes with his blood on the barrack walls: "Andreas Rapaport—lived sixteen years."

There is the nine-year-old who knows he knows "a lot," but "won't learn any more."

There is the defendant Boger, who finds a child eating an apple, grabs him by the legs, smashes his head against the wall, and calmly picks up the apple to eat it an hour later.

There is the son of an SS man on duty who comes to the camp

to visit his father. But a child is a child, and the rule of this particular place is that all children must die. Thus he must wear a sign around his neck "so they wouldn't grab him, and into the gas oven with him."

There is the prisoner who holds the selectees to be killed by the "medical orderly" Klehr with phenol injections. The door opens and in comes the prisoner's father. When all is over: "I cried and had to carry out my father myself." The next day, Klehr asks him why he had cried, and Klehr, on being told, "would have let him live." Why hadn't the prisoner told him? Could it be that he was afraid of him, Klehr? What a mistake. Klehr was in such a good mood.

Finally, there is the woman witness who had come to Frankfurt from Miami because she had read the papers and seen the name of Dr. Lucas: "the man who murdered my mother and family, interests me." She tells how it happened. She had arrived from Hungary in May 1944. "I held a baby in my arms. They said that mothers could stay with their children, and therefore my mother gave me the baby and dressed me so as to make me look older. [The mother held a third child by the hand.] When Dr. Lucas saw me he probably realized that the baby was not mine. He took it from me and threw it to my mother." The court immediately knows the truth. "Did you perhaps have the courage to save the witness?" Lucas, after a pause, denies everything. And the woman, apparently still ignorant of the rules of Auschwitz— where all mothers with children were gassed upon arrival—leaves the courtroom, unaware that she who had sought out the murderer of her family had faced the savior of her own life. This is what happens when men decide to stand the world on its head.

1966

HOME TO ROOST

We have come here together to celebrate a birthday party, the two hundredth birthday not of America but of the Republic of the United States, and I fear we could not have chosen a less appropriate moment. The crises of the Republic, of this form of government, and its institutions of liberty could be detected for decades, ever since what appears to us today as a mini-crisis was triggered by Joe McCarthy. A number of occurrences followed which testified to an increasing disarray in the very foundations of our political life: to be sure the episode itself was soon forgotten, but its consequence was the destruction of a reliable and devoted civil service body, something relatively new in this country, probably the most important achievement of the long Roosevelt administration. It was in the aftermath of this period that the "ugly American" appeared on the scene of *foreign* relations; he was then hardly noticeable in our domestic life, except in a growing inability to correct errors and repair damages.

Immediately thereafter a small number of thoughtful spectators began to have doubts whether our form of government would be able to withstand the onslaught of this century's inimical forces and survive the year 2000—the first to utter such doubts publicly, if I remember rightly, was John Kennedy. But the general mood of the country remained cheerful and no one was prepared, not even after Watergate, for the recent cataclysm of events, tumbling over one another, cascading like a Niagara Falls of history whose sweeping force leaves everybody, spectators who try to reflect on it and actors who try to slow it down, equally numbed and paralyzed. The swiftness of this process is such that even to remember in some order "what happened when" demands a serious effort; indeed "anything that is four minutes old is as ancient as Egypt" (Russell Baker).

No doubt the cataclysm of events that numbs us is due to a large extent to a strange but in history by no means unknown coincidence of occurrences, each of which has a different meaning and a different cause. Our defeat in Vietnam—by no means a "peace with honor" but on the contrary an outright humiliating defeat, the helter-skelter evacuation by helicopter with its unforgettable scenes of a war of all against all, certainly the worst possible of the administration's four options to which we added gratuitously our last public-relations stunt, the baby airlift, the "rescue" of the only part of the South Vietnamese people who were entirely safe—the defeat by itself could hardly have resulted in so great a shock; it was a certainty for years, expected by many since the Tet offensive.

That "Vietnamization" would not work could have surprised nobody; it was a public-relations slogan to excuse the evacuation of American troops who, ridden by drugs, corruption, desertions, and plain rebellion, could no longer be left there. What came as a surprise was the way Thieu himself, without even consulting his protectors in Washington, managed to accelerate the disintegration of his government to such an extent that the victors were unable to fight and conquer; what they found, when they could make contact with an enemy who fled more rapidly than they could pursue him, was not an army in retreat but an unbelievable rout of a mob of soldiers and civilians on a rampage of gigantic proportions.

However, the point is that this disaster in Southeast Asia occurred almost simultaneously with the ruin of the foreign policy of the United States—the disaster in Cyprus and possible loss of two former allies, Turkey and Greece, the coup in Portugal and its uncertain consequences, the debacle in the Middle East, the rise to prominence of the Arab states. It coincided in addition with our manifold domestic troubles: inflation, devaluation of currency, the plight of our cities, the climbing rate of unemployment and of crime. Add to this the aftermath of Watergate, which I think is by no means behind us, the trouble with NATO, the near bankruptcy of Italy and England, the conflict with India, and the uncertainties of détente, especially in view of the proliferation of nuclear arms, and compare it for a moment with our position at the end of World War II, and you will agree that among the many unprecedented events of this century the swift decline in political power* of the United States should be given due consideration. It, too, is almost unprecedented.

We may very well stand at one of those decisive turning points of history which separate whole eras from each other. For contemporaries entangled, as we are, in the inexorable demands of daily life, the dividing lines between eras may be hardly visible when they are crossed; only after people stumble over them do the lines grow into walls which irretrievably shut off the past.

At such moments in history when the writing on the wall becomes too frightening, most people flee to the reassurance of day-to-day life with its unchanging pressing demands. And this temptation today is all the stronger, since any long-range view of history, another favorite escape route, is not very encouraging

---

*The reader should bear in mind Arendt's sharp distinction between military *strength*, which depends on the implements of violence, and *political power*, which is generated by the political will of the people acting together on matters that concern them in common.—Ed.

either: the American institutions of liberty, founded two hundred years ago, have survived longer than any comparable glories in history. These highlights of man's historical record have rightfully become the paradigmatic models of our tradition of political thought; but we should not forget that, chronologically speaking, they were always exceptions. As such they survive splendidly in thought to illuminate the thinking and doing of men in darker times. No one knows the future, and all we can say with certainty at this rather solemn moment is no matter how it will end, these two hundred years of Liberty with all its ups and downs have earned Herodotus' "due meed of glory."

However, the time for this long-range view and the glorification inherent in remembrance has not yet come, and the occasion quite naturally tempts us to recapture, as has been proposed, "the extraordinary quality of thought, speech and action" of the Founders. This, I am inclined to believe, might have been impossible under the best of circumstances because of the truly "extraordinary" quality of these men. It is precisely because people are aware of the fearful distance that separates us from our beginnings that so many embark upon a search for the roots, the "deeper causes" of what happened. It is in the nature of roots and "deeper causes" that they are hidden by the appearances which they are supposed to have caused. They are not open to inspection and analysis but can be reached only by the uncertain way of interpretation and speculation. The content of such speculations is often far-fetched and almost always based on assumptions which are prior to an impartial examination of the factual record—there exists a plethora of *theories* about the "deeper" cause for the outbreak of the first or second World War based not on the melancholy wisdom of hindsight but on the speculations grown into convictions about the nature and fate of capitalism or socialism, of the Industrial or post–Industrial Age, the role of science and technology, and so on. But such theories are even more severely limited by the implied demands of the audience to which they are addressed. They must be *plausible*, that is, they must contain statements that most reasonable men at the particular time can accept; they cannot require an acceptance of the unbelievable.

I think that most people who have watched the frantic, panic-stricken end of the Vietnam war thought that what they saw on their television screens was "unbelievable," as indeed it was. It is this aspect of reality, which cannot be anticipated by either hope or fear, that we celebrate when Fortuna smiles and that we curse when misfortune strikes. All speculation about deeper causes returns from the shock of reality to what seems plausible and can be explained in terms of what reasonable men think is possible. Those who challenge these plausibilities, the bearers of bad tidings, who insist on "telling it as it is," have never been welcomed and often not been tolerated at all. If it is in the nature of appearances to hide "deeper" causes, it is in the nature of speculation about such hidden causes to hide and to make us forget the stark, naked brutality of facts, of things as they are.

This natural human tendency has grown to gigantic proportions during the last decade when our whole political scene was ruled by the habits and prescriptions of what is euphemistically called public relations, that is, by the "wisdom" of Madison Avenue. It is the wisdom of the functionaries of a consumer society who advertise its goods to a public, the larger part of which spends much more time in consuming its wares than it takes to produce them. Madison Avenue's function is to help distribute the merchandise, and its interest is focused less and less on the needs of the consumer and more and more on the need of the merchan-

JUDGMENT

dise to be consumed in larger and larger quantities. If abundance
and superabundance were the original goals of Marx's dream of a
classless society in which the natural surplus of human labor—
that is, the fact that labor stimulated by human needs always produces more than is necessary for the individual survival of the
laborer and the survival of his family—then we live the reality of
the socialist and communist dream, except that this dream has
been realized beyond the wildest fantasies of its author through
the advancement of technology whose provisional last stage is
automation; the noble dream has changed into something closely
resembling a nightmare.

Those who wish to speculate about the "deeper" cause underlying the factual change of an early producer society into a consumer society that could keep going only by changing into a huge
economy of waste, would do well to turn to Lewis Mumford's
recent reflections in the *New Yorker*. For it is indeed only too true
that the "premise underlying this whole age," its capitalist as well
as its socialist development, has been "the doctrine of Progress."
"Progress," Mumford says, "was a tractor that laid its own
roadbed and left no permanent imprint of its own tracks, nor did
it move toward an imaginable and humanly desirable destination.
The going is the goal,'" but not because there was an inherent
beauty or meaningfulness in the "going." Rather to stop going, to
stop wasting, to stop consuming more and more, quicker and
quicker, to say at any given moment enough is enough would
spell immediate doom. This progress, accompanied by the incessant noise of the advertising agencies, went on at the expense of
the world we live in, and of the objects with their built-in obsoles-
cence, which we no longer use but abuse, misuse, and throw away.
The recent sudden awakening to the threats to our environment is
the first ray of hope in this development, although nobody, as far

262

as I can see, has yet found a means to stop this runaway economy without causing a really major breakdown.

Much more decisive, however, than these social and economic consequences is the fact that Madison Avenue tactics under the name of public relations have been permitted to invade our political life. The Pentagon Papers not only showed in detail "the picture of the world's greatest superpower killing or seriously injuring a thousand noncombatants a week, while trying to pound a tiny backward nation into submission on an issue whose merits are hotly disputed"—a picture which in Robert McNamara's carefully measured words was certainly "not a pretty one." The papers also proved beyond doubt and in tedious repetition that this not very honorable and not very rational enterprise was exclusively guided by the needs of a superpower to create for itself an *image* which would *convince* the world that it was indeed "the mightiest power on earth."

The ultimate aim of this terribly destructive war, which Johnson let loose in 1965, was neither power nor profit, not even anything so real as influence in Asia to serve particular tangible interests for the sake of which prestige, an appropriate image, was needed and purposefully used. This was not imperialist politics with its urge to expand and annex. The terrible truth to be gleaned from the story told in these papers was that the only permanent goal had become the *image* itself, which was debated in countless memoranda and "options," that is, in the "scenarios" and their "audiences," the very language borrowed from the theater. For the ultimate aim, all "options" were but short-term interchangeable means, until finally, when all signs pointed to defeat, this whole official outfit strained its remarkable intellectual resources on finding ways and means to avoid *admitting* defeat and to keep the *image* of the "mightiest power on earth" intact. It was at this moment, of course, that the administration was bound to clash head-on with the press and find out that free and uncorrupt correspondents are a greater threat to image-making than foreign conspiracies or actual enemies of the United States. This clash certainly was triggered by the simultaneous publication of the Pentagon Papers in the *New York Times* and the *Washington Post*, probably the greatest journalistic scoop of the century, but it was actually unavoidable so long as newspapermen were willing to insist on their right to publish "all the news that's fit to print."

Image-making as global policy is indeed something new in the huge arsenal of human follies recorded in history, but lying as such is neither new nor necessarily foolish in politics. Lies have always been regarded as justifiable in emergencies, lies that concerned specific secrets, especially in military matters, which had to be shielded against the enemy. This was not lying on principle, it was the jealously guarded prerogative of a small number of men reserved for extraordinary circumstances, whereas image-making, the seemingly harmless lying of Madison Avenue, was permitted to proliferate throughout the ranks of all governmental services, military and civilian—the phony body counts of the "search-and-destroy" missions, the doctored after-damage reports of the air force, the constant progress reports to Washington, in the case of Ambassador Martin continuing up to the moment when he boarded the helicopter to be evacuated. These lies hid no secrets from friend or enemy; nor were they intended to. They were meant to manipulate Congress and to persuade the people of the United States.

Lying as a way of life is also no novelty in politics, at least not in our century. It was quite successful in countries under the rule of total domination, where the lying was guided not by an image but by an ideology. Its success as we all know was overwhelming but depended on *terror*, not on hidden persuasion, and its result is far from encouraging: quite apart from all other considerations, to a large extent this lying on principle is the reason that Soviet Russia is still a kind of underdeveloped and underpopulated country.

In our context, the decisive aspect of this lying on principle is that it can work only through terror, that is, through the invasion of the political processes by sheer criminality. This is what happened in Germany and Russia on a gigantic scale during the thirties and forties; when the government of two great powers was in the hands of mass murderers. When the end came, with the defeat and suicide of Hitler and the sudden death of Stalin, a political kind of image-making was introduced in both countries, though in very different ways, to cover up the unbelievable record of the past. The Adenauer regime in Germany felt it had to cover up the fact that Hitler had not only been helped by some "war criminals" but supported by a majority of the German people, and Khrushchev in his famous speech on the Twentieth Party Congress pretended that it all had been the consequence of the unfortunate "personality cult" of Stalin. In both instances, this lying was what we today would call a cover-up, and it was felt to be necessary to enable the people to return from a monstrous past that had left countless criminals in the country and to recover some kind of normality.

As far as Germany was concerned, the strategy was highly successful and the country actually recovered quickly, whereas in Russia the change was not back to anything we would call normal but a return to despotism; and here we should not forget that a change from total domination with its millions of entirely innocent victims to a tyrannical regime which persecutes only its opposition can perhaps best be understood as something which is normal in the framework of Russian history. Today the most serious consequence of the terrible disasters of the thirties and forties in Europe is that this form of criminality with its bloodbaths has remained the conscious or unconscious standard by which we measure what is permitted or prohibited in politics. Public opinion is dangerously inclined to condone not crime in the streets but all political transgressions short of murder.

Watergate signified the intrusion of criminality into the political processes of this country, but compared to what had already happened in this terrible century its manifestations—blatant lying, as in the Tonkin resolution, to manipulate Congress, a number of third-rate burglaries, the excessive lying to cover up the burglaries, the harassment of citizens through the Internal Revenue Service, the attempt to organize a Secret Service exclusively at the command of the executive—were so mild that it was always difficult to take them altogether seriously. This was especially true for spectators and commentators from abroad because none of them came from countries where a constitution is actually the basic law of the land, as it has been here for two hundred years. So certain transgressions which in this country are actually criminal are not felt in other countries to be crimes.

But even we who are citizens, and who as citizens have been in opposition to the administration at least since 1965, have our difficulties in this respect after the selective publication of the Nixon tapes. Reading them, we feel that we overestimated Nixon as well as the Nixon administration—though we certainly did not overestimate the disastrous results of our Asian adventure. Nixon's actions misled us because we suspected that we were confronted with a calculated assault on the basic law of the land, with an attempt to abolish the Constitution and the institutions of liberty. In retrospect it looks as though there existed no such grand schemes but "only" the firm resolve to do away with any *law*, constitutional or not, that stood in the way of shifting designs inspired by greed and vindictiveness rather than by the drive for power or any coherent political program. In other words, it is as though a bunch of con men, rather untalented Mafiosi, had succeeded in appropriating to themselves the government of "the mightiest power on earth." It is in line with such considerations that the credibility gap, which the administration tells us threatens our relations with foreign countries, who allegedly no longer trust our commitments, is actually threatening domestic rather than international affairs. Whatever the causes for the erosion of American power, the antics of the Nixon administration with its conviction that dirty tricks are all you need to be successful in any enterprise are hardly among them. All this, to be sure, is not very consoling, but it is still the case that Nixon's crimes were a far cry from that sort of criminality with which we were inclined to compare it. Still, there are a few parallels which, I think, may rightfully claim our attention.

There is first the very uncomfortable fact that there were quite a number of men around Nixon who did not belong to the inner circle of his cronies and were not hand-picked by him, but who nevertheless stuck with him, some to the bitter end, even though they knew enough about the "horror stories" in the White House to preclude their mere manipulation. It is true that he himself never trusted them, but how could *they* trust this man who had proved throughout a long and not very honorable public career that he could *not* be trusted? The same uncomfortable question could of course, and with more justification, be asked about the men who surrounded and helped Hitler and Stalin. Men with genuinely criminal instincts acting under compulsion are not frequent, and they are less common among politicians and statesmen for the simple reason that their particular business, the business in the public realm, demands publicity, and criminals as a rule have no great desire to go public. The trouble, I think, is less that power corrupts than that the *aura* of power, its glamorous trappings, more than power itself, *attracts;* for all those men we have known in this century to have abused power to a blatantly criminal extent were corrupt long before they attained power. What the helpers needed to become accomplices in criminal activities was permissiveness, the assurance that they would be above the law. We don't know anything solid about these matters; but all speculations about an inherent tension between power and character suffer from a tendency to equate indiscriminately born criminals with those who only rush to help once it has become clear to them that public opinion or "executive privilege" will protect them from being punished.

As far as the criminals themselves are concerned, the chief common weakness in their character seems to be the rather naïve assumption that all people are actually like them, that their flawed character is part and parcel of the human condition stripped of hypocrisy and conventional clichés. Nixon's greatest mistake—aside from not burning the tapes in time—was to have misjudged the incorruptibility of the courts and the press.

The cascade of events in the last few weeks almost succeeded for a moment in tearing to shreds the tissue of lies created by the Nixon administration and the web of the image-makers that had preceded it. Events brought out the undisguised facts in their brutal force, tumbling out into a heap of rubble; for a moment, it looked as though all the chickens had come home to roost together. But for people who had lived for so long in the euphoric mood of "nothing succeeds like success," the logical consequence that "nothing fails like failure" was not easy to accept. And thus it was perhaps only natural that the first reaction of the Ford administration was to try a new image that could at least attenuate the failure, attenuate the admission of defeat.

Under the assumption that "the greatest power on earth" lacked the inner strength to live with defeat, and under the pretext that the country was threatened by a new isolationism, of which there were no signs, the administration embarked upon a policy of recriminations against Congress, and we were offered, like so many countries before us, the stab-in-the-back legend, generally invented by generals who have lost a war and most cogently argued in our case by General William Westmoreland and General Maxwell Taylor.

President Ford himself has offered a broader view than these generals. Noticing that time under all circumstances has the peculiarity of marching *forward,* he admonished us repeatedly to do as time does, he warned us that to look backward could only lead to mutual recriminations—forgetting for the moment that he had refused to give unconditional amnesty, the time-honored means to heal the wounds of a divided nation. He told us to do what he had not done, namely, to forget the past and to open cheerfully a new chapter of history. Compared to the sophisticated ways in which for many years unpleasant facts were swept under the rug of imagery, this is a startling return to the oldest methods of mankind for getting rid of unpleasant realities—*oblivion.* No doubt, if it were successful, it would work better than all the images that tried to be substitutes for reality. Let us forget Vietnam, let us forget Watergate, let us forget the cover-up and the cover-up of the cover-up enforced by the premature presidential pardon for the chief actor in this affair, who even today refuses to admit any wrongdoing; *not amnesty but amnesia will heal all our wounds.*

One of the discoveries of totalitarian government was the method of digging giant holes in which to bury unwelcome facts and events, a huge enterprise which could be achieved only by killing millions of people who had been the actors in or the witnesses of the past. For the past was condemned to be forgotten as though it had never been. To be sure, nobody for a moment wanted to follow the merciless logic of these past rulers, especially since, as we now know, they did not succeed. In our case, not terror but persuasion enforced by pressure and the manipulation of public opinion is supposed to succeed where terror failed. Public opinion at first did not show itself to be very amenable to such attempts by the Executive; the first response to what happened was a rapidly increasing stream of articles and books about "Vietnam" and "Watergate," most of which were eager not so much to tell us the facts as to find out and teach us the lessons we are supposed to learn from our recent past, quoting again and again the old adage that "those who do not learn the lessons of history are condemned to repeat it."

Well, if history—as distinct from the historians who derive the most heterogeneous lessons from their interpretations of history—has any lessons to teach us, this Pythian oracle seems to me more cryptic and obscure than the notoriously unreliable prophecies of the Delphic Apollo. I rather believe with Faulkner, "The past is never dead, it's not even past," and this for the simple reason that the world we live in at any moment *is* the world of the past; it consists of the monuments and the relics of what has been done by men for better or worse; its facts are always what has *become* (as the Latin origin of the word: *fieri—factum est* suggests). In other words, it is quite true that the past *haunts* us; it is the past's function to haunt us who are present and wish to live in the world as it really is, that is, has *become* what it is now.

I said before that in the cataclysm of recent events it was as though "all the chickens had come home to roost," and I used this common expression because it indicates the boomerang effect, the unexpected ruinous backfiring of evil deeds on the doer, of which imperialist politicians of former generations were so afraid. Indeed anticipating this effect actually restrained them decisively from whatever they were doing in faraway lands to strange and foreign people. Let us not count our blessings, but in quick and certainly not exhaustive form mention some of the most obvious ruinous effects for which it would be wise to blame no scapegoats, foreign or domestic, but only ourselves. Let us start with the economy whose sudden turn from boom to depression nobody predicted, and which the latest events in New York City so sadly and ominously dramatized.

Let me first say the obvious: inflation and currency devaluation are inevitable after lost wars, and only our unwillingness to admit a disastrous defeat leads and misleads us into a futile search for "deeper causes." Only victory together with acquisition of new territories and reparations in a peace settlement, can make up for the entirely unproductive expenses of war. In the case of the war which we have lost, this would be impossible anyhow since we did not intend to expand, and even offered (though apparently never intended to pay) North Vietnam two and a half billion dollars for the reconstruction of the country. For those eager to "learn" from history, there is the trite lesson that even the extravagantly rich can go bankrupt. But there is, of course, more to the sudden crisis that has overcome us.

The Great Depression of the thirties, which spread from the United States to all of Europe, was in no country brought under control or followed by a normal recovery—the New Deal in America was no less impotent in this respect than the notoriously ineffective *Notverordnungen*, the emergency measures of the dying Weimar Republic. The Depression was ended only by sudden and politically necessitated changes to a war economy, first in Germany, where Hitler had liquidated the Depression and its unemployment by 1936, and then with the outbreak of the War, in the United States. This tremendously important fact was noticeable to everybody, but it was immediately covered up by a great number of complicated economic theories, so that public opinion remained unconcerned. Seymour Melman is, as far as I know, the only writer of any consequence to make this point repeatedly (see *American Capitalism in Decline*, which, according to a critic in the *New York Times Book Review*, "presents enough data to float three books this size"), and his work remains entirely outside the mainstream of economic theory. But while this basic fact, very frightening in itself, was overlooked in nearly all public debates, it resulted almost immediately in the more or less commonly shared conviction that manufacturing "companies are in business not to produce goods but to provide jobs."

This maxim may have had its origin in the Pentagon, but it certainly has meanwhile spread all over the country. It is true that the war economy as the savior from unemployment and depression was followed by the large-scale use of the various inventions which we sum up under the label of automation, and which, as was dutifully pointed out fifteen or twenty years ago, should have meant a brutal loss of jobs. But the debate over automation and unemployment quickly disappeared for the simple reason that featherbedding and similar practices partly, but only partly, enforced by the great power of the unions, have seemed to take care of the problem. Today it is almost universally accepted that we must make cars to keep jobs, not to move people about.

It is no secret that the billions of dollars demanded by the Pentagon for the armaments industry are necessary not for "national security" but for keeping the economy from collapsing. At a time when war as a rational means of politics has become a kind of luxury justifiable only for small powers, arms trade and arms production have become the fastest growing business, and the United States is "easily the world's largest arms merchant." As Canada's prime minister Pierre Trudeau, when criticized recently for selling arms to the United States that were eventually used in Vietnam, sadly stated, it has all become a choice "between dirty hands and empty bellies."

Under these circumstances, it is entirely true that, as Melman states, "inefficiency [has been elevated] into a national purpose," and what has come home to roost in this particular case is the hectic and unfortunately highly successful policy of "solving" very real problems by clever gimmicks which are only successful enough to make the problems temporarily disappear.

Perhaps it is a sign of a reawakening sense for reality that the economic crisis, highlighted by the possible bankruptcy of the country's largest city, has done more to push Watergate into the background than all the various attempts of two administrations put together. What still persists, and still haunts us, is the astounding aftermath of Mr. Nixon's enforced resignation. Mr. Ford, an unelected president, appointed by Mr. Nixon himself because he was one of his strongest supporters in Congress, was greeted with wild enthusiasm. "In a few days, almost in a few hours, Gerald Ford dispelled the miasma that hung so long over the White House; and the sun, so to speak, started shining in Washington again," said Arthur Schlesinger, certainly one of the last among the intellectuals one would have expected to nurture secret longings for the man on horseback. That was indeed how a great many Americans instinctively reacted. Mr. Schlesinger may have changed his mind after Ford's premature pardon, but what then happened showed how well attuned he had been to the mood of the country in his hasty evaluation. Mr. Nixon had to resign because he was sure to be indicted for the cover-up of Watergate; a normal reaction of those concerned with the "horror stories" in the White House would have been to follow up by asking who actually instigated this affair which then had to be covered up. But so far as I know this question was asked and seriously pursued by one lone article, by Mary McCarthy in the *New York Review of Books*. Those who had already been indicted and convicted for their roles in the cover-up were overwhelmed with very high offers from publishers, the press and television, and the campuses to tell their story. No one doubts that all these stories will be self-serving, most of all the story Nixon himself plans to publish, for which his agent thinks he can easily get a $2 million advance. These offers, I am sorry to say, are by no means politically motivated; they reflect the market and its demand for "positive images"—that is, its quest for more lies and fabrications, this time to justify the cover-up and to rehabilitate the criminals.

What comes home to roost now is this long education in imagery, which seems no less habit-forming than drugs. Nothing in my opinion told us more about this addiction than the public reaction, on the street, as well as in Congress, to our "victory" in Cambodia, in the opinion of many "just what the doctor ordered" (Sulzberger) to heal the wounds of the Vietnam defeat. Indeed, " ' 'Twas a famous victory!' " as James Reston aptly quoted in the *New York Times;* and let us hope that this was finally the nadir of the erosion of power in this country, the nadir of self-confidence when victory over one of the tiniest and most helpless countries could cheer the inhabitants of what only a few decades ago really was the "mightiest power on earth."

Ladies and Gentlemen, while we now slowly emerge from under the rubble of the events of the last few years, let us not forget these years of aberration lest we become wholly unworthy of the glorious beginnings two hundred years ago. When the facts come home to roost, let us try at least to make them welcome. Let us try not to escape into some utopias—images, theories, or sheer follies. It was the greatness of this Republic to give due account for the sake of freedom to the best in men and to the worst.

1975

NOTES

SOME QUESTIONS OF MORAL PHILOSOPHY

1. The behavior of the *individual* is at stake in moral matters and this came out in courtroom procedures where the question was no longer, Was he a big or small cog? but Why did he consent to become a cog at all? What happened to his conscience? Why did it not function, or function the other way round? And why could no Nazi be found in postwar Germany? Why could it be turned about a second time, simply because of defeat? (Hannah Arendt, "Basic Moral Propositions")

2. Immanuel Kant, *Foundations of the Metaphysics of Morals*, trans. Lewis White Beck, Library of Liberal Arts (Indianapolis: Bobbs-Merrill, 1959), 20.—Ed.

3. Immanuel Kant, *Die Religion innerhalb der Grenzen der blossen Vernunft*, in *Immanuel Kant's Sämtliche Werke*, ed. G. Hertenstein, vol. 6 (Leipzig: Leopold Voss, 1868), 132–133.—Ed.

4. Friedrich Nietzsche, *Werke in Drei Bänden*, vol. 3 (München: Carl Hanser Verlag, 1956), 484. Walter Kaufman translates this passage as follows: "Naïveté: as if morality could survive when the *God* who sanctions it is missing. The 'beyond' absolutely necessary if faith in morality is to be maintained." *Will to Power*, no. 253 (New York: Random House, 1967), 147.—Ed.

5. Immanuel Kant, *Critique of Pure Reason*, trans. Norman Kemp Smith (New York: St. Martin's Press, 1965), A819, 644.—Ed.

6. Immanuel Kant, *Lectures on Ethics*, translated by Louis Infield, with foreword by Lewis White Beck (Indianapolis: Hackett Publishing Company, 1963), 51.—Ed.

7. Immanuel Kant, *Critique of Practical Reason*, trans. Lewis White Beck, Library of Liberal Arts (Indianapolis: Bobbs-Merrill, 1956), 166.—Ed.

8. Immanuel Kant, "Perpetual Peace," in *On History*, ed. Lewis White Beck, Library of Liberal Arts (Indianapolis: Bobbs-Merrill, 1963), 112.—Ed.

9. In Kant, there is the problem of whence to derive obligation: it can't be derived from some transcendence outside man, even though without the hope for an intelligible world, all moral obligations could turn out to be *Hirngespinste* (phantasms). (For they make themselves felt only within man, and as far as their objective validity goes, even a nation of devils or a consummate villain could act according to them. They are dictates of right reason.) A transcendent source would deprive man of his

autonomy, that he follows only the law within himself, which gives him his dignity. Hence, duty could be an "empty concept," for to the question: And why should I do my duty? there is only the answer: Because it is my duty. And the presupposition that to do otherwise I stand in contradiction to myself has not the same force of argument in Kant, because reason is not the same thing as thinking, and thinking is not understood as an intercourse of myself with myself. The obligation in Kant derives from the *dictamen rationis,* a dictate of reason. And this dictate is as unanswerable as other rational truths, such as mathematical truths, which are always taken as the example. ("Basic Moral Propositions")

10. There are always a few with whom it [the pressure to conform with those others in Nazi society] did not work. And we are concerned in this course with them. What prevented them from acting as everyone else did? Their noble nature (as Plato would suggest)? What does this nobility consist of? We follow Plato and recognize them as those to whom certain moral propositions are self-evident. But why? First, who were they? Those who conformed to the new order were by no means those who were revolutionary, who were rebels, etc. Obviously not, for they were the overwhelming majority. The collapse consisted in the yielding of those social groups which had not doubted and had never raised rebellious slogans. They were what Sartre calls "*les salauds*" and whom he identifies with the paragons of virtue in respectable society.

Those who resisted could be found in all walks of life, among poor and entirely uneducated people as among members of good and high society. They said very little and the argument was always the same. There was no *conflict,* no struggle, the evil was no temptation. They did not say, we are afraid of an all-seeing and avenging god, not even when they were religious; and it would not have helped because the religions had become quite nicely adjusted too. They simply said, I can't, I'd rather die, for life would not be worthwhile when I had done it.

Hence we are concerned with the behavior of common people, not of Nazis or convinced Bolsheviks, not with saints and heroes, and not with born criminals. For if there is any such thing as what we call morality for want of a better term, it certainly concerns such common people and common happenings. ("Basic Moral Propositions")

11. You don't need Kant's philosophy to arrive at this conclusion. I'll give you another more recent example which, from altogether different presuppositions, arrives at exactly the same conclusions. A recent author, George A. Schrader ("Responsibility and Existence," *Nomos,* vol. 3), finds himself in the old difficulty: even if moral truth were self-evident, moral obligation—that you should act according to what you know is right—is neither self-evident nor can it be proved conclusively. Hence, he tries to transform all moral imperatives not into simple propositions but into ontological statements, obviously in the hope that being, or existence itself, will provide a binding force which we otherwise can find only in the power of divine commandments. The result is that what we usually call right or wrong turns out to be adequate or inadequate behavior. Interestingly enough, our author, somehow following Heidegger, starts with the fact that man has not made

himself, but owes his existence, which was given to him as a free gift. From this he concludes that man is answerable, responsible by definition: "To be a man is to be responsible to oneself for oneself." Well, to whom else would one be responsible? But isn't it rather obvious that the statement of the fact of not having chosen life might mean exactly the opposite: since I have not made myself, and if my existence has been given to me as a free gift I may count it among my possessions and do with it as I please. But let us disregard this counterargument and also the reappearance of the self as the ultimate standard, and proceed to the next assertion: "To state this is in no wise to recommend what a man *ought* to be in some ideal sense, but simply to state what he *is* and *must be*." From which it would follow that if the discrepancy between the "must be" and the actual behavior is great enough, man ceases to be man. If we could afford the luxury to call immoral conduct simply nonhuman conduct, then our problems would indeed be at an end. But they are not, as you'll see immediately from one of our author's key illustrations, the mistreatment of a dog. It is "morally and cognitively wrong" to treat a dog as though it were a stone. What is involved is a "misrepresentation" of an object, a cognitive error. Not for a moment does it occur to our author that if I treat a dog like a stone, either I behave like a stone, or, what is more likely, I want to cause pain. No cognitive error is involved; on the contrary, if I did not know that a dog is *not* a stone, I would never be tempted to mistreat it.

12. The self for whom it is better to suffer than to do wrong is actually not so much this entity of I-am-I *(Richard III)* as it is an activity. What is at stake is the capacity of thinking matters through by myself, and neither the I-am (which first of all is one and not two-in-one—in acting you are *one*, in the world you appear as *one*), nor the possible results. Socrates did not teach, he had no knowledge; he was engaged in an unending process, a process that depended upon whatever was proposed to get him started. In *Charmides* (165b): "Critias, you act as though I professed to know the answers to the questions I ask you, and could give them to you if I wished. It isn't so. I inquire with you into whatever is proposed just because I don't myself have any knowledge." He repeats this frequently, also in *Gorgias* (506a). Hence, the emphasis is not on knowledge, on acquisition, but on an activity. (Politically, Socrates seems to have believed that not knowledge but knowing how to think will make the Athenians better, more likely to resist the tyrant, etc. Incidentally, Socrates' trial turns about this point: Socrates did not teach new gods but he taught how to question everything. For those who take the nonresults of such questioning for results, this idol-shattering enterprise can become very dangerous. No one who knows how to think will ever again be able simply to obey and to conform, not because of a rebellious spirit but because of the habit of examining everything. In the *Apology* Socrates' last answer to the judges was, I can't give up *examining*. Why couldn't he do it in silence? The priority of *dialegesthai* over *dianoeisthai*. ("Basic Moral Propositions")

13. Friedrich Nietzsche, "Draft of a Letter to Paul Rée" (1882), in *The Portable Nietzsche*, selected and translated by Walter Kaufman (New York: Viking Press, 1954), 102.—Ed.

14. In "Basic Moral Propositions" Arendt defined "four fundamental, ever-recurring moments" of conscience:

My conscience is (a) witness; (b) my faculty of judging, i.e., of telling right from wrong; (c) what sits in judgment in myself over myself; and (d) a voice in myself, as against the biblical voice of God from without.

The word, *con-scientia, syn-eidenai,* was originally consciousness, and only the German language has two different words for moral conscience and consciousness. *Con-scientia:* I know together with my self, or while I know I am aware that I know. *Syn-eidenai:* always or mostly in Plato and Aristotle with myself—*emautō, hautois,* etc. In Greek the word was not used in a specifically moral way, although I can be conscious of bad deeds, and this consciousness (*synesis* in Euripides) may be very unpleasant. This consciousness can be understood as testifying to my existence. To the extent that I am aware of myself I know that I am. If I am not aware of myself I don't know if I am at all. In Augustine, and later in Descartes, the question of reality, including my own, was raised. Augustine's answer was that I may doubt whether anything exists at all, but I cannot doubt that I doubt.

Here you see already the two-in-one, the splitting up. I can testify about myself. The first time we find *conscientia* in terminological use in Cicero it has this meaning (*De officiis* 3.44): when I am under oath for something that is hidden from all men, I should remember that I have a god as witness. According to Cicero this means that "my mind is my witness" and "the god himself has bestowed upon man nothing more divine." (In this sense we find in Egypt, 1,500 years before Christ, a royal servant recounting his services and saying, "My heart told me to do all this. It was an excellent witness.") The point is *witness for what is hidden.* Thus in the New Testament, Rom. 2.14 ff., regarding the "secrets of man," Paul speaks of conscience bearing witness and of thoughts which are in conflict with each other, deliberating in man, which "accuse and excuse one another" as in a courtroom. In 2 Cor. 1.12 *syneidēsis* is testimony. In Seneca: A sacred spirit watching and guarding our evil and good deeds. Hence, conscience was closely connected throughout the Middle Ages with God, who knows the secrets of men's hearts (Matt. 6.4).

During the Middle Ages, there was usually a sharp distinction between conscience as (a) self-consciousness, and (b) the faculty of telling right from wrong according to an innate law.

The voice of conscience is also very old, not only because we find it in the Old Testament, where God speaks to man constantly, but primarily, of course, because of Socrates' daimon. A daimon is something between a god and a mortal whom every man has as his companion. It is a voice which comes from without and cannot be answered—very different from *conscientia.* And this voice never tells me what to do but only prevents me or warns me away from doing.

15. "The goal given by reason may conflict with the goal given by desire. In this case, it is again reason which decides. Reason is a higher faculty, and goals given by reason belong to a higher order. The assumption is that I will listen to reason, that reason masters or rules the desires. Reason does not say, Thou shalt not, but Better not." ("Basic Moral Propositions")

Notes

16. At this point it becomes clear that neither reason nor desire are free, properly speaking. But the will is—as the faculty of choosing. Moreover, reason reveals what is common to all men qua men, desire is common to all living organisms. Only the will is entirely my own. By willing I decide. And this is the faculty of freedom. ("Basic Moral Propositions")

17. In "Basic Moral Propositions" Arendt considered the possibility that Aristotle's *prohairesis* could be understood as a sort of will:

Qualification of the statement that there was no will in antiquity: *prohaireses* in the *Nicomachean Ethics,* especially Book 3, chapters 2–3. The word signifies a stretching out into the future, taking or choosing ahead. Its definition is: *bouleutikē orexis tōn eph hēmin,* a deliberating appetite with respect to what is in our power (1113a10).

Aristotle is uncertain about this faculty. He always tries to reduce it to desire and reason. For instance, he says that appetite and the logos are origins of *prohairesis* (*Nicomachean Ethics* 1139a31), and that *prohairesis* has in common *dianoia* and *orexis* (*Movement of Animals* 700b18–23). Most important in the *Nicomachean Ethics,* he says that *prohairesis* is not for the goal but for the means (1112b11). Its opposite is *boulēsis tou telous* (1111b27). Here, the goal is figured out by deliberation. But in the *Rhetoric* we blame and praise according to *prohairesis* and not according to *ergon* or *praxis.* All badness resides in *prohairesis.*

Only once, in *Metaphysics* 1013a21, is *prohairesis* the beginning of *praxis.* What is lost in other definitions is the stretching out into the future. If we take our clue from that, we conclude that will, as the faculty that stretches out into the future, is the movement of all action. This function of the will has in itself an element of deliberation as well as appetite. If we compare will in this respect with other faculties, desire stretches out into the world as it is given now, in the present; memory stretches out into the past. Reason somehow tries to go beyond these temporalities. It tries to go into a timeless space, where numbers, for instance, are forever what they are. Then reason becomes the greatest of the faculties because it deals with timeless things.

18. It is worth noting that in the "Willing" volume of *The Life of the Mind* Arendt's position is quite different. There she also says that Epictetus is concerned only with inner freedom, but sees that he indeed has a conception of the will, one that is fully active, "omnipotent," and "almighty" ("Willing" 73–83).—Ed.

19. Here the question arises: and whom does the will command? The desires? Not at all, it commands itself to control the desires.

Hence, the will is split in itself into a part that commands and another that obeys. The will "doth not command entirely, therefore what it commandeth, is not done." For the truth of the matter is: "It was I who willed, I who nilled, *I, I myself (ego, ego eram).* I neither willed entirely, nor nilled entirely, and therefore was rent asunder" (*Confessions* 8.10). This *ego, ego eram* (it was I, indeed I) should remind you of the Socratic "Being One it would be better for me to be at odds with the whole world than with myself." But even though I-am-I, there are "two wills," one who wills and commands, one who resists and counter-wills, and therefore "it is no monstrous thing partly to will, partly to nill." It may not be monstrous and it is not a contest between opposing principles—as though we "had two minds, one good, the other evil." The conflict comes up only when the will begins to operate, not before. It is in the nature of the will. But this is a conflict and not a silent intercourse with myself. Again, I am two-in-one but now whatever I do, even if I behave very well or very badly, there is conflict. The proof is that the same happens when "both wills are bad." The problem is always how to will with "an entire will"—as I "spoke, I all but performed. I all but did it, and did it not." We now have four wills all operating at the same time paralyzing each other, "held in suspense."

At this point arises the question: why should God have given me a will? We turn to *De libero arbitrio*. The question is two-fold: Why was will given if grace is needed to get out of self-created predicaments? And why is free will given since by it we can sin? Only the second question is asked explicitly. The answer is that without free will we could not live rightly.

Another question arises: Why was not some other faculty given? A faculty like justice which no one can use wrongly? (2.18) The answer is that there can be no right acting except by the free choice of the will. To put it differently, only will is entirely in our power, only through willpower are we ourselves. Or (1.12), the will is such a great good because all you need to have it is to will: *velle solum opus est ut habeatur*. Or, it is by will that we deserve a happy or an unhappy life. From which it follows that if someone wills to will rightly, he attains a thing so great with such ease that having what he has willed is nothing other than the fact of willing it. But if the will is split within itself, isn't it then perhaps in the nature of the will to originate this movement toward the bad, and if this is so, is it not by nature and hence by necessity that we sin? The answer is yes, perhaps, but how do you then explain the fact that we blame and praise? For the mind is made the servant of desire by nothing but its own will; it is not the servant of desire by virtue of desire or by weakness. The last question: if our bad acts are voluntary, how does that accord with God's foreknowledge? The answer is that God is not the author of everything he knows. By his foreknowledge he does not force us.

From 3.5 to 3.17 the dialogue becomes a monologue. The predicament has become so great that Augustine finds it necessary to say: Never should sinful souls move you to say that it were better they were not or that they should be other than they are. (Remember Jesus' *skandalon* [Luke 17.2]: Betrayal and offenses against the little ones, i.e., those you have in your power.) For Augustine, this is as though you willed it. And his answer is that being is such a good that you can't will it not to be; you can't think nothingness. The interlocutor comes back in chapter 17: "I am asking for the cause of the will." But is not this a question ad infinitum? "Will you not perhaps inquire again for the cause of that cause if we find it?" For the question is wrong. The will is the only thing that can't have a cause prior to itself. What could be the cause of the will prior to the will? For either the will is its own cause or it is no will. We are here confronted with a simple fact. Whereupon Augustine comes to Romans 7 and Galatians 5. And the philosophical discourse is finished. ("Basic Moral Propositions")

20. Hence, freedom is the voluntary renunciation of will. ("Basic Moral Propositions")

21. What we have lost sight of entirely is the will as arbiter, that which chooses freely. Free choice meant free from desire. Where desire intervened, the choice was prejudged. The arbiter was originally the man who approached an occurrence as unconcerned spectator. He was an eyewitness, and as such noncommitted. Because of his unconcern he was held to be capable of impartial judgment. Hence, freedom of will as *liberum arbitrium* never starts something new, it is always confronted with things as they are. It is the faculty of judgment.

If this is the case, however, how could it ever be allowed to be among my willing faculties? Answer: (a) If it is assumed that the ultimate goal of the will is given by reason as the highest good, then (in Aquinas) we are free only in the choice of the means. And this choosing is then the function of *liberum arbitrium*. However, precisely in willing the means, the will is not free. Every goal implies the means with which to achieve it. These are prejudged; there are only better or worse, more adequate or less adequate means. A matter of deliberation rather than of willing. Only in the marginal case where I may say, in order to reach this goal I must employ means which are so bad that it is better not to reach the goal, is the willing faculty involved; (b) There is another possibility: the will reaches not only into the future, but it is also the faculty by which we can affirm and deny. And in this respect, there is indeed an element of willing in all judgments. I can say yes or no to what is. In Augustine: *Amo: volo ut sis.* My affirmation of what or who is, relates me to that which is anyhow, as my denial alienates me from it. In this sense the world is *dilectores mundi.* Or the love of the world constitutes the world for me, fits me into it. ("Basic Moral Propositions")

THINKING AND MORAL CONSIDERATIONS

1. See my *Eichmann in Jerusalem,* 2nd edition, 252.

2. Quoted from the posthumously published notes to Kant's lectures on metaphysics, *Akademie Ausgabe,* vol. 18, no. 5636.

3. Carnap's statement that metaphysics is no more "meaningful" than poetry certainly runs counter to the claims made by metaphysicians; but these, like Carnap's own evaluation, may be based on an underestimation of poetry. Heidegger, whom Carnap singled out for attack, countered (though not explicitly) by stating that thinking and poetry (*denken* and *dichten*) were closely related; they were not identical but sprang from the same root. And Aristotle, whom so far no one has accused of writing "mere" poetry, was of the same opinion: philosophy and poetry somehow belong together; they are of equal weight (*Poetics* 1451b5). On the other hand, there is Wittgenstein's famous aphorism, "What we cannot speak of we must be silent about" (*Tractatus,* last sentence). If taken seriously, it would apply not just to what lies beyond sense experience but, on the contrary, most of all to objects of sensation. For nothing we see, hear, or touch can be adequately described in words. When we say, "The water is cold," neither the water nor the cold are spoken of as they are given to the senses. And was it not precisely the discovery of this discrepancy between words, the medium in which we think, and the world of appearances, the

medium in which we live, that led to philosophy and metaphysics in the first place? Except that in the beginning—with Parmenides and Heraclitus—it was thinking, be it as *nous* or as *logos*, that was supposed to reach true Being, whereas at the end the emphasis shifted from speech to appearance, hence to sense perception and the implements with which we can extend and sharpen our bodily senses. It seems only natural that an emphasis on speech will discriminate against appearances and the emphasis on sensation against thinking.

4. It seems noteworthy that we find the same insight in its obvious simplicity at the beginning of this thinking in terms of two worlds, the sensual and the supersensual. Democritus presents us with a neat little dialogue between the mind, the organ for the supersensual, and the senses. Sense perceptions are illusions, he says; they change according to the conditions of our body; sweet, bitter, color, and such exist only *nomō*, by convention among men, and not *physei*, according to true nature behind the appearances—thus speaks the mind. Whereupon the senses answer: "Wretched mind! Do you overthrow us while you take from us your evidence [*pisteis*, everything you can trust]? Our overthrow will be your downfall" (fragments B125, B9). In other words, once the always precarious balance between the two worlds is lost, no matter whether the "true world" abolishes the "apparent one" or vice versa, the whole framework of references, in which our thinking was used to orienting itself, breaks down. In these terms, nothing seems to make much sense anymore.

5. *Critique of Pure Reason* B30.

6. *Akademie Ausgabe*, vol. 18, no. 4849.

7. *Akademie Ausgabe*, vol. 16, no. 6900.

8. In the eleventh book of *On the Trinity*, Augustine describes vividly the transformation an object given to the senses must undergo to be fit to be an object of thought. Sense perception—"the vision which was without when the sense was formed by a sensible body"—is succeeded by a "similar vision within," an image destined to make present the "absent body" in representation. This image, the representation of something absent, is stored in memory and becomes a thought object, a "vision in thought," as soon as it is willfully remembered, whereby it is decisive that "what remains in the memory," that is, the re-presentation, is "one thing, and that something else arises when we remember" (chapter 3). Hence, "what is hidden and retained in memory is one thing, and what is impressed by it in the thought of the one remembering is another thing" (chapter 8). Augustine is well aware that thinking "in fact goes even further," beyond the realm of all possible imagination, "as when our reason proclaims the infinity of number which no vision in the thought of corporeal things has yet grasped" or when reason "teaches us that even the tiniest bodies can be divided infinitely" (chapter 18).

Augustine here seems to suggest that reason can reach out to the totally absent only because the mind, by virtue of imagination and its re-presentations, knows how to make present what is absent and how to handle these absences in remembrance, that is, in thought.

9. *Introduction to Metaphysics* (New York, 1961), 11.

10. Kant, *Akademie Ausgabe,* vol. 18, nos. 5019 and 5036.

11. *Phaedo* 64, and Diogenes Laertius 7.21.

12. I paraphrase the passages: *Seventh Letter* 341b–343a.

13. *Dante and Philosophy* (New York, 1949, 1963), 267.

14. Ibid., 273. For the whole discussion of the passage, see 270 ff.

15. Diehl, frag. 16.

16. *Meno* 80.

17. Xenophon, *Memorabilia* 4.6.15, 4.4.9.

18. In this as in other respects, Socrates says in the *Apology* very nearly the opposite to what Plato made him say in the "improved apology" of the *Phaedo.* In the first instance, he explained why he should live and, incidentally, why he was not afraid to die although life was "very dear" to him; in the second, the whole emphasis is on how burdensome life is and how happy he was to die.

19. *Sophist* 258.

20. Xenophon, op. cit., 4.3.14.

21. *Apology* 30, 38.

22. *Lysis* 204b–c.

23. In the funeral oration, Thucydides 2.40.

24. *Symposium* 177.

25. I shall quote here only the view held by Democritus, because he was a contemporary of Socrates. He thought of *logos,* speech, as the "shadow" of action, whereby shadow is meant to distinguish real things from mere semblances; hence he said "one must avoid speaking of evil deeds," depriving them, as it were, of their shadow, their manifestation. (See fragments 145 and 190.) Ignoring evil will turn it into a mere semblance.

26. *Sophist* 254d—see Martin Heidegger, *Identity and Difference* (New York, 1969), 23–41.

27. *Theaetetus* 189e ff., and *Sophist* 263e.

The Deputy: GUILT BY SILENCE?

1. Guenther Lewy's "Pius XII, the Jews and the German Catholic Church," *Commentary* (February, 1964) later became part of Lewy's major work *The Catholic Church and Nazi Germany* (New York: McGraw-Hill, 1964).

AUSCHWITZ ON TRIAL

1. Sybille Bedford, *Observer* (London), January 5, 1964.

2. See *Economist* (London), July 23, 1966.

INDEX

Abel, 73
Achilles, 144
Action
    distinction between thought and,
        105–6
    moral distinguished from political,
        112
Action Française, 222
Acts of state argument, 37–39
Adams, John, 153
Adeimantus, 87, 88
Adenauer, Konrad, 34, 35, 55, 236, 245,
    265
Aeschylus, 151
Alcibiades, 176
American Capitalism in Decline
    (Melman), 272
American Philosophical Society, xxxiii,
    xxxiv
American Society of Christian Ethics,
    xxvi–xxvii
Antimiscegenation laws, xxxiv, 194 n.,
    202–3
Apollo, 151
    temple of, 76
Apology (Plato), 102, 286
Aquinas, Thomas, 64–66, 73, 119, 170
Arab states, 259
Arendt, Hannah
    arrest in Berlin (1933), x n.
    Augustine and, xxv

"Auschwitz on Trial" (1966), xxxvi,
    227–56
    on becoming U.S. citizen, 3–4
    on Churchill, 49–50
    "Collective Responsibility" (1968),
        xx, xxxiii–xxxiv, 147–58
    "Crisis Character of Modern
        Society, The" (1966), vii–viii
    "The Deputy: Guilt by Silence?"
        (1964), xx, xxxvi, 214–26
    *Eichmann in Jerusalem: A Report on
        the Banality of Evil,* xi–xvi, xx,
        xxxiv, 17–18, 59
    on European background, 4–5
    experience as Jew, xi–xii
    "Home to Roost" (1975), ix, viii,
        xxxiii, 257–75
    The Human Condition, xv
    leaves Europe, 3, 5
    The Life of the Mind, xvii, 282
    on Nazi conquest of Denmark, 5–7
    Nietzsche and, xviii
    The Origins of Totalitarianism, xv
    "Personal Responsibility Under
        Dictatorship" (1964), xiv, xxxiii,
        17–48
    "Prologue" (1975), xxxii, xxxiii,
        3–14
    on public recognition, 7–14
    "Reflections on Little Rock" (1959),
        xxxiv–xxxv, 193–213

Index

remarks to American Society of
Christian Ethics (1973),
xxvi–xxviii
"Some Questions of Moral
Philosophy" (1965–1966), xiii n.,
xvii, xxvii, xxix, xxxiii, 49–146
Sonning Prize awarded to, xxxii
on Stalin regime, 52–53
"Thinking and Moral
Considerations" (1971), xvii, xxix,
xxxiii, 159–89
on Zionism, xii n.
Aristotle, 46, 64–65, 92, 98, 171,
280–82, 285
Armaments industry, 273
Atomic bomb, x
Auden, W. H., 7, 10, 159
Augustine, xxv, xxvii, 22, 113, 120–21,
127, 130, 131, 133, 136, 280,
283–84, 286
Aumeier, 238
Auschwitz concentration camp, 43,
216
Frankfurt trial, 227–56
"Auschwitz on Trial" (Arendt), xxxvi
text of (1966), 227–56
Automation, debate over, 272

Bach, Johann Sebastian, 96
Baer, Richard, 236, 240
Baker, Russell, 258
Baretzki, 235, 253
"Basic Moral Propositions" (Arendt),
xxxiii
Bauer, Fritz, 229, 246
Bedford, Sybille, 253
Bednarek, 248, 253, 254
Belgium, 219, 221
Bentham, Jeremy, 133
Bergson, Henri, 9, 10
Beria, Lavrenti, 34
*Between Friends: The Correspondence of
Hannah Arendt and Mary*

McCarthy 1949–1975 (ed.
Brightman), xxxiv n.
Beyond Good and Evil (Nietzsche), 99,
123–24, 127, 131–32, 134
Bible, the, 73–74, 115–16, 152, 281
Billy Budd (Melville), 74
Bischoff, 237
Black Americans, school desegregation
and, 193–95, 197, 201–4, 210, 212,
213
Boger, Wilhelm, 229, 233, 235–36, 238,
240, 253, 255
Bohr, Niels, xxxii
Bolshevism, xix, 218–19, 222
Boredom, 98
Braham, R. L., xvi n.
Breitwieser, 246
Brightman, Carol, xxxiv n.
Broad, Pery, 233, 234, 243
Broad Report, 233, 234, 243
Brothers Karamazov, The (Dostoevsky),
63
Brown v. Board of Education, xxxv n.,
194, 197, 201
Buber, Martin, 29
Bucher, Minister of Justice, 228

Caesar, Julius, 144
Cain, 73
Calhoun, C., xxxv n.
Callicles, 83, 87, 90, 181, 182
Cambodia, 274
Capesius, 236, 253
Carnap, Rudolf, 285
Categorical imperative, of Kant, 61–62,
69–71, 77, 80, 108, 153, 157
Catholic Church, xxxvi, 20, 21, 37, 59,
214–19, 222, 225
Catholic Church and Nazi Germany, The
(Lewy), 287
Catholic Encyclopedia (Germany), 222
Catholic Jews, 214, 215, 224–25
Cato, 99

Index

Index

"Ein Deutscher klagt den Papst an"
(Weltsch), 20 n.
Einsatzkommando, 239
Eligibility for public office, 204–5
Ellison, Ralph, xxxv
Enghien, duc d', 39
Epictetus, 114–15, 282
Epicureans, 65
Epicurus, 8
Equality principle, 199–200, 209
Ethics (Spinoza), 67
Euthyphro (Plato), 66, 86, 170
Evil, nature of, xv–xvii, 72–75, 79, 82,
94–95, 101, 110–12, 124–27,
159–61, 179–80, 186–88
Exclusiveness, rule of, 208
Executive privilege, 268

Faubus, Orville, 202
Faulkner, William, viii, 199, 202, 270
Final Solution (*see* Nazi Germany)
Finland, 219
Finnberg, Emil, 239–40, 251
Flacke, Oberscharführer, 252
Ford, Gerald R., 269, 273–74
Forgiveness, 89, 95, 125
*Foundations of the Metaphysics of
Morals* (Kant), 71
Founding Fathers, 4, 89, 260
France, 215, 216, 221
Francis of Assisi, St., 76, 135
Frankfurter Allgemeine Zeitung
(newspaper), 228
Frankfurter Hefte, 220
Frankfurt trial, 227–56
Free association, 205–7, 212
Freedom, 114, 118–19, 128, 133, 154–55
French Revolution, xxvii, 20

Gay Science (Nietzsche), 135
Genealogy of Morals (Nietzsche), 73
Genocide (*see* Nazi Germany)

Gilson, Etienne, 169–70
Gioacchino da Fiore, 20
Glaucon, 87, 88
Globke, Hans, 236, 238
"God is dead" propositions, 161–62
Gorgias (Plato), 82–87, 89–90, 91, 93,
180–81, 280
Grabner, 248
Graham, Robert A., 219
Great Britain, 259
Great Depression, 271, 272
Greece, 51, 70, 99, 259
Group formation, 205
Guilt, collective, 21, 28–29, 59, 147–58
Gurian, Waldemar, 220, 221

Hamlet (Shakespeare), 27–28
Hand, Learned, xxxv n.
*Hannah Arendt and the Meaning of
Politics* (ed. Calhoun and
McGowan), xxxv n.
Happiness, 129–31
Heer, Friedrich, 220, 225–26
Hegel, Georg Wilhelm Friedrich, 9, 20,
74, 126, 177
Heidegger, Martin, xxv n., 9, 10, 166,
175, 279, 285
Heraclitus, 285
Herodotus, 260
Heydrich, Reinhard, 238
Himmler, Heinrich, 39, 40, 238, 240,
243, 248
Hippias Major, 185–86
Hitler, Adolf, xii, xxxvi, 20, 21, 24, 30,
35, 42, 54, 58, 153, 155, 178, 222,
223, 225, 237, 238, 244, 265, 267,
272
Hitler and the Christians (Gurian), 221
Hochhuth, Rolf, xxxvi, 20, 37, 59,
214–17, 220, 223, 225
Höcker, Adjutant, 236, 240
Hofmann, Camp Commandant, 236,
238

Index

ML   12/03